# TERRORISM AND THE LIBERAL STATE

*By the same author*

SOCIAL MOVEMENT
POLITICAL TERRORISM

# TERRORISM AND THE LIBERAL STATE

PAUL WILKINSON

First published 1977 by
THE MACMILLAN PRESS LTD
London and Basingstoke
Associated companies in Delhi Dublin
Hong Kong Johannesburg Lagos Melbourne
New York Singapore and Tokyo

ISBN 0 333 19123 4 (hard cover)
0 333 22770 0 (paper cover)

Printed in Great Britain by
LOWE AND BRYDONE PRINTERS LIMITED
Thetford, Norfolk

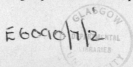

For Susan

# CONTENTS

*Prefatory Note*                                                    ix

PART I: FORCE, VIOLENCE, ORDER AND THE LIBERAL STATE

    I.    The Liberal Tradition in Political Philosophy          3
    II.   The Bases of Political Obligation                      12
   III.  The Rule of Law                                        16
   IV.  The Role of Force                                      18
    V.   Sanction, Punishment and Deterrence                    20
   VI.  Violence Defined                                       23
  VII.  Modes of Conflict, Opposition and Protest              24
 VIII.  Political Violence: Characteristics and Typology        30
   IX.  Causes of Political Violence in Liberal States         34
    X.   Can Political Violence ever be Morally Justified
           in a Liberal State?                                  38
   XI.  The Proper Use of Force in the Liberal State           41
  XII.  Terror and Terrorism: Concepts, Characteristics
           and Typology                                         47
 XIII.  Terrorism and Criminality                              65

PART II: INTERNAL TERRORISM AND THE LIBERAL STATE

 XIV.  The Philosophy of Terror                               71
  XV.  The Terrorist Threat to Liberal Societies              80
 XVI.  The Roots of Terrorism                                 93
XVII.  Terrorist Ideologies and Beliefs                       96

XVIII.   Vulnerabilities of Liberal Societies              102

XIX.   Terrorist Strategy and Tactics                   106

XX.   General Problems of Internal Defence against
         Terrorism                                     114

XXI.   General Principles of Counter-terrorist Strategy   121

XXII.   The Role of Intelligence                        132

XXIII.   Countering 'Spasm' Terrorism                    139

XXIV.   Army's Role in Combating 'Spasm' Terrorism      147

XXV.   Countering Incipient Civil War                   150


PART III: INTERNATIONAL TERRORISM

XXVI.   International and Transnational Terrorism        173

XXVII.   Force and Violence in International Relations    175

XXVIII.   International Terrorism and International
           Relations                                    177

XXIX.   Underlying Political and Strategic Causes        181

XXX.   Vulnerabilities: Targets, Technology and Tolerance  188

XXXI.   Precipitative Causes                            193

XXXII.   Effects of International Terrorism              195

XXXIII.   Potential Threats                              198

XXXIV.   The Hijacking Problem                           206

XXXV.   Diplomatic Kidnappings and Attacks              224

XXXVI.   Barricade and Hostage Situations               229

XXXVII.   General Measures against International Terrorism  231


Notes and References                                   235
Index                                                  249

# PREFATORY NOTE

There have been encouraging signs over the past few years of a growth of scholarly interest in the phenomenon of political terrorism.[1] Surely it is not entirely coincidence that this has occurred when the incidence of terrorism in many parts of the world has been dramatically increasing.[2] It has never been my view that it is improper or demeaning for academics to interest themselves in the urgent practical problems of the day. Indeed in discussing the problem of terrorism with members of the public, politicians, officials, members of security forces and fellow academics, one is impressed by the widespread desire for serious analysis and long-term thinking concerning the nature of terrorist phenomena, their causes, effects and policy implications for Western governments and societies. The present book is an attempt to contribute to this analysis and to stimulate further debate through an investigation of the problem of terrorism from a liberal democratic perspective, and to suggest some practicable and effective means of tackling it.

It will come as no surprise to the reader to learn that in the colourful aviary of contemporary Academia many shriek and squawk against any project of this kind. Some, while admitting the fact of terrorism in the contemporary world, want its defenestration from the ivory tower either because of academic snobbery or plain squeamishness. One is reminded of the widespread academic prejudice against war studies. War, like terrorism, is a nasty, bloody, messy business which, some wish to argue, should only be studied by universities under the *cache sexe* of 'Peace' or 'Conflict' studies. Yet another group hold to a position of invincible ignorance about terrorism; they hold that the word has no meaning but is simply a pejorative for freedom fighting or rebellion disapproved of by the authorities. It would be foolish to deny that the word has been abused in this way. For example, the South African government tend to designate all those who actively oppose them, by whatever means, as 'terrorists'. But the mere fact of propagandist abuse of a political term surely does not justify dropping it altogether from our vocabulary. Should we drop the word 'democracy' because of the way it has been used by the so-called 'People's Democracies'? Or is the term 'socialist' to be consigned to oblivion because of its appropriation by Hitler's National Socialist party? As I try to make clear in the conceptual discussion in Part I, there are quite clear *differentiae* between the intent, aims and psychological effects of terrorism and those of other forms of violence such as the collective violence of riots and revolutionary uprisings and conventional war. It is an elementary but common mistake, for example, to equate terrorism with guerrilla war. As a matter of history many guerrilla struggles have been fought without recourse to the tactics of terrorism, and, as will be discussed later, many guerrilla leaders have been explicitly opposed to any policy of terrorisation both on grounds of expediency and morality.

Those who claim to eschew the word 'terrorism' on the grounds that it is contentious and implies value judgement[3] are by so doing dodging a whole set of issues: (i) they implicitly abandon the essential conceptual basis and framework for analysis of state terror and terroristic agencies and practices; (ii) should we simply ignore the very explicit theorists and manuals prescribing systematic terrorism as a political weapon and spelling out appropriate tactics and techniques?; (iii) what other terms do they suggest we use to differentiate between those governments, political leaders and revolutionaries who do favour and practice such methods from those who do not? It is surely ridiculously ostrich-like to hide our heads from this whole ugly area of historical experience?

A more fundamental opposition is expressed, predictably, by the small groups of anti-liberal democratic intellectuals and ideologues. They often have a sophisticated awareness of the possible political uses of terrorism, and generally offer terrorist movements a promising recruiting ground, a revolutionary ideology or programme and leadership. Even if they do not actually plan and promote acts of terrorism, they are likely to encourage and condone acts of violence, destruction, disruption and intimidation damaging to the liberal democratic system they so loathe. Whereas I may hope to communicate with some sceptical and reflective members of the first group it would be delusive to hope to get through to the hard-core allies, apologists and front men of terrorist movements. I suppose it is little use pointing out that 'post-revolutionary' régimes have also proved vulnerable to calculated terrorisation by powerful political and para-military movements or that citizens in 'revolutionary' societies also have basic human needs for security against murder, injury and destruction whether at the hands of the ruling party or its agencies or of private terrorist factions. One can only assume that Communists and their fellow-travellers who remain unmoved by the testimony of *The First Circle* or *The Gulag Archipelago*, who cannot or will not listen to the cries of generations of victims of Soviet tyranny, have blotted out all sense of individual rights and freedoms. By suppressing all human feeling or sympathy for individuals in the name of that deadly abstraction, 'revolutionary justice', they have strangled their own humanity.

A main concern of the present work is to try to improve our understanding of the problem of terrorism against the whole background of contemporary international relations and continuing ideological conflict. It is necessary, therefore, to examine the extent to which some, though by no means all, terrorist movements and campaigns are promoted, aided and deployed as auxiliary weapons by revolutionary movements and as modes of unconventional and surrogate war by some states. It will be shown that the Soviet Union has a considerable record of involvement in this type of conflict, and that this has important consequences for Western internal and external defence policy and strategy. However, the reader should be reassured that the author does not seek to present any general conspiracy theory or cold war *grand simplification* to 'explain' contemporary terrorist phenomena. On the contrary, terrorism is a very clear manifestation of the intensifying multipolarity of international conflicts, of the almost infinite variety of actual and potential ideological, religious, ethnic, particularistic, secessionist and international sources of terrorist conflict that beset us. Terrorism is not the monopoly of any ideology or cause; in many countries and circumstances (for example in Italy, Spain, Brazil and Argentina) neo-fascist and ultra-rightist terrorist groups constitute a growing menace. Indeed Mussolini and Hitler can claim the dubious distinction of having pioneered many techniques and tactics of terrorisation as an auxiliary weapon for seizing and consolidating power.

Theorising about political violence and about terrorism in particular raises fundamental and complex ethical issues. Can terrorism

ever be morally justifiable in an operative liberal democratic
society? If not, may it nevertheless be justifiable against totalitarian
or authoritarian dictatorships, or against a foreign conqueror? Is
there some argument analogous to the case for the 'just war' which
may be used to justify terrorist violence under certain circumstances?
There are some enormous questions to be posed about the practice of
terrorism itself. Should there be some kind of terrorist 'ethic', or
rules about the limits of violence that is to be used? Can terrorism be
selective, precise and discriminate? Who is to decide, and on what
basis are they to decide, who shall be the recipients (victims) of
terrorist 'justice'? In liberal democratic societies acute ethical
problems arise concerning the appropriate treatment of convicted
terrorists who have been attempting through terror to blackmail and
intimidate a government, group or community which has majority
legitimacy and support into conceding to their political demands.
Does their claim to have a political motivation entitle them to
special treatment or status in the judicial process? Should the lives of
convicted terrorists dedicated to making war on society be forfeit?
These are a few of the ethical questions that will be discussed
recurrently throughout the present work.

However, there is another kind of theoretical complexity involved. Complexities, ambiguities and uncertainties in the international system, in particular the fluctuating relations between
domestic and international political forces, raise baffling problems of
empirical theory. Are current trends in terrorism symptomatic of an
increasing swing away from bipolarity to multipolarity, and of a
relative weakening of super-power capacity to mould international
relations? Terrorism can be interpreted as a desperate response of
the growing number of weak or powerless groups challenging the
rigidities of frontiers, power and resource distribution underpinned
by the current international system. A French theorist has asserted
'Terrorism is the weapon of the weak pretending to be strong.' We
must go on to ask whether the weak are gaining strength at the expense of the strong or vice versa? Is terrorism, particularly in its international and transnational manifestations, a true harbinger of
wider and far more sanguinary and dangerous revolutionary
struggles by movements claiming to represent the poor and under-
privileged of the Third World against the rich states of the First
World? Or, on the other hand, is the very desperation and the
fanatical, almost suicidal style of the transnational terrorist

brotherhoods indicative of their weakness, vulnerability and ultimate political irrelevance? Could they really survive a concerted
campaign by the international community to outlaw and eliminate
them?

By contrast many indigenous terrorist struggles at regional and
national levels are by no means so clearly asymmetrical in character.
In some cases (particularly where external powers are acting as their
sponsors), revolutionary movements engaging in terrorism may acquire the resources, weapons and popular base equalling or even sur-
passing the resources of the target régime.

These ambiguities and contradictions should warn us against any
premature general theory or model of the causes, inception and
development of terrorism. For in reality there are many terrorisms,
each calling for different theories, models and approaches from the
scholar seeking to relate these phenomena to other dimensions of
political change. Therefore the primary tasks must be: to clarify and
refine the concept of political terrorism; to establish a working
typology of political terrorism; and, most difficult of all, to relate
terrorism to other modes of violence and to the basic political
values, structures and processes of liberal democracy. These tasks are
attempted in Part I of the present work.

Part II, the heart of the book, deals with the special problems of
revolutionary and sub-revolutionary political terrorism in liberal
democracies. It discusses the underlying and precipitative causes of
terrorism in liberal states and assesses influential causal and
developmental theories and models of terrorism under these conditions. The ideologies, aims, beliefs, strategies, tactics, organisational structures, recruitment and logistics of terrorist groups are
identified and their influence and efficacy are analysed. Considerable attention is given in this section to evaluating both the implications of terrorism for liberal democratic states and the most
practicable and potentially effective strategies of prevention,
deterrence, internal and external defence and counter-offensive open
to governments and security forces. Attention is given to the lessons
of recent experience of anti-terrorist campaigns regarding the administrative, police, military and psychological resources, tactics,
equipments, security, judicial and political measures most appropriate to the varying intensities of anti-terrorist operations, ranging from isolated bombings and assassinations to major anti-terrorist
emergencies. I conclude this section by highlighting what in my

view are the most serious dangers and mistakes that may threaten the success of anti-terrorist operations by liberal states: under-reaction, political inertia and the disintegration of the state; over-reaction, indiscriminate repression and the loss of popular support and legitimacy.

Liberal democracies are particularly vulnerable to infiltration and attack by international and transnational terrorists and it is with this particular challenge that Part III is concerned. The specific problems of skyjacking, diplomatic kidnappings, embassy attacks and assassinations and possible national, bilateral, regional and international counter-measures and co-operative action against these forms of terrorism are examined.

It will be clear from the foregoing that this book does not offer a general historical narrative of terrorist movements and campaigns, a survey of empirical data or a guide to the literature. Readers should refer elsewhere for these.[4] My aim has been to concentrate on debating theory, analysis, strategy and policy, and in order to give the main lines of argument sharper definition I have tried to keep cross-references and academic apparatus to an unobtrusive minimum.

The study of terrorism is still relatively new and undeveloped, younger by far than the study of civil violence and revolution. In a field with so few wise men to follow, the contributions of Professors Feliks Gross, Joseph Roucek and Eugene Walter shine like beacons, and all succeeding students of terrorism rest heavily in their debt. I should also like to pay tribute, in this connection, to that pioneering triumvir of British experts on terrorism: Brian Crozier, Robert Moss and Dr Richard Clutterbuck. The superb quality of their contributions is internationally recognised though inadequately acknowledged in British Academia. I wish to thank all three for their generous encouragement, insights and assistance, all of which I have drawn on freely. Shaie Selzer of Macmillan has been remarkable for his patience and kind forbearance. Needless to say, none of the above is responsible for the faults and errors in what follows.

*Cardiff*                                                    PAUL WILKINSON
*1977*

# PART I
# FORCE, VIOLENCE, ORDER AND THE LIBERAL STATE

'Justice without Force is impotent: Force without Justice is a tyranny.'

Blaise Pascal, *Pensées*

'Free speech, raised in protest, is the life-blood of democracy, yet the freer the speech the more likely it is to inflame its audience to violence. But violence can kill democracy, for if given rein it will destroy the democracy that licensed it; while to curb it freedom itself may have to be restricted, and democracy thus impaled on the other horn of the dilemma. Any nation which so orders its affairs as to achieve a maximum of freedom of speech with a maximum of freedom from public disorder may fairly claim a prize among the highest achievements of the human race. In terms of individual happiness it surely ranks higher than a successful landing on the moon. How has the prize been won? Can it be held?'

T. A. Critchley, *The Conquest of Violence*

# I
# THE LIBERAL TRADITION IN
# POLITICAL PHILOSOPHY

The term 'state' in my title has been chosen quite deliberately in order to exploit its *triple sens*: a given territory and its inhabitants; a system of government and laws; and, more colloquially, the general condition and outlook of liberal values, institutions and citizens. Aristotle drew attention to the danger of terminological confusion in his discussion of the question of the continuity of the state. If the constitution of a particular people and territory changes from oligarchy or tyranny to democracy does it become a new state?

> On the one hand we may say that the identity of the state remains the same so long as there is continuity of race; for, as we call a river by the same name, although different water passes into and out of it all the time, so we ought to speak of the state as the same state, although one generation of people dies and another is born. On the other hand it might be said that while we speak of the population as being the same for the reasons stated, we ought to say that the state is different. For, since the state is an association of citizens in a constitution, when the constitution of the citizens changes and becomes different in kind, the state also does. We may compare this with a chorus, which may at one time perform in a tragedy and at another in a comedy and so be different in kind, yet all the while be composed of the same persons... If this is right, it would seem that the criterion of continuity or continued identity ought to be *constitution* rather than race.[1]

Aristotle's decision to give primacy to the constitution of the *polis*, that is, to the form of government and laws of the state, as the criterion of continuity provided the basis not only for Aristotle's pioneering comparative study of constitutions but for the whole development of political science up to the modern age. And in accordance with this tradition political theorists and analysts have regarded the liberal democratic state as a separate genus, characterised by distinctive constitutional arrangements, which has been confined to the relatively recent historical experience of a minority of modern states.

However, while it is very important to be able to identify and explain the crucial differences between the modern liberal state and the various forms of autocracy, tyranny, and totalitarianism, it is also valuable to recognise the continuities between liberal and pre-liberal political orders, the mixed nature of modern liberal democratic constitutions, and the relatively early origins of liberal political ideas, which can certainly be traced back to the classical and medieval political philosophers, and which find their richest modern expression in the works of Locke, Montesquieu, Madison, de Tocqueville and Mill.

A major difficulty encountered by those studying the liberal tradition in political philosophy stems from its multifarious and eclectic nature. Those who attempt to nail down a precise definition of liberal principles and doctrines are on a wild goose chase, for liberal political thought lacks the systematic character of an ideology. There are, for example, basic disagreements within the tradition concerning metaphysical assumptions, doctrines of man, the origins and appropriate purposes and forms of government and laws, the bases of political obligation, and the desirable balance between the rights and duties of government and individual citizens. However, my main purpose in the present work is not to attempt to survey the complex historiography of liberalism or to examine comprehensively its substantive doctrinal controversies. My more limited aim here is to correct what I regard as a dangerous imbalance in contemporary accounts of liberal political theory. Most contemporary debates on liberalism concentrate on its individualist and libertarian elements at the expense of its doctrines of government, law and authority. The stress is almost exclusively placed upon the extension of rights, democracy and 'participation' (a notoriously ambiguous slogan enjoying a recent vogue as a panacea for the ills of liberal democracy) at the cost of any attention to obligations, duties, law, authority and order. In short there is a grave danger of neglecting the basic truth that liberal democratic rights all ultimately depend upon the viability of the liberal state. For, as Locke argues in a famous passage, 'in all states of created beings, capable of laws, where there is no law there is no freedom. For liberty is to be free from restraint and violence from others; which cannot be where there is no law; and is not, as we are told, a liberty for every man to do what he lists.'[2] The classic liberal political philosophers' writings are indeed *primarily* concerned with building up a theory of the liberal state, its origins, establishment and constitution. Inevitably they wrestle with the problems of securing governmental legitimacy and authority, political obligation and order. Both explicitly and implicitly they seek to determine the necessary and legitimate functions of state coercion, and to devise adequate safeguards against private and factional violence which might undermine the authority, security and peace of the commonwealth.

Not all liberal theorists share a belief in the Christian doctrine of man, and very few contemporary liberals profess a belief in Natural Law. Nevertheless the earthy realism of the liberal view of human nature as neither wholly good and perfectible nor wholly and irredeemably bad, has much in common with classical and medieval attitudes. This is perhaps less surprising when one recalls that the medieval and renaissance philosophers were steeped in classical writings on politics, especially Aristotle, and it is significant that the leading seventeenth and eighteenth century political theorists refer endlessly to the Greek and Roman histories and writings on constitutions.

For the classic liberal thinkers as for Aristotle and Aquinas it is because Man's pride and wilfulness lead him, on occasion, to harm others deliberately and even to behave with cruelty and barbarity, that government is necessary. Madison put the matter concisely: 'But what is government itself but the greatest of all reflections on human nature? If men were angels, no government would be necessary. If angels were to govern men, neither external or internal controls on government would be necessary.'[3] Christian thinkers spoke of the Fall of Man and Original Sin: 'Video meliora proboque, Deteriora sequor' (I know and respect what is right, but I do what is wrong). Secular liberal theorists today generally assume that human beings have imperfect knowledge, imperfect altruism and imperfect rationality. This liberal assumption of human fallibility has three important implications which find their parallel in the

theological implications of the belief that all men are sinners: (i) the
idea of moral equality which was expressed in theological terms as
'all men are equal in the sight of God'; (ii) the possibility of moral
self-improvement by learning and following rules of good conduct
(in theological terms the hope of redemption by faith, prayer and
good works); and (iii) and potentially most disturbing in its political
implications, it follows that rulers cannot be exempt from mortal
fallibility and moral responsibility. That is to say that rulers could
also be criticised for moral failings, and that it might even be
legitimate and necessary to disobey a bad or tyrannical ruler, or
even to resist him and seek his overthrow.

The notions of moral equality, and moral responsibility and accountability of rulers are key elements in the political philosophy of
Aristotle. In Book III of *Politics* he makes a clear distinction
between despotic rule characterised by the servile relationship of
subjects to the ruler, and 'another kind of rule – that exercised
among men who are free and equal in birth. This we call
"constitutional" or "political" rule.'⁴ For Aristotle, therefore, a
truly political association can only be enjoyed by a republic of moral
equals, that is of citizens, all of whom are entitled to participate in
the business of government. Numerous critics have pointed to the
uglier side of Athenian democracy, its dependence upon the large
non-citizen population of slaves, women and those of foreign birth.
Indeed there is an ironic twist in the fact that Aristotle did not, as a
Macedonian, enjoy citizen status in Athens. He counted as *metoikos*
in the very *polis* he so admired. Nevertheless the idea of morally
equal citizens each regarded as morally and legally entitled to share
in ruling the affairs of the *polis* was a truly revolutionary conception
'rediscovered' with devastating consequences by the radical theorists
and revolutionaries of England, Holland, America and France in the
seventeenth and eighteenth centuries.

The long-term implications of the quest for moral and political
equality are still reverberating. Demands for equal legal and political
rights, and for the abolition of privileges and discrimination on
grounds of race, religion, class or sex are still explosive sources of
protest and discontent, and constitute clear evidence, if any is needed, that liberal political ideas still constitute a real revolutionary
force in the world. However, one must recognise also that socialist
doctrines of equality, and the demand for more equal distribution of
wealth and material resources are a far more potent source of revolu-

tion among the poor and hungry masses of the developing and developed world than liberal ideas. Well before modern socialist thought developed, liberal thinkers as diverse as Rousseau, Madison and Mill had followed Aristotle in identifying gross inequalities in the distribution of property and wealth as a major source of political instability. None of the liberal theorists, however — not even the sensible J. S. Mill in his wide-ranging *Political Economy* — proposed any practical measures to rectify this situation.

In truth, liberalism, despite its enormous advances in the political sphere by the late nineteenth century, remained trapped in a crude Free Trade and *laissez-faire* economic outlook. In some countries moral and political liberalism have been pushed to the very limits of popular tolerance, for example in the realms of sexual behaviour, penological reform and obscenity laws. But it is the socialist thinkers and movements who have concentrated the attack on economic inequalities and who have campaigned for radical reforms in the economic system.

Liberal thinkers have consistently emphasised the moral value of the individual. They share with the Judaeo—Christian tradition the humanist doctrine of man which views the individual as a free-willing agent endowed with reason and moral responsibility. And it is on the basis of this belief in the moral value and equality of individuals that liberal philosophers asserted the general human rights to life, liberty and the pursuit of happiness, and to the numerous civil and legal rights and freedoms that are codified in many modern constitutions.

The true antithesis of the liberal state with its constitutional government, rule of law and protection of individual rights and liberties, is the tyranny. Aristotle describes the worst kind of tyrant as the one who rules entirely outside the law to suit his own interest and pleasure rather than to serve the interests of the people. 'No one', he concludes, 'willingly submits to such a government if he is a free man.'[5]

Aquinas, in his discussion of tyranny, echoes Aristotle's view: 'Tyrannical government is unjust because it is not directed to the common good but to the private good of the ruler.'[6] He then makes the extraordinarily modern claim that 'the overthrow of such government is not strictly sedition, unless perhaps when accompanied by such disorder that the community suffers greater harm than from the tryannical government'.[7] Aquinas has strong claim to be counted the first liberal political theorist in the modern sense, for according to his theory of authority the permanent constitution (*modus*) of a community should be ultimately determined by the people. His justification of popular rebellion against tyranny anticipates Locke's by over 400 years.

Locke makes his own antipathy to tyranny very plain. Having defined tyranny as 'the exercise of power beyond right, which no body can have a right to', he argues 'whosoever in authority exceeds the power given him by the law, and makes use of the force he has under his command to compass that upon the subject which the law allows not, ceases in that to be a magistrate, and acting without authority may be opposed, as any other man who by force invades the right of another.'[8]

It is important to underline the fact that the liberal political philosophers all express their principled opposition to despotic and tyrannical forms of government, and that this marked a crucial difference between them and those political philosophers from Thrasymachus to Machiavelli and Hobbes who have taken a more equivocal or even favourable view of tyrannical power. Machiavelli, for example, in *The Prince*, cannot conceal his admiration for the skill, nerve and cunning of self-made tyrants like Agathocles the Sicilian. Agathocles made himself ruler of Syracuse by tricking all the Senators and wealthy men of Syracuse into attending an assembly and then having his soldiers murder them. Machiavelli concedes that Agathocles achieved power by wickedness rather than by fortune or virtue. Yet he praises him for his strength and 'greatness of mind' in gaining and keeping power. *The Prince* can be reasonably interpreted, indeed, as a kind of manual in techniques of effective despotism: trickery, force, fraud and the breaking of promises. Machiavelli simply takes for granted that the successful Prince of his age will rule by ruthless and cunning Realpolitik.

Hobbes's position is often misunderstood, and there have even been recent attempts to interpret him as a liberal political philosopher.[9] Yet this is odd because Hobbes made his position much more starkly clear than most political philosophers have before or since. For Hobbes the greatest good was Order defined as a state of civil peace, and the greatest evil was civil conflict or anarchy, 'a condition of Warre' of all against all. He was prepared to pay the price of submission to an absolute despot in order to guarantee civil peace. In his discussion of Covenants and Laws in Chapter XV of

*Leviathan* he insists upon a Thrasymachian ultra-positivist position regarding the basis of justice. Justice is what the ruler shall determine it to be. There can be no injustice when there is no Commonwealth. And in a Commonwealth all that is covenanted under the coercive power of the sovereign is *ipso facto* just.

The major proposition of *Leviathan* is that all men should place their natural propensity for competitive hostility under severe limits by simultaneously agreeing to surrender their natural rights to unlimited freedom of action and to accept the sovereign authority of Leviathan. In Hobbes's exposition the notion of the Covenant is a covenient literary device for establishing the essential contractual foundations of Hobbes's Commonwealth, the vital artefact to secure social peace. Hobbes is determined to secure a perpetual and secure order. Hence there must be a ruler with sufficient power to coerce all the subjects of the Commonwealth to obey its laws. Hobbes thus claims that social peace and freedom from constant fear of death, injury or dispossession is really conditional upon this once-for-all agreement: 'a covenant of every man with every man, in such manner, as if every man should say to every man, I authorize and give up my right of governing myself, to this man, or to this assembly of men, on this condition, that thou give up thy right to him, and authorize all his actions in like manner.'[10].

It is quite clear from *Leviathan* that Hobbes believed 'Peace without subjection' was unattainable. Security and order could only be achieved by men if they submitted to a common power 'to keep them all in awe'. The price of social peace was a once-and-for-all submission to 'that great Leviathan. . .that Mortall God'. Hobbes is most insistent that the power of this 'Mortall God', whether embodied in a sovereign person or assembly, was absolute over the affairs of its subjects. The constitutional form implicit in the covenant is not limited and representative government in any sense. It is surely an understatement to describe it as merely 'authoritarian' in character.[11] Hobbes accords Leviathan the power of absolute despotism, and he understood as clearly as Montesquieu that the principle of despotic rule is *fear*. For he accords the sovereign 'the use of so much Power and Strength conferred on him, that by terror thereof, he is inabled to forme the wills of them all, to Peace at home, and mutuall ayd against their enemies abroad'.[12]

Leviathan's political power over his subjects is absolute and perpetual. Even in cases where a commonwealth is *instituted* by covenant rather than acquired by force of arms subjects have no right individually or collectively to attempt to renounce their allegiance or dispose of the sovereign. The sovereign is given the *unconditional* right to make the laws, interpret and administer them, and to punish those who fail to observe them. Moreover the sovereign has sole right to determine all matters of internal and external policy. There is no room in such a system for political or civil liberties. Hobbes hammers home the point

> that nothing the Soveraign Representative can doe to a Subject on what pretence soever, can properly be called Injustice, or Injury; because every Subject is Author of every act the Soveraign doth; so that he never wanteth Right to any thing, otherwise, than as he himself is the subject of God, and bound thereby to observe the laws of Nature. And therefore it may, and doth often happen in common-wealths, that a Subject may be put to death, by the command of the Soveraign Power; and yet neither doe the other wrong.[13]

The only freedom of action left to the individual is not a liberty enjoyed as of right but that residual area of private life permitted by the sovereign and on which the law is silent 'such as is the Liberty to buy, and sell, and otherwise contract with one another; to choose their own aboad, their own diet, their own trade of life, and institute their children as they themselves think fit; and the like'.[14] We may certainly exonerate Hobbes, on this account, from advocating totalitarian control of society and individual. But it is hard to see what possible grounds exist for Michael Oakeshott's bizarre claim that 'Hobbes, without being himself a liberal, had in him more of the philosophy of liberalism than most of its professed defenders'.[15]

Nothing more clearly demonstrates the gulf dividing Hobbes's constitution of despotism from the representative and limited government of Locke than their attitudes towards tyranny. Hobbes is quite categorical that rebellion against the sovereign can never be justified. The political obligation only ceases when the sovereign's power is itself destroyed by internal or external enemies and subjects are compelled to look elsewhere for protection. Because rebellion is outlawed even tyranny must be borne. In Chapter XXIX of *Leviathan* Hobbes indicates his wish to make a clean break with classical and medieval doctrines of tyrannicide which appeared to justify sedition under certain circumstances. He warns against 'the Venime' of 'Democraticall writers' and what he terms '*Tyrannophobia* or feare of being strongly governed'.[16] And in his 'Review and Conclusion' he even attempts to argue that there is really no such thing as tyranny: it is, he claims, simply a pejorative for sovereignty:

> And because the name of Tyranny, signifieth nothing more, nor lesse, than the name of Soveraignty, be it in one, or many men, saving that they that use the former word, are understood to be angry with them they call Tyrants; I think the toleration of a professed hatred of Tyranny, is a Toleration of hatred to Commonwealth in generall, and another evill seed, not differing much from the former.[17]

Thus with a splendid early example of 'double-think' Hobbes concludes that those who hate tyranny must be enemies of the state.

We have already noted that Locke accepted the Aristotelian definition of tyranny, as the exercise of power beyond right. Locke's liberal model of civil government is essentially an attempt to promote a settled government of laws and clearly defined and limited powers in place of arbitary rule based on the whim and pleasure of the ruler. Locke's version of the social contract is therefore different from Hobbes's covenant in certain crucial respects. It is a compact of morally equal citizens all of whom have a permanent stake and interest in the civil society. Furthermore the contract imposes reciprocal obligations on both government and citizens. The sovereign legislative assembly, elected by the majority of the citizens, has a fiduciary responsibility for observing and administering the laws authorised by popular consent. For their part, citizens have a duty of allegiance to the legally constituted sovereign and must obey its laws and commands. What if an individual or faction attempts to seize power from the legally constituted sovereign assembly or to encroach upon or to subvert its powers and authority or uses illegal powers? In such circumstances Locke is prepared to admit that force may be opposed to 'unjust and unlawful force'.[18] He is prepared to defend stoutly the proposition that 'the people are absolved from obedience when illegal attempts are made upon their liberties or properties'.[19] Locke argues:

The end of government is the good of mankind; and which is best for mankind, that the people should always be exposed to the boundless will of tyranny, or that the rulers should be sometimes liable to be opposed when they grow exorbitant in the use of their power, and employ it for the destruction, and not the preservation, of the properties of their people?[20]

This is a concise statement of the classical liberal opposition to tyranny and despotism, encapsulating the liberal rationale that underpinned the English, American and French revolutions of the seventeenth and eighteenth centuries.

But it is clearly inadequate to try to define liberal political philosophy purely negatively in terms of its principled opposition to absolutism and despotism. We need to identify the positive features of the liberal state as they emerge in modern liberal theory. How was the Aristotelian golden mean to be secured? What form of constitution could provide most effectively a secure foundation of order, laws and liberties? Madison stated the basic problem very simply:

In framing a government which is to be administered by men over men, the great difficulty lies in this: you must first enable the government to control the governed; and in the next place oblige it to control itself. A dependence on the people is, no doubt, the primary control on the government; but experience has taught mankind the necessity of auxiliary precautions.[21]

## II
# THE BASES OF POLITICAL OBLIGATION

The primary foundation of the liberal state is the political obligation and support willed by its citizens. What is the basis of general political obligation in the liberal state? We have noted that in the traditional despotism or tyranny the ruler-ruled relationship is analogous to that of master and servant. According to absolutist doctrine subjects obey primarily out of fear of the consequences of disobedience, because they go in terror or awe of their Mortal God.

Yet even Hobbes's account of the original covenant instituting a Commonwealth does not provide a convincing rationale for obedience. Why should a majority necessarily agree that the securing of social peace is the greatest good? Men might equally well determine that they preferred to pursue other values, even at the cost of continuing conflict. In any event, once the Leviathan is established men have little option but to obey.

Liberal doctrines of general political obligation are necessarily grounded not only on prudence and habit, but also on appeals to *reason*. Perhaps the most obvious of these is the argument from utility. The *philosophes*, the *économistes*, and later the Scottish philosophical radicals, and the English utilitarians, all rehearsed the reasons why government was essential to the welfare of society: it prevented men from becoming slaves to the passions of others, provided for internal peace and defence against external enemies, and regulated both domestic and foreign trade and commerce. It might be argued that this utilitarian ground for political obligation has been weakened in the modern era due to the proven incapacity of many states to provide the essential energy resources, raw materials, and even essential food supplies required by their populations. One encounters much loose discussion of the alleged obsolescence of the nation-state as a fundamental unit of political organisation, and of radical proposals for reform of the international system by means of new forms of international organisation and regional integration.[22] I cannot pursue this at length here. Nevertheless it is relevant to the present discussion to point out that, for good or ill, the state is now the fundamental general-purpose political organisation for the whole human race. We are stuck with it until such time as other more effective forms of organisation may be evolved. In any case the liberal theorist can legitimately argue that most contemporary liberal democracies rank among the more effective states in the world in terms of providing for the essential needs and welfare of their citizens. Perhaps we should aim therefore at encouraging more states to follow the liberal model rather than try to abandon the state altogether. A third strong argument in favour of the continuing relevance and significance of the liberal state, in my view, is that most recent developments and experiments in international organisation and regional integration (for example, the U.N. and the European Economic Community) have been largely instigated, sustained and financed by the liberal democracies.

Movements towards internationalism can be seen, therefore, as a sign of the political creativity and co-operative capacities of certain states, and are not necessarily signs that the state has outlived its usefulness.

Other liberal justifications for political obligation may be identified with specific liberal philosophers. Locke's social contract theory argued that men should obey the law because they had promised to do so either explicitly or tacitly in their consent to the social contract. They have, so to speak, renounced their natural power of perfect freedom and agreed to accept the settled rules of the community. A necessary condition for the establishment of a civil society or commonwealth is the willingness of its members individually and collectively to accept its laws, adjudications and punishments as authoritative and binding. Locke's insistence on unanimity of consent to the establishment of the body politic raises extraordinary difficulties which have been discussed at length by Locke's critics. Once the social compact is made every man who has consented 'puts himself under an obligation to everyone of that society to submit to the determination of the majority, and to be concluded by it'.[23] Locke realises that a unanimity requirement for legislative decisions would make government unworkable, though he does countenance the possibility of express agreement that decisions may require the consent of an agreed number greater than a majority. But suppose certain individuals or factions become aggrieved at the decisions of the majority in the civil society. Under what circumstances, if any, may they rescind their consent to the social contract? May minorities secede from the civil society? If so must they seek exile abroad, or may they claim an inalienable right to remain on their property? Other critics have emphasised the ahistorical and fictional nature of Locke's account of the original social contract. Perhaps the founding of the United States is the sole historical example of a constitution being established in a manner remotely resembling Locke's compact?

It is nevertheless possible, while rejecting social contract theory in its original form, to extract from it certain important truths about the reciprocal character of obligations and responsibilities of citizens and government in the liberal society. These truths have rarely been more cogently stated than by John Stuart Mill in *On Liberty*:

Though society is not founded on a contract, and though no

good purpose is answered by inventing a contract in order to deduce social obligations from it, every one who receives the protection of society owes a return for the benefit, and the fact of living in society renders it indispensable that each should be bound to observe a certain line of conduct towards the rest. This conduct consists, first, in not injuring the interests of one another; or rather certain interests, which, either by express legal provision or by tacit understanding, ought to be considered as rights; and secondly in each person's bearing his share (to be fixed on some equitable principle) of the labours and sacrifices incurred for defending the society or its members from injury and molestation. These conditions society is justified in enforcing at all costs to those who endeavour to withold fulfilment. [24]

Given the difficulties encountered by social contract theories of political obligation it is perhaps fortunate that modern doctrines of representation and democratic participation also provide strong grounds for obligation to the liberal state, in addition to the general grounds of utility. Where citizens have the opportunity to elect representatives to a sovereign legislature on the basis of universal suffrage and free elections it can be argued that such participation implicitly obliges them to abide by the decisions of a government enjoying majority support among the electorate. If this were not the case it would make nonsense of democratic procedures. Naturally this claim begs many questions about the fairness of different systems of representation, the frequent occurrence of minority governments, and the problem of whether certain entrenched rights or powers can or should be secured for minority ethnic or religious groups. The means agreed to meet these kinds of difficulties will naturally vary between political systems in the light of historical traditions, attitudes and political and social conditions. Very often the political viability of a liberal state will indeed depend upon meeting the basic conditions and needs of militant and powerful minorities. However, if and when these conditions can be met the principles of universal rights of democratic participation and democratic majoritarianism as the basis of decision-making do provide the most powerful basis of general political obligation.

Experience suggests that such principles offer a far better foundation than fear, coercion and habit, for ultimately the obligation to abide by the democratic decisions of the community in which one is a full participant is a moral one, and is not mere obedience out of expediency. And it is in keeping with liberal theory to regard political obligation not only as a species of moral obligation but also as conditional rather than absolute. Thus the individual citizen might, in certain circumstances, decide that an over-riding moral obligation justified refusal to obey a particular law or command which went against conscience. This notion that human law must not conflict with more universal moral principles or laws is clearly closely akin to the idea of Natural Law, but it does not necessarily follow that such rules can only exist if they are grounded on Divine Law.

# III
# THE RULE OF LAW

The second major foundation of any liberal state is the supremacy of its rule of law. As we have already noted Locke looked to the legislative assembly to be the lynchpin of the civil government that was to replace the government of men by the government of laws. He viewed the legislature as the vehicle and guardian of the popular will and interest of the community: the executive was to be under the control of the representative assembly and the latter was to be responsible to the people. Perhaps Locke's lofty expectations of the legislative power led him to overstate the case for legislative supremacy and to overestimate its inherent incorruptibility and benevolence:

> A man, as has been proved, cannot subject himself to the arbitrary power of another; and having, in the state of nature, no arbitrary power over the life, liberty, or possession of another, but only so much as the law of nature gave him for the preservation of himself and the rest of mankind, this is all he doth, or can give up to the commonwealth, and by it to the legislative power, so that the legislative can have no more than this.[25]

Locke clearly derived from Natural Law the rule of property law that no one can convey to another a greater right than he has himself. From this he tries to deduce that no one can transfer to another absolute power over himself. Of course the analogy is false because power over others is not a tangible possession dependent upon titles of ownership: it is a complex and volatile function of economic, moral and political relations. There is a disarming innocence in Locke's assumption that the legislature of his civil society will be immune to the pursuit of power after power.

Nevertheless Locke does take care to specify guiding principles for the legislative branch of government:

> First, They are to govern by promulgated established laws, not to be varied in particular cases, but to have one rule for rich and poor, for the favourite at Court, and the countryman at plough.
> Secondly, These laws also ought to be designed for no other end ultimately but the good of the people.
> Thirdly, They must not raises taxes on the property of the people without the consent of the people given by themselves or their deputies . . .
> Fourthly, The legislative neither must nor can transfer the power of making laws to anybody else, or place it anywhere but where the people have.[26]

However, the rule of law depends on far more than the making and promulgation of laws. In complex societies with complex systems of law there must be specialist institutions, processes, and personnel to interpret, adjudicate and administer the law. It has been a constant theme in liberal discussion to emphasise the vital necessity of an independent and impartial judiciary protected from political control and interference. Indeed this must surely be a precondition for any operative rule of law.

The judiciary is far and away the weakest and most vulnerable of the departments of government: it lacks the power of sword or of purse and depends upon the executive to enforce its judgements. Montesquieu concludes that 'there is no liberty if the power of judging be not separated from the legislative and executive powers'.[27] Alexander Hamilton argues, in *Federalist Paper No. 78*, that it is especially vital to secure the independence of the courts in a limited constitution. For where the branches of government are expressly prohibited certain powers the courts must take on the additional role of guarding against breaches of the constitution by the legislative and executive departments.

There have, of course, been impassioned debates as to the most effective means of guaranteeing judicial independence, and the extent to which it may have been eroded. But recent judicial decisions in America, for example, concerning the Watergate conspiracy, and in Britain, regarding the Thameside education issue, would seem firmly to disprove claims that judicial independence has been subverted by corruption and political interference. The principles of rule of law and judicial independence are still an essential part of both the theory *and* practice of the modern liberal state.

# IV
# THE ROLE OF FORCE

The third main foundation of the liberal state is the right use of the state's monopoly of legitimate force in order to preserve internal peace and order, to enforce the law, and to defend the community against external enemies. As we have already noted, liberal theorists have not been prepared to sacrifice all liberties and rights for the sake of order. Tyranny and slavery are for them too high a price for peace. Nevertheless they agree in recognising that order or internal peace is a precondition for the establishment of a workable civil society and for social progress. Not all Hobbes's English contemporaries espoused his absolutism but they shared his consciousness of the agonies and dangers of civil strife. Like Ulysses in *Troilus and Cressida* they were haunted by the spectre of disorder turning into social disintegration:

> There everything includes itself in power
> Power into will, will into appetite;
> And appetite, an universal wolf,
> So doubly seconded with will and power,
> Must make perforce an universal prey,
> And last eat up himself.

The fear of anarchy and civil war that had haunted the English imagination in the sixteenth and seventeenth centuries began to recede by the mid-eighteenth century. It was rekindled again by the violence and terror of the revolutionary events in France and by the dire warnings of Burke. But by the mid-nineteenth century, despite revolutions in Europe and civil war in America, English liberalism had become remarkably complacent about the problem of maintaining internal peace. John Stuart Mill hardly touches on the matter in his lengthy essay *Considerations on Representative Government*. He does briefly define order as the preservation of peace by the ending of private violence, and declares it to be a precondition for representative government and for social progress. But he implies that the problem of order has already been solved in Britain and shows no inkling that it might be a constant or recurring challenge.

By the mid-twentieth century the British people might perhaps legitimately have claimed that Mill's confidence was largely justified. There had, after all, been no civil war or major civil violence in mainland Britain in the century following the publication of Mill's essary (1861).

Present-day Britain, as T. A. Critchley observed in the shrewd and prescient remarks quoted in the epigraphs above, can no longer safely assume that civil violence has been conquered once and for all. By the mid-1970s many liberal democracies had become targets for campaigns of political violence and terrorism. And Britain had on its hands a particularly bitter and desperate terrorist campaign by the Provisional I.R.A. It is true that liberal democratic government is an invention that can make recourse to violence unnecessary. Unfortunately the very liberties and restraints of liberal democracy also make it a more accessible and tempting target for violence. We shall later be examining the reasons why this should be so, the nature of the threats posed, and the options for response by liberal democratic governments and societies. The point I wish to stress here is that there are very real internal threats to the survival of order in the modern liberal state: it would be foolishly irresponsible, in the light of recent experience, to assume that internal order, even in the most traditionally stable liberal democracies, is the *sine qua non*. It is more than ever necessary to discuss the question of the right use of force to preserve the integrity of the liberal state itself. I use the term force in the traditional sense to mean the legitimate and legally authorised coercive power of the state. Violence is the term I shall use to denote the unauthorised and illegal use of coercive power, whether by the state, by factions or individuals.

Locke expressed particular concern about the danger from the executive using illegal coercion against the people: 'I say using force upon the people without authority, and contrary to the trust put in him that does so, is a state of war with the people, who have a right to reinstate their legislative in the exercise of their power. . . In all states and conditions the true remedy of force without authority is to oppose force to it.' The experience of the many liberal democracies that have been the victims of military *coups* in Europe and Latin America seems to indicate that it is generally very difficult for the legislative authorities to organise effective resistance once the military moves to take over the state power. The only lasting protection against this particular form of violence is to ensure that the armed forces and police are thoroughly controlled by, and are accountable to, the democratically responsible civil government. Thus there is a double necessity for the liberal state to maintain a monopoly of coercive power within its territory: it must be in a position to suppress the violence of any armed factions or private groups within the state, and it must be able to ensure that it will not be destroyed by its own guns being turned against it.

Yet one cannot pretend that these nostrums resolve all the dilemmas posed by the state's dependence on force. For what if the whole machinery of state be turned against the people, and dictatorship emerge from behind the stalking-horse of legality? It follows from the principle of the state's monopoly of force that if the state power is captured by a dictatorship the people will be left without weapons to resist it. Classic liberal theory argues for popular resistance against tyranny, but leaves the citizens helpless to effect it. This dilemma has been accentuated by the development of modern weapons technology which has created an enormous and ever-increasing gap between the military power of the state and the military potential of popular resistance.


# V

# SANCTION, PUNISHMENT AND DETERRENCE

Internal use of force by the liberal state has another vital function. The state must ensure that the law is enforced. 'It is essential to the idea of a law', argues Hamilton, 'that it be attended with a sanction; or, in other words, a penalty or punishment for disobedience, the resolutions or commands which pretend to be laws will, in fact, amount to nothing more than advice or recommendation.'[28]

States cannot choose their citizens, and, in the nature of things, all states will have to deal with a percentage of criminally inclined, unreasonable and selfish members of the population. It is this basically unselective nature of the political community that makes it so essential that the law should be backed up by the sanction of force. Sometimes moral pressure and ostracism suffices to induce conformity to rules. According to most accounts such methods are, for example, extensively used in Communist China. But no modern state, not even China, has been able to dispense entirely with imprisonment and other physical sanctions against law-breakers.

The somewhat pious hopes of utopians that society might progress to such a state of loving harmony that ideas of crime and punishment could be discarded do not accord with the realist view of human nature underlying liberal philosophy. It man is neither beast nor angel but a free-willing agent bearing the burden and freedom of moral responsibility for his actions he must surely be free to decide to break the law. We must, of course, accept the possibility of unintended infringements of the law through ignorance: in such cases there is no criminal intent although a crime may have been committed in the eyes of the law. It follows from the notion of individual moral responsibility that one has a right to punishment for breaking the law, a penalty appropriate to the scale of punishments laid down for the offence in question. Now before the armchair radicals begin to scream about the absurdity of 'a right to punishment' let us recall that this is indeed the logical basis of that method of protest known as civil disobedience. The aim of those committing civil disobedience is to demonstrate the intensity of their moral objection to a particular law or policy, and their willingness to bear the martyrdom of prosecution, conviction and punishment in order to get the law or policy changed. It is a form of moral pressure freely undertaken by free men. Hence the notion of punishment is a necessary concomitant of the value of personal freedom.

There is not space here to include a lengthy disquisition on punishment.[29] It is worth observing, however, that the debate concerning justifications for punishment has been somewhat clouded by obsession with the argument from deterrence, the idea that the risk of punishment actively discourages criminals or potential criminals from committing offences. It is well known that it is difficult, if not impossible, to calculate precisely the extent to which particular punishments discourage or fail to discourage particular offences (witness the conflicting evidence concerning the effectiveness of capital punishment as a deterrent against murder). Far stronger than the argument from deterrence of particular classes of criminals is the case that the existence of punishments acts as a general preventive against law-breaking by society in general. The grave visage presented by the whole system of law and punishment soon enters the awareness of every new generation. Most children become socialised or inducted into the whole notion of formal punishment very early in life in home and school. Suppose one were to remove the whole back-up of punishment from the legal system. In my submission this would be to run the grave risk of removing all respect for legally constituted authority. The ordinary man-in-the-street would no longer take the laws of the country seriously, and society would have taken another step closer to disintegration. Thus there is a powerful argument for the retention of punishments as legal sanctions in the liberal state: their existence can be seen to reinforce and sustain the process whereby society as a whole learns to be law-abiding.

A further possible argument from social utility is that, even if only in a small number of cases, experience of punishment may have a reformative or rehabilitative influence on the criminal. It is not necessary to show that this is effective in the case of the majority of criminals. However if it can be shown, as some have confidently claimed,[30] that rehabilitation and reformation of character has taken place directly as the result of the penal process, and that restoration of the individual to a useful and law-abiding life in society could not have been achieved in any other way, then this powerfully reinforces the case for the continuing value of punishment in the liberal society.

The retributive argument for punishment seems to me the least convincing and is surely highly unattractive. For the idea that society should wreak vengeance on an individual for his crime seems even more primitive and barbaric than *lex talionis*. After all the latter was a crude and fairly effective device for resolving disputes in a primitive legal system. Vengeance for vengeance's sake, however, is an appeal to the basest passions of cruelty and hatred and a recipe for perpetual violence and counter-violence more closely resembling a blood feud than a system of law.

# VI
# VIOLENCE DEFINED

I have argued earlier in favour of maintaining the traditional distinction in usage between force and violence as authorised and unauthorised forms of coercion. A more adequate definition of violence must now be attempted for, as Raymond Williams sensibly reminds us, this term 'needs early specific definition, if it is not (as in yet another sense), to be done violence to — to be wrenched from its meaning or significance.'[31] Much difficulty and confusion arises from rhetorical and figurative uses of the term, for example to describe severe poverty, underprivilege and discrimination. Of course for many people in the world these are the most desperately urgent problems and it is understandable that their leaders and spokesmen often resort to fiery and violent language. Is it not preferable that they restrict their violence to language? Experience suggests this is too sanguine a view. Even the leaders of avowedly non-violent movements have found it difficult to contain and control the effects of emotive propaganda. Others, of course, have no such inhibitions and freely resort to such means to incite and intensify hatred and to encourage physical violence.

The U.S. National Commission report on violence, unfortunately in my view, dropped the distinction between force as the legitimate use of state power to prevent, restrain or punish breaches of the law, and violence which lacks the legitimation of constitutional and legal sanction and which is therefore essentially arbitrary. However it made a valuable move to greater precision by its insistence on defining violence as direct, or threatened physical injury or damage.

In the present study violence is defined as the illegitimate use or threatened use of coercion resulting, or intended to result in, the death, injury, restraint or intimidation of persons or the destruction or seizure of property. This definition has several advantages: it does not confuse the capacity to inflict violence with its actual infliction, and it implies a clear distinction between physical violence and aggressive and emotive rhetoric. In my view, it is vital to make these distinctions clear if there is to be serious public discourse or scholarly investigation concerning the problem of violence.


# VII
# MODES OF CONFLICT, OPPOSITION AND PROTEST

When violence is defined in this more precise way it can readily be distinguished from a whole range of non-violent modes of political conflict ranging from political dissent and argument and informal and formalised opposition, to party and electoral competition, lobbying, protest and demonstration, conscientious objection and civil disobedience.

Pluralist liberal theory recognised the inevitability of faction and interest and made them the very stuff of constitutional government:

> The latent causes of faction are thus sown in the nature of man; and we see them everywhere brought into different degrees of activity, according to the different circumstances of civil society. . . The regulation of these various and interfering interests forms the principal task of modern legislation and involves the spirit of party and faction in the necessary and ordinary operations of government.[32]

Yet Madison also believed that one must guard against the mischievous effects of faction. Anticipating the fears of de Tocqueville and J. S. Mill concerning the possible tyranny of the majority, he argued that the most potentially dangerous development would occur 'when a majority is included in a faction'. Such a faction could capture control of the government and 'sacrifice to its ruling passion or interest both the public good and the rights of other citizens'.[33] But he believed that this danger was less likely to occur under a republican and federal constitution in which, he assumed, a wider variety of parties and interests would be able to check and balance each other at national and local levels. Hence hegemony by a single party, interest or sect could be avoided.

The history of modern liberal democracies to a surprising extent bears out Madison's confident optimism. And the forces of political pluralism have brought other side-benefits which went largely un-recognised in Madison's somewhat jaundiced assessment of factions and parties. The competition between parties for national con-stituencies of support among an increasingly politically informed and sophisticated public helped to encourage more effective national policies, leadership and efficient government. At least electorates now had some measure of choice of programmes and government personnel. Moreover formalised party opposition in the legislature became a major instrument, in combination with extra-parliamentary lobbying and consultation, for subjecting the government of the day to constant surveillance and criticism. Even at the levels of policy debate, the constant clash and testing of ideas, and day-to-day scrutiny of the conduct of administration, the existence of a mul-tiplicity of parties and groups can be seen to serve an invaluable function for liberal democracy.

And yet, critics of liberal democracy will maintain, the success of all these parliamentary and electoral methods depends upon the willingness of all members of the society to accept the ultimate decisions of government and legislature as authoritative and binding for all. But does not the system break down when a vocal majority or minority group in the community refuse to accept or abide by a particular law or policy determined by the government? Are there any alternatives to violent confrontation in such circumstances? Many crypto-revolutionaries are all too ready in such crises to prepare for the death dance of democracy. Almost invariably their cries of doom are shown to be premature. For the great strength of liberal democracies is their capacity for peaceful internal change. Governments and parties constantly adapt and move their positions in response to the winds and storms of a changing environment and opinion. The internal dynamics of large-scale opinion changes and the influence of changing popular attitudes and events on policy-makers are as yet too little understood by social scientists. But the toughness of liberal democratic systems in grave crises in the past can be attested to by historians. Time and again doom has been predicted as a result of some fresh economic cataclysm, some major shift in power or a reverse in foreign policy, and yet the crises have been weathered and the vultures of doom have returned hungrily to their perches.

The real secret of the inner political resilience and adaptability of liberal democracies, so often overlooked, is their capacity to tolerate, respond to, and harness the forces of popular protest and discontent. Modes of conflict exist which are essentially non-violent, un-institutionalised and spontaneous, and which can afford even the most disadvantaged groups in society powerful levers of political, moral and even economic pressure upon government leaders and élite groups. Such means include, for example, strike action, go-slows, and works to rule by industrial workers. (It should be recalled that strikes and other forms of trade union pressure have been used effectively not only to win concessions and rights from specific employers, but also as a means of opposing government legislation, as was the case with the Industrial Relations Act in Britain.) Mass economic boycotts have been used successfully, for example by the civil rights movement in the United States. A now time-honoured and powerfully influential mode of political and moral pressure is the mass campaign of marches, processions, demonstrations, mass meetings and sit-ins, inevitably coupled with massive media publicity and pressure on government personnel and political parties. A recent successful example was the campaign against American participation in the Vietnam War. Modern media technology has vastly augmented and intensified the potential impact of such mass campaigns of protest and reform, but the underlying conceptions of grass-roots moral and political crusading have been a feature of western political systems since the days of the anti-slavery and franchise reform movements of the nineteenth century. All these great reform movements achieved their purposes by non-violent protest. (Those violent incidents that did occur in the course of these campaigns were essentially caused by peripheral hooliganism or by over-reaction and panic by the authorities.)

And suppose these well-tried methods of political and moral pressure fail, what then? There are still two further non-violent courses open to those individuals or groups who wish to oppose and resist particular laws or policies of government on grounds of moral conviction or conscience: conscientious objection and civil disobedience. Conscientious objection is an individual refusal to obey a particular policy, law or command on the ground that compliance would entail an action contrary to the objector's moral or religious beliefs. It is an inherently non-violent means of individual resistance to authority, though it may, on occasion, stimulate a violent or repressive response by the authorities or by members of the community hostile to the objector's position. Civil disobedience may be employed by individuals or groups for one or more of the following purposes: to signify their principled opposition to particular laws or commands by deliberately flouting the laws concerned; as a means of dramatising a more general moral or political protest concerning an issue quite unconnected with the particular laws disobeyed; as a general tactic of passive resistance, for example a general refusal to co-operate with the forces of an occupying power.

It is clear that none of these tactics entails violence by those who adopt them, though there may be strong grounds for assuming that they will provoke a violent response. Conscientious objection and limited acts of civil disobedience directed against specific policies or laws do not involve a comprehensive rejection of legal authority. Indeed their very efficacy as tactics of moral pressure *depends* upon the due processes of law and punishment taking place in order to convey the message of moral sacrifice and 'martyrdom'. The third type of civil disobedience distinguished above, mass passive resistance, is, on the other hand, potentially a far more serious and direct form of challenge to authority. It has been canvassed as a potentially valuable weapon for revolutionaries, and as technique of territorial defence.[34]

Civil disobedience on a large scale becomes revolutionary when it is used to overthrow an existing system and establish a revolutionary régime, and when it is employed to coerce opposing and uncommitted elements into submitting to the revolutionary will. In the context of civil disobedience in a liberal state van den Haag's distinction between persuasive and coercive civil disobedience is therefore quite crucial.[35] Persuasive civil disobedience, however embarrassing or inconvenient it may be for the authorities, is a legitimate and tolerable expression of extreme dissent in a free society. Free men and women may surely choose to break the law in the hope of persuading their fellow citizens to change their views or to alter laws. And *provided* that those who take this course are prepared to accept the punishments meted out for their offences by due process of law, and provided that they do not attempt to coerce or intimidate their fellow citizens, then no contradiction with liberal democratic principle is implied. In a free society there is surely an implicit right to choose to break the law. But the resort to political violence, blackmail and intimidation, *is* incompatible with the rule of law and with liberal democratic theory. Coercive civil disobedience threatens to subvert the authority of the legally elected government and replace it by the will of an illegal minority.

I entirely agree with van den Haag's conclusion that civil disobedience cannot be justified 'if the issue is of less than overwhelming moral importance or if persuasion by legal means is possible and not altogether hopeless'.[36] It is striking, however, that the stringent conditions van den Haag stipulates as justification for civil disobedience are by no means as rare as he seems to imply in modern liberal democracies. Van den Haag claims that the citizen is only morally justified in deliberately disobeying legitimate authority if:

a) the protested law is morally intolerable to him; b) it is not likely to be remedied otherwise; c) the effects of the law are not revokable by probable or possible later correction; d) the totality of the expected effects of civil disobedience under the circumstances is, in his view, morally preferable to the totality of expected effects of any of the courses available under the law.[37]

The sad fact is that these conditions hold for numerous minority groups, particularly ethnic minorities, within the liberal democratic states. In situations of strained or worsening communal relations, and where there is danger of protracted communal conflicts, many group militants *will tend to perceive their situation* in van den Haag's terms even if this does not square with objective reality. In such conflict situations it is surely far preferable that they should canalise their protest into non-violent persuasive civil disobedience than into mayhem and destruction.

In sum I wish to argue that an operative liberal democratic society must learn to afford and tolerate high levels of protest, turbulence and extra-parliamentary agitation. In a complex society, with rapidly changing needs and political demands and slow-moving and frequently insensitive bureaucracy and political leadership, protest is more than simply a safety valve: it should be regarded as a valuable mode of political communication, criticism and democratic consultation in its own right. In the case of a liberal democratic government with politically shrewd, intelligent and imaginative leadership, peaceful protest and agitation should be seen as a legitimate and vital part of the engine of social reform.

Let us make no mistake: the alternatives can offer only a bleak and bloody future for the liberal state. If liberal democratic governments and societies try to suppress or ignore deeply felt needs and grievances then peaceful protests and agitation and passive civil disobedience are likely to give way rapidly to political violence. There are, of course, many vivid examples of a malignant growth of political violence and terrorism afflicting contemporary liberal states in varying degrees and forms.

In liberal democratic societies, where the rule of law and the full range of civil rights and liberties pertain, we are accustomed to assume that there will be no popular basis of support for violent rebellion or revolution. Campaigns of violence in such societies are generally attributed to tiny conspiratorial groups or criminal psychopaths. Frequently this is actually the case. But it would be foolish to overlook the fact that in many liberal states certain minority groups claim to have long-standing grievances against the majority institutions or against other groups. It is these aggrieved and allegedly underprivileged and alienated groups that constitute the potential constituencies for urban guerrilla movements. Such movements become a serious threat as soon as they begin to attract a degree of mass support, sympathy and tacit collaboration in particular strata.

It should therefore be a major objective of liberal states to identify and defuse such conflict situations long before they threaten to enter a violent phase. All legal means of opposition and pressure, and all available channels of communication and peaceful bargaining, should be employed in an effort to determine legitimate grievances and to remedy them by effective action. We should broaden our concept of internal defence to include the prompt and effective tackling of the problems of minorities. This is one positive way of helping to ensure that liberal states avoid the tragedies of generalised violence, terrorism and civil war which are so hard to stop and which can destroy the democratic system itself.

# VIII
# POLITICAL VIOLENCE:
# CHARACTERISTICS AND
# TYPOLOGY

We must now consider more closely the nature of the problem of political violence in the liberal state. Political violence is either the deliberate infliction or threat of infliction of physical injury or damage for political ends, or it is violence which occurs unintentionally in the course of severe political conflicts. We are still dealing with an extremely broad range of phenomena. It would surely be an act of sheer folly rather than mere hubris to attempt to explain all forms of political violence, ranging, say, from the intimidation of a professor for his alleged political views to acts of international war, in terms of a single grand scientific theory. We must bear in mind the enormous differences in scale, intensity, duration and effects, between small group violence and the large-scale collective violence of modern total war, which can engulf continents.

The social anthropologist Edmund Leach has suggested that we can usefully distinguish three aspects of human behaviour: (i) natural biological activities of the human body; (ii) technical actions (to alter the physical state of the external world); and (iii) expressive actions.[38] Violence does not really fit neatly under any of these heads for though individual acts may be interpreted as having a purely instrumental or symbolic significance, the *context* of collective violence is far more complex and is less susceptible to such simple distinctions. Wars, revolutions and riots have the character of cataclasms or even of cataclysms for many of those caught up in them. Many are swept along by these tides of violence and destruction and are literally driven into fighting for the defence of family and community. Critics have roundly attacked Lorenz's theory of the 'aggressive instinct'[39] and the crude determinism and social darwinist assumptions of works such as Trotter's *The Instincts of the Herd in Peace and War*. Fromm's hypothesis of an individual flight instinct[40] would seem more credible. Yet at very least one must allow that much intra-specific violence takes place in the context of a generalised *collective* violence in which a whole community or group feels impelled to make a violent response to attacks by a perceived enemy.

Political violence is particularly difficult to classify and analyse because it frequently involves the interaction and effects of the actions of many persons and collectives involving a multiplicity of motivations, psychological effects and subjective evaluations, among those involved. Hence, although it is often claimed that an act of violence is trying to 'say something',[41] violence is a singularly clumsy and ambiguous mode of communication. It is one thing to convey hatred, vengeance and rage: it is quite another to communicate a more complex political message about power structures, and constitutional and policy issues. The purely symbolic or expressive act of violence is rare, for even 'propaganda of the deed' often strikes down victims, harms innocents and damages property. And generally such acts stimulate further violence and counterviolence. Therefore most political violence serves both instrumental and expressive functions simultaneously. Almost invariably the 'price' of relaying a message of terror to a 'target audience' is the death, injury or dispossession of victims whose rights and liberties have been arbitrarily curtailed by the perpetrators of violence.

Two further general characteristics of violence render it a peculiarly dangerous disease for a political community, and one which is especially difficult to cure. First, it is extremely difficult for its promoters and perpetrators to control. The wrong targets may be hit. Opponents and third parties may respond in unanticipated ways, and what had been planned as small attacks with limited objectives may provoke a much wider conflict or general repression. Second, many of the immediate physical effects of political violence – death, maiming, destruction – are irreversible and cannot be atoned. Hence reconciliation and compromise, the cement of normal politics, becomes less and less attainable the longer political violence continues.

It is perhaps due to the generality and ambiguity of the concept that few attempts have been made to produce a comprehensive typology of political violence. One of the most valuable and much-discussed is the scheme proposed by Professor Samuel Huntington.[42] I have sought to utilise some of his suggestions in the framework sketched below.

The basis of the typology adopted in Table 1 is the scale and intensity of the political violence. By *scale* is meant the total numbers of persons involved, the physical extent of their area of operation, the political stakes involved in the conflict, and the significance of the level of violence in the international system. Major indicators of *intensity* would be the duration of the violence, the number of casualties caused, and the amount of fire-power and weaponry employed.

Two 'ladders', each consisting of seven 'rungs' of scale and intensity, are identified, one for mass violence and the other for small group political violence. An 'escalation ladder' model is clearly implied, suggesting that violence is likely to escalate rung by rung to higher levels of intensity. No theory is offered at this juncture to explain the causes or dynamics of escalation or de-escalation. Nor do I wish, at this stage, to attempt to theorise about the possible interrelationships between the two sets of scales. While analogies may be discernable there is no ground on our present knowledge for assuming that small group violence is either causally related to levels of mass violence (or vice versa), or that in any developmental model

Table 1

*Escalation ladders showing the rising scale of intensities of mass and small group political violence*

| Mass Political Violence | Small Group Political Violence |
| --- | --- |
| Riots and street violence | Isolated acts of sabotage or attacks on property |
| Armed rebellion or resistance | Isolated assassination attempts |
| Revolution or counter-revolution | Political gang warfare and feuds |
| State or mass terror and repression | Political terrorism |
| Civil war | Localised or small-scale guerrilla operations |
| Limited war | International or transnational terrorism |
| Nuclear war | Guerrilla raids on foreign states |

of mass violence, small group violence necessarily precedes the former (or vice versa).

A very different kind of typology is proposed in Table 2. It is based on the different major general political purposes or aims that political violence may serve. In this case there is no model or relationship between the types implicit. As some of the terms are not

Table 2

*Classification of types of political violence by general aims or purposes*

| Type | General Aims or Purposes |
|---|---|
| 1. Inter-communal | Defence or furtherance of alleged group interests in conflicts with rival ethnic or religious groups |
| 2. Remonstrative | Expression of anger and protest: can be used to persuade government to remedy grievances |
| 3. Praetorian | Used to coerce changes in government leadership and policy |
| 4. Repression | Quelling actual or potential opposition and dissent |
| 5. Resistance | To oppose and prevent a government establishing authority and executing its laws |
| 6. Terroristic | Use of systematic murder and destruction, or threats of murder and destruction to terrorise targets or victims into conceding the terrorists' political aims |
| 7. Revolutionary<br>8. Counter-revolutionary | Overthrow of existing political system and its replacement by a new régime: note that leaders of this type of violence are often prepared to exploit all types of political violence, including war |
| 9. War | To gain political ends by means of military victory over opponents |

self-explanatory, column 2 gives brief definitions of the aims involved. Needless to say, these types of political violence are rarely
to be found in their pure form in the real world. Most violent states,
movements or groups employ violence simultaneously at several
different levels for their political ends. For example terroristic
violence is a thread running through modern war, revolution and internal political struggles in the contemporary history of many countries. And in many régimes concurrent traditions of inter-communal,
remonstrative, praetorian and repressive violence have wrought
endemic instability. There is clearly a need for sub-typologies under
these very general heads, and some contributions on these lines are
offered in later sections of the present work. In particular, attention
is given to the concept and typology of terrorism, as a vital
preparatory step to the closer analysis of terrorism in Parts II and
III.


# IX
# CAUSES OF POLITICAL VIOLENCE
# IN LIBERAL STATES

Terrorism is clearly only one of the many possible types of political
violence that can erupt in a liberal state. It is one of the forms which
sometimes quite tiny groups may use to attack even the most stable
liberal states, those enjoying a high degree of popular support and
legitimacy. But first I shall briefly consider the underlying causes of
political violence in liberal states, the tangled problem of justification, and the identification of those general principles of internal
defence against violence which liberal democratic theory affords.

It has already been emphasised that the most serious threats of
violence facing liberal states internally are those which directly en-
danger the survival and stability of the liberal constitution itself, and
those which indirectly and cumulatively undermine the state's
authority and support through major defiance of law and order and
by endangering the lives of citizens to the point where confidence in
the authorities is eroded. In reasonably secure and well-established
liberal democracies these really dangerous levels of internal political
violence are only likely to occur if there is mass disaffection among

large sectors of the population, combined with large-scale popular support for resort to violence in defiance of the state. How invaluable it would be if we could satisfactorily explain how mass disaffection and willingness to resort to violence occurs! Unfortunately, many of the so-called theories of collective violence turn out to be nothing more than crude models, merely positing a possible relationship between variables. Others are merely statements of the *correlates* of human violence, or checklists of fertile conditions for violence or of possible precipitating or triggering situations. Most attempts to construct a social scientific theory of collective violence either totally neglect or gravely underestimate the influence of differing ideologies, beliefs and perceptions in inciting hatred and hostility and in the instigation of political conflict.

Arguably the most influential theoretical approach in modern social-science theory of the causes of violence has developed on the basis of the work of the psychologist, Dr John Dollard. Dollard, a product of the American Purposive Psychology School (inspired by the earlier work of McDougall and Lloyd Morgan), produced, in 1939, a theory of frustration–aggression. He claimed to have proved that humans only become violent if they are frustrated in their efforts to attain a particular goal: severe frustration leads to anger and anger to acts of aggressive violence. Initially, Dollard and his collaborators used the term 'frustration' in the narrower sense of the hindering or interrupting of an actual process of goal-attainment already embarked upon. More recently the term has been employed much more loosely by the relative deprivation theorists to cover any case of unrealised desire or need. Hence one of the major exponents of relative deprivation theory defines relative deprivation as:

Actors' perception of discrepancy between their value expectations and their environment's apparent value capabilities. Value expectations are the goods and conditions of life to which people believe they are justifiably entitled. The referents of value capabilities are to be found largely in the social and physical environment: they are the conditions that determine people's perceived chances of getting or keeping the values they legitimately expect to obtain.[43]

We have left the caution and precision of Dollard's original laboratory experiments far behind. For it becomes clear that whatever the notions of a collective sense of frustration or relative deprivation may convey to us, they are not precisely definable or objectively measurable qualities. Collective rage and violence are not necessarily a summation of individual frustrations but may, in large part, be a function of changing ideologies, beliefs and historical conditions which so materially affect social conceptions of justice and legitimacy. It is not really surprising, in the light of these imprecise and unproven initial assumptions, that relative deprivation theory is quite unable to explain how this ill-defined collective frustration and anger becomes converted into specific manifestations of political violence. In truth it provides only a very crude model concerning the causation of collective violence, but does not approach meeting the requirements for a scientific theory.

Of course it has been realised, since ancient times, that a sense of suddenly worsening deprivation, injustice or oppression, is often a major precondition of political violence. But the idea of a revolution of rising expectations in which a people's sense of deprivation and outrage may increase *despite* objective improvements in their material situation as a result of a dramatic raising of hopes, is relatively modern. De Tocqueville, in *L'Ancien Régime et la Révolution,* was probably the first to articulate this hypothesis:

> It is not always by going from bad to worse that a country falls into a revolution. It happens most frequently that a people, which had supported the most crushing laws without complaint, and apparently as if they were unfelt, throws them off with violence as soon as the burden begins to be diminished. The state of things destroyed by a revolution is almost always somewhat better than that which immediately preceded it; and experience has shown that the most dangerous moment for a bad government is usually that when it enters upon the work of reform . . . The evils which were endured with patience so long as they were inevitable seem intolerable as soon as a hope can be entertained of escaping from them. The abuses which are removed seem to lay bare those which remain, and to render the sense of them more acute; the evil has decreased, it is true, but the perception of the evil is more keen.[44]

Four basic models of relative deprivation have been explored and refined by modern theorists:[45] (i) capabilities remaining static while expectations rise; (ii) rising capabilities overtaken by rising expectations; (iii) the so-called J-curve situation, in which capabilities keep pace with expectations for a period and then suddenly drop behind; and (iv) general socio-economic malaise which may cause a dramatic fall in capabilities while expectations remain constant. It is easy to see that all the conditions posited might have potentially destabilising consequences for a political system. But the relative deprivation literature still has little to tell us about *how* the crucial changes in expectations are actually caused. Nor does it satisfactorily relate levels of relative deprivation to major political conflicts, or to changes in the distribution of political power.

Some writers on relative deprivation theory shrewdly broaden their concept of deprivation to encompass political values and rights. Some would argue that this form of deprivation is more likely than any other factor to lead to political violence. Feliks Gross, for example, gives high priority to the role of mass perceptions of ethnic and political oppression and injustice, and he argues that historically it is periods of intense politico-ideological tensions rather than those marked by inequalities which are most conducive to violence.[46] And T. A. Critchley concludes his discussion of causes of political violence in Britain by emphasising this point: 'Whenever in a civilised state a substantial section of the community has reason to feel, on racial, social, or religious grounds, that it is under-privileged or otherwise deprived of elementary political rights, its protest is likely to take the form of direct action.'[47]

I wish to suggest that there is no advantage in trying to conflate all forms of perceived deprivation and injustice under the umbrella of relative deprivation. For there simply is no general theory which satisfactorily relates or explains these perceptions of grievance and injustice. A more modest but, I hope, practical proposal is that we frankly recognise the lack of any adequate general scientific theory of the necessary and sufficient conditions for political violence. It is possible, however, to identify some of the most frequent contributory causes of internal political violence, constantly recurring in the recorded history of political conflict and challenging both our attention and our powers of explanation and analysis: (i) ethnic conflicts, hatreds, discrimination and oppression; (ii) religious and ideological conflicts, hatreds, discrimination and oppression; (iii) socio-economic relative deprivation; (iv) stresses and strains of rapid modernisation tending to accentuate (iii);[48] (v) perceived political inequalities, infringements of rights, injustice or oppression; (vi) lack of adequate channels for peaceful communication of protests, grievances and demands (e.g. denial of franchise or other rights of participation, representation or access to media); (vii) existence of a tradition of violence, disaffection and popular turbulence; (viii) the availability of a revolutionary leadership equipped with a potentially attractive ideology;[49] (ix) weakness and ineptness of the government, police and judicial organs (e.g. under-reaction, over-reaction); (x) erosion of confidence in the régime, its values and institutions afflicting all levels of the population including the government; (xi) deep divisions within governing élites and leadership groups.[50] I shall be referring back to this checklist of general causes of internal political violence later in the discussion, and will also give separate consideration to the more specific causes of terrorist violence in particular. It may be objected here that it is unreal to distinguish between the causes of political violence and criminal violence. There is much evidence that the two are frequently interlinked and to some extent feed each other, with political groups and underworld associates exploiting each other in conditions of protracted civil strife. However, I believe it would be dangerous to confuse the underlying causes of the two. The history of crime yields copious examples of periods in which intensive criminal activities have proliferated without any accompanying political conflict or instability. Crime for private gain seems to result from far more deep-seated, discrete and universal features of the human condition. We shall later consider the linkages that exist between war, revolution, repression, terrorism and criminality.

# X
# CAN POLITICAL VIOLENCE EVER BE MORALLY JUSTIFIED IN A LIBERAL STATE?

To partially explain acts of political violence is not necessarily to justify them. Under what circumstances, if any, is resort to political violence justified within an operative liberal democracy? The categorical 'no' given by T. H. Green in his *Lectures on Political*

*Obligation* in answer to this question is too facile, too much a product perhaps of that smug complacency of Victorian England which, we have earlier noted, was also reflected in the writings of Mill. Perhaps we should forgive the natural pride of the mid and late Victorians in what they generally regarded as their model of progressive constitutional democracy. But, alas, there are large pockets of injustice, discrimination, under-privilege and exploitation in even the greatest of democracies. And can we really say to those who do not enjoy the *basic* civil rights (e.g. the franchise, equality under the law) 'You who are outside the political community of citizens yet dwell and labour in our midst have no moral right to take direct action to secure democratic rights'? Had the slaves of the American South no moral right to rebel against their owners and the system that exploited them? Those who are the subjects of a liberal state, but who are not admitted to its rights of citizenship cannot be morally bound to obedience to the state. They are not bound by political obligation for they have not been accorded any rights by the state.

It may be objected that a state in which the majority does not enjoy citizenship is not in any case a liberal democracy in the true sense of these terms. It may be that a ruling group, as is the case with the whites in South Africa, accord themselves the rights of an Athenian minority confining democratic procedures and participation to their own minority affairs. But it does not follow that in such conditions the subject majority population owes any duty of obedience to their rulers, whatever massive resources the latter may employ to coerce their obedience. It may be argued that on prudential grounds the majority may be well advised to avoid confrontation when the forces of the state enjoy a huge power advantage. Majority leaders need to weigh the chances of victory for their just rebellion against the possible loss of life that might ensue from defeat and retribution at the hands of the régime.

In strict terms where a majority is subjected to tyrannical or despotic rule by a minority the minority is imposing its sovereignty by violence and therefore can be legitimately opposed by the force of just rebellion or resistance by the majority. By definition such a purely coercive régime cannot be a lawful liberal democratic state, and therefore majority opposition to it cannot be regarded as seditious or violent according to the liberal democratic principles we have earlier defined.

There are at least two sets of circumstances, however, in which a *prima facie* case can be made for the morally justifiable resort to political violence by a minority within a liberal democratic state. Firstly, there is the case of the minority whose basic rights and liberties are denied or taken away by arbitrary action of the government or its agencies. A clearcut example is the case of the U.S. citizens of Japanese descent illegally interned by the U.S. authorities in clear violation of the Constitution. The second case arises when one minority is attacked by another minority and does not receive adequate protection from the state and its forces of law and order. In such circumstances the attacked minority community may have little alternative but to resort to violence in order to defend itself. Both these situations of political violence result from the gross ineptitude or dereliction of the state. Fortunately such conditions have been the exception rather than the rule in most Western liberal democracies.

When, as is generally the case in liberal democracies, aggrieved minorities enjoy full protection and rights of participation in the liberal state, and their enjoyment of these rights is not under attack either by the state or by other groups or factions, violence for political ends *cannot* be morally justified. It can never be right for minorities — however intensely they may desire to realise particular aims or to redress specific grievances — to use violence to try to coerce the majority or the government into submitting to their demands. They are entitled to use to the full the normal channels of democratic argument, opposition and lobbying through the political parties, pressure groups, the media and peaceful protest. But they must limit themselves to persuasion, negotiation and peaceful bargaining. And if persuasion through the ballot box, lobbying and peaceful demonstration ultimately fails to win the minority's objectives, then, according to the tested principles of liberal democracy, they must abide by the democratic decision of the majority.

Except in the very extreme and rare cases we have already identified, therefore, political violence in a liberal democratic state must be regarded as intolerable. If violence becomes the accepted or normal means for groups to gain political objectives within a state one can say goodbye to liberal democracy. To be effective a liberal state must not foster civil violence: it must conquer it.

## XI
# THE PROPER USE OF FORCE IN THE LIBERAL STATE

We have seen that there are circumstances when it is not only justifiable for the state and citizens to use force but also positively obligatory. Citizens have a duty, for example, to assist the state in defence of the community against external attack. And there are clear obligations to defend and uphold the constitution and enforce the laws. It has been observed earlier in this discussion that there may also be circumstances in which the citizens may have a moral obligation to use force unilaterally against leaders or state officials who have seriously derogated from, subverted, or overturned the liberal democratic constitution. The problem of the right use of force, however, raises not only issues of moral legitimacy and legality but also some difficult questions concerning the *way* in which force should be employed. Who should be entrusted with the execution of force? How *much* force should be used?

In the case of external attack the normal agency of the state responsible for defence is the armed forces, and in a democracy both government and citizens will expect these defence forces to use whatever force is required to repel attack and defeat the enemy. Moreover it is a cardinal and long-standing principle of democratic government that the armed services should be firmly under ultimate civil control by the democratically responsible government. But responsibility for tasks of internal security has been a matter of serious contention in many liberal states. Should the civil police take on the job as a natural extension of their police law-enforcement function? Should responsibility be shared by police and army, the latter being called in to tackle the more serious outbreaks of political violence and unrest? Or should there be a 'third force', on the model of the French C.R.S., specially designated, trained and equipped to tackle domestic political violence? The precise formula adopted has tended to vary widely in accordance with constitutional and juridical traditions. Clear advantage may be gained from a tradition of unarmed police using low-profile and gentle methods and maintaining public support and sympathetic co-operation. These benefits must, however, be weighed against the concomitant lack of decisive physical superiority and firepower necessary to defeat armed insurgents. Britain's police services have moved, in the last fifteen years, to a much more sophisticated combination of traditional unarmed policing together with specialist and armed police units. In all liberal democracies the army is regarded as the last line of defence against internal disorders, and various constitutional and legal formulas exist to invoke their aid to the civil power in severe disturbances and emergencies. However, whatever the balance of forces deployed by the state to deal with internal violence (and we shall be examining some of their alleged merits and disadvantages later), there are certain basic principles which must govern the use of such force by the liberal state.

First and foremost security agencies must operate entirely within the framework of law. If they defy the rule of law under the pretence of protecting it they undermine the integrity, authority and public respect for the law which is essential to the continuance of constitutional democracy. Some individual sections and members of police and security forces will be tempted to accrete extra-legal powers and to hide behind the shield of 'superior orders' and 'security interests'. Others may unwittingly be misled, in the absence of clearly defined legal responsibilities and procedures, into taking actions which expose them to civil actions and public prosecutions. The most evil and dangerous consequence that may follow from repeated overturning of the rule of law is the establishment of the power-hungry security apparatus which acquires an appetite for extra-judicial reprisal. Alas Solzhenitsyn was too sanguine in assuming that 'the only punitive organ in human history that combined in one set of hands investigation, arrest, interrogation, prosecution, trial and execution of the verdict' was the Cheka.[51] Democracies have no magical immunity against such cancerous growths, and their citizens and political leaders have a duty to ensure that police and security services operate within the constitution and the law. It is noteworthy that the recent Church Committee investigation into the U.S. Secret Services' activities, while admitting the difficult problems entailed in firm political control and surveillance of such operations, repeatedly spells out the importance of this lesson for the health of the U.S. political system.

The clear corollary of operating within the rule of law is the maintenance of absolutely clear and firm democratic control over police and security services and operations. Some modern counter-insurgency specialists constantly reiterate their demand for these services to be kept under a single unified control.[52] Whereas a case may be made out for this on the grounds of economy of resources, secrecy and effectiveness, we should also recognise the dangers inherent in such a unified structure. There are obvious traditional weaknesses of administrative centralisation such as bureaucratic remoteness, insensitivity and cumbersome decision-making procedures. Additional dangers may stem from a 'monopolist' security organisation abusing its power, losing its identification with local communities, and forfeiting invaluable popular trust and support.

The other major principle governing the right use of force by the liberal state is the doctrine of *minimal force*. This principle has been the predominant guide to the British police forces in the matter of political violence, throughout their history. In essence it has meant the use of the minimum force necessary to deter, restrain, or, if necessary, contain violence, and to preserve public order. To exercise the police function with such restraint inevitably calls for superb discipline and professionalism, a studied impartiality and neutrality in matters of political controversy, and considerable patience and moral courage.

Minimal force does not simply apply to crowd control and potentially violent or disruptive demonstrations and processions. The essential principle can also be applied to armed response to armed violence. In such circumstances the aims of minimal force must be to protect the public, to bring about the rapid disarming and peaceful surrender of the armed persons involved, and to bring them before the courts on criminal charges. Contrast the purely military aim in time of war of identifying the enemy and shooting them on sight. One of the reasons why soldiers find it so onerous and unnatural to take on a constabulary minimal-force role is that it is essentially alien to their military training and ethos.

But can minimal force really work effectively when the security forces face a sizable number of heavily armed and ruthless insurgents? Historical experience indicates that liberal states need to react much more positively and forcefully to defeat armed revolutionaries, guerrillas and terrorists. In what is, after all, an internal war situation, the forces of the state have to be empowered to take war measures, to go over to the offensive and to use all military means necessary to defeat a direct challenge to the survival of the state. I would argue that the doctrine of minimal force is only really effective in circumstances where there is a relatively high degree of political consensus and social cohesion, co-operation and discipline. It fails to work where large sections of the population deny the legitimacy of the state, and where many view the police and army as alien, hostile and oppressive. T. A. Critchley vividly conveys the minimal force ethos traditional in the British constabulary:

> From the start, when they were first practising non-violent methods of crowd control against the Reform Bill demonstrators and the Chartists, the police have been wholly dependent for their success on the continuing approval and goodwill of the public, and they are now as mild as it is possible for them to be while yet remaining a force capable of protecting people against criminals and governments against minority groups. They rely on a controlled application of force, scrupulously careful to offer no provocation. The *bona fides* of protestors are taken for granted, unless there is proof to the contrary.
>
> The police – it cannot be stated too often – have never been, and are not today, a *corps d'élite* arrogantly lording it over the population. They regard themselves, and rightly, as citizens in uniform. [53]

It could be argued that recent experience of industrial picketing and demonstrations has borne out the value of the minimal force doctrine in the context of political protest and crowd control in mainland Britain. Clearly, of course, it has not sufficed for many years in Northern Ireland. And it is worth asking whether minimal force doctrine now has not in fact a declining relevance, even in mainland U.K., owing to the effects of major long-term social changes.

In explaining the relative internal peace that prevailed between mid-nineteenth and mid-twentieth century in Britain, Critchley stresses the following factors: (i) traditional British self-discipline; (ii) the decline of socio-economic motives for violence as popular demands were met; (iii) secularisation and the declining sharpness of religious differences; (iv) the virtual absence of racial prejudice; (v) the creation of a professional unarmed police on good terms with the general public; (vi) the growing availability of peaceful means of airing grievances and campaigning for demands (for example, trade unions, the popular Press and the franchise). There is some evidence for believing that conditions (i), (ii) and (iv) are increasingly less operative and that we should now be prepared for violence and disruption on the part of some radically alienated and increasingly hostile groups in our society. Critchley shrewdly observes, in a footnote, that 'a police force can hardly be disarmed until the populace which it serves has been disarmed'.[54] And he concedes that the United States has long needed its armed police to control an armed population. But, in the light of the presence of highly armed and desperate groups within British society, should we not question the assumptions underlying our own police posture and policy?

Nor is it simply a question of dangers of armed attacks and terrorism. Is there sufficient *minimal* force available to the state to contain really serious riots and disturbances? At a time of general economic crisis, when there is a call for swingeing cuts in public expenditure, obviously many voices will be heard resisting any increase in expenditure on police services, and a few will argue for cutting them back. It is important to remember that the community tends to get the kind of police service it deserves both in terms of public support and control, and the amount the community is prepared to spend on manpower and equipment. For example, the ceilings laid down for the full-time police establishment in major British cities are almost certainly too low. Just let us suppose that disturbances caused by major industrial picketing confrontations coincided with a number of terrorist bombing attacks involving the clearing of a busy shopping centre, and were accompanied by a serious outbreak of gang or race rioting in another quarter of the same city. How could any of our already overstretched police forces cope single-handed with such a situation? Of course, there is a system for injecting reserves from neighbouring forces and from the Special Constabulary and army in such emergencies. But suppose the emergency conditions become more widespread, affecting whole regions? This may sound like an obsessively gloomy scenario. But we should remember the large number of British cities that have been affected by a general worsening in race relations, and the rapidity with which industrial confrontation can spread, as for example in 1972, through the use of flying columns of pickets and national tactics of industrial disruption.

There is also a grave shortage of equipment and special skills and training in the riot control field. Shields, riot control helmets, water cannon and tear gas which are the stock in trade of many American and continental European police forces are going to be needed extensively in Britain in coming decades. These basic requirements will need to be supplemented by newer developments in riot control technology, such as improved armoured personnel carriers for the security forces and new temporarily incapacitating gases for crowd dispersal which have no permanently injurious side effects.[55] The unpleasant fact is that unless resources such as these are made rapidly and widely available to our police, the latter simply will not have the level of minimal force necessary to contain riots and disturbances that are likely to occur, despite the best efforts of government and social services, in our multi-ethnic and conflict-ridden, overcrowded cities. And it would be in circumstances where the police were clearly unable to cope that a government would be likely to take the grave step of calling in the army to aid the civil power in a widening range of situations of disorder. Alternatively there might be such strong political pressures in favour of establishing a special third force to deal with the disorders that they would prove politically irresistible.

In sum, I am arguing that while the doctrine of minimal force is a sensible and comfortably reassuring one for a democracy, we should be constantly critically re-examining our level of force in the light of changing threats and potentialities of violence within society. There is no room for complacency about the resources of the British police, for although there have been impressive improvements in their anti-terrorist capability and organisation they are woefully underprepared for the type of mass urban violence and race riots that, for example, afflicted American cities in the late 1960s, and which now loom in many British cities. And such outbreaks could well be accompanied by, or become a breeding ground for, political terrorism and other forms of political violence.

There is another reason why we should be conscious of the limitations of minimal force doctrine. We must avoid falling into the habit of believing that the possession of adequate force for legal sanctions and defence is sufficient unto the day, a panacea for all forms of social and political violence. Force may restrain or punish or defend but it cannot reconcile and heal:

Who overcomes
By force, hath overcome but half his foe.[56]

Positive political co-operation and unification require the building of allegiances, loyalties, trust and confidence and greater mutual understanding. Force cannot bring these things about, though certainly a restrained and humane use of force is less likely to destroy positive political co-operation than unrestrained and overwhelming force. But the necessary vehicles for bringing about positive political progress must be effective communication, dialogue and mutual education. To restore a parched and stricken political community one needs to irrigate it by replenishing or creating afresh the vital channels of political culture. As Fraser and others have shown,[57] the rigid segregation of schooling on sectarian lines and the enclosed, almost tribal, worlds of the conflicting groups in Northern Ireland help to perpetuate fresh generational sub-cultures of hatred and violence that wrack that province. The recent history of political violence in Ireland and many other countries shows very clearly that while force alone may succeed in *containing* violence in such conditions, for a time at any rate, it cannot really permanently end it. And a peaceful political settlement is meaningless if it is just a constitutional or legal formula lacking the basis of any genuine political goodwill and moral legitimacy among the people.

# XII
# TERROR AND TERRORISM:
# CONCEPTS, CHARACTERISTICS
# AND TYPOLOGY

We must now consider the slippery and much-abused concepts of terror and terrorism and their complex and often ambiguous relation to other forms of political violence and to criminality. Terror, to state a truism, is a subjective experience: we all have different 'thresholds' of extreme fear and tend to be more easily terrified by certain experiences, images and threats than by others. It is the interplay of these subjective factors and individual irrational, and often unconscious, responses that makes the state of terror, extreme fear or dread a peculiarly difficult concept for empirical social scientists to handle. It has been the tendency recently in the social sciences to shy away from the study of phenomena that are extremely difficult to define and almost impossible to measure. Furthermore the concepts of terror and terrorism have obviously very strong evaluative and emotive connotations.

Historians and political philosophers have not been so ready, however, to ignore the many real and significant individual and collective experiences of a state of terror. Nor have they neglected to study those leaders, régimes and movements responsible for developing explicit theories and policies of terrorism, or to attempt to assess the socio-economic and political conditions and consequences of terror.[58] For our purposes, however, it will be useful to make two preliminary distinctions: (i) between terror and terrorism; and (ii) between political terrorism and other forms of terrorism.

Much of our experience of terror is the unintended or epiphenomenal by-product of other happenings which are beyond our power to predict or control. Indeed inability to understand what is happening, say in a sudden automobile collision or a fire, is in itself a cause of more intense fear. And outbreaks of cataclysmic mass violence such as wars and revolutions inevitably bring a vast amount of epiphenomenal terror in their wake. This large-scale, and often sanguinary, epiphenomenal terror, should, of course, be clearly distinguished from the systematic régimes of terror which, for example, succeeded the French and Russian Revolutions. As E. V. Walter has shown, in a pioneering analysis,[59] régimes and processes of terror are phenomena of quite ancient lineage, and they are deliberately maintained even when it can be shown that they have counter-productive effects on the society in question. I wish therefore to maintain the distinction between epiphenomenal or incidental terror of the kind that frequently accompanies mass violence and the systematic terrorism of groups or régimes of terror in which the use of terror as a mode of psychological warfare is explicitly intended and planned.

Terrorism may not be politically motivated. Criminals have used it to obtain ransom and for other forms of private gain. Psychopaths have terrorised from motives they themselves may not fully understand. The bored, sadistic and weak-minded may terrorise to express their frustrations and hatreds in acts of symbolic protest and revenge against society: an appalling aesthetic explanation was attempted by Taillhade: 'Qu'importe les victimes, si le geste est beau!' Matters are complicated by the fact that criminals and psychopaths sometimes clothe themselves in political slogans of justification, and by the well-known propensity of terrorist movements to recruit assistance from, and to collaborate with, the criminal underworld.

However it is politically motivated terrorism with which the present work is primarily concerned. Political terrorism may be briefly defined as coercive intimidation. It is the systematic use of murder and destruction, and the threat of murder and destruction in order to terrorise individuals, groups, communities or governments into conceding to the terrorists' political demands. It is one of the oldest techniques of psychological warfare. A primary target for terrorisation is selected; the objective, or message to be conveyed, is determined; and credibility is established by convincing the target that the threat can actually be carried out. The victim or victims of the actual act of terrorist violence may or may not be the primary target, and the effects of relatively small amounts of violence will tend to be quite disproportionate in terms of the number of people terrorised: [60] in the words of an ancient Chinese proverb, 'Kill one, frighten ten thousand.'[61] As a modern American analyst has put it, the terrorist wants a lot of people watching rather than a lot of people dead. [62] Though this may hold for the relatively rare cases of 'pure' terrorism, such as mass hostage situations, repressive and revolutionary terror often result in the massacre of large numbers of people. Furthermore, strategic theories of terror as a psychological weapon assume a logic and symmetry in the rationale of the terrorist which is generally lacking in the real world. Terrorists are more often than not consumed with hatred against a perceived class or race 'enemy', and often deliberately attempt mass slaughter in public. Indeed this was advocated by the pioneer German terrorist theorist, Johannes Most, in the 1880s. It is a great mistake to assume that political terrorists will conform to some minimum standard of rationality and humanity. Clausewitz once remarked that war has its own language but not its own logic. The same is true of terrorism which is, after all, a kind of unconventional war.

We would do well to question not only the assumed rationality of the terrorists, but also the strategic rationale of terror as a weapon. It is easy to see how a terrorist can terrorise individual victims into submission when the latter are unarmed, captive and entirely at the mercy of the terrorists. But how can the terrorist be certain as to the effects of his act of violence on his primary target, his chosen audience? The target audience may well be frightened but this may galvanise them into self-defence or counter-measures against the source of terror. Far from automatically leading to a climate of collapse in which the primary target is prepared to surrender to the terrorists' demands, terrorism may lead to mobilisation and hardening of resolve to resist their demands and eliminate the terrorism. Terrorism, as someone has shrewdly remarked, is a faulty weapon that often backfires. Those who instigate it may find it leads to a wave of outrage and revulsion against them sweeping aside any latent or actual base of public support and sympathy for the terrorists' political cause. Or, in other conditions, it may lead to unanticipated spontaneous counter-violence and terror with vigilante or rival groups. Terrorists may then find themselves sucked into a kind of inter-communal or inter-movement struggle which effectively neutralises their effectiveness in influencing long-term constitutional or policy changes. Terrorists can also, paradoxically, be the unwitting agents providing the justification and the opportunity for governments and security forces to acquire the far-reaching emergency powers and systems of control which may be used to permanently suppress or exclude the terrorists' political movement from power.

In short, the theory of terrorism as a political weapon is based upon a number of assumptions about human behaviour which are either false or unproven: (i) that persons faced with threats to life and limb will ultimately always surrender their allegiances, principles or beliefs to save themselves; (ii) that terrorism invariably leads to terrorisation of the target and victims; and (iii) that consequently when they have been exposed to a given quotient of coercive intimidation they will inevitably suffer a collapse of will and submit to their persecutors. There is clearly a close parallel here with the theory of torture, i.e. that everyone has a final breaking point at which they will be prepared to tell all rather than suffer more. But again the torturer—tortured relationship is an individual one whereas the theory of terrorism posits a *collective* process of collapse and breakdown of will. In any case the historical evidence is clear that torture does not 'work' effectively on all individuals: some individuals have a far higher resistance to it than others, and some can certainly succeed in witholding information they do not wish to impart.[63]

There is ample historical evidence that terror alone is not generally an effective weapon for bringing about the overthrow of dictatorships or democracies. The few cases where terrorism played a major part in bringing sweeping political changes have arisen in certain colonial independence struggles against foreign rule, as in the case of the ending of the Palestine Mandate after the terrorist campaigns of Irgun and Stern, and the EOKA campaign in Cyprus. Even in these rare cases special conditions prevailed that made terrorism a more potent weapon: (i) due to humanitarian and judicial restraints the occupying power was unwilling to carry through draconian measures to wipe out the terrorist organisations; (ii) in each case there were inter-communal power struggles within the colony which rendered a peaceful diplomatic settlement and withdrawal difficult if not nigh impossible; (iii) the terrorists who succeeded in these conditions (as in Aden up until 1968) enjoyed massive if not solid support from their own ethnic groups, and this created an almost impenetrable barrier for the intelligence branches on which the government security forces depended for success, and a vast reservoir of active and tacit collaboration and support for the terrorist operatives. Even taking into account the influence of terrorism as an auxiliary tactic in revolutionary and independence struggles, and in the rise of fascism between the First and Second World War, the overall track record of terrorism in attaining major political objectives is abysmal.

Yet, in spite of the record, political terrorism as a form of undeclared clandestine warfare continues to be emulated by individuals, small factions, secret societies, political parties, mass movements, religious organisations, armies, police, intelligence and security services, penal systems, and, of course, governments, around the world. It has not been confined to any specific regions, cultures or periods, and there is rich anthropological evidence that terrorism has been employed by relatively primitive cultures. Why should this be? And why does it survive even in the most advanced and sophisticated industrial societies, haunting us in ever new forms? Before trying to investigate the roots of terrorism it is surely vitally important to distinguish the salient characteristics of terroristic violence from other forms with which it is so freely confused. A Boston Irishman, speaking on British television, defined a terrorist as 'anyone the British do not like'. Others use the word as a synonym for 'insurgent' or 'guerrilla'. As I have argued at length elsewhere these loose usages of the term as a mere pejorative label or slogan only serve to confuse public debate. Certainly they are useless for the purposes of scholarly analysis. In an earlier work I have argued that:

> Guerrillas may fight with small numbers and often inadequate weaponry, but they can and often do fight according to conventions of war, taking and exchanging prisoners and respecting the rights of non-combatants. Terrorists place no limits on means employed and frequently resort to widespread assassination, the waging of 'general terror' upon the indigenous civilian population, and even killing of innocent foreigners who may never have visited the country of the revolutionaries.[64]

In other words, although many guerrillas have employed terrorism or have been supported by terrorist cells and factions, terrorism cannot be equated with guerrilla war in general. Terrorism is a special mode or process of violence which has at least three basic elements: the terroristic aims of its perpetrators, their *modus operandi* in deploying particular forms of violence to achieve those aims, and the psychological effects of terrorist violence upon the victims and the target audience.

Terroristic violence has the following salient characteristics.

(1) It is inherently indiscriminate in its effects. Terrorists often profess to use terrorism selectively and rationally and claim to be able to predict precisely the effects of their attacks. Obviously terrorists may choose to follow a policy of selective assassination or kidnapping aimed at key politicians or officials or members of the security forces in preference to massacre of large numbers of the general public. Yet even when terrorists claim to select individual targets they do so, of necessity, clandestinely and according to their own idiosyncratic codes. No one can be certain that they will not be the next victim.[65] It is of the very nature of this kind of violence that the terrorists, in order to terrorise their audience, strike like lightning in the dark.

(2) Terrorism is essentially arbitrary and unpredictable, both in the minds of its victims and audience and in its effects upon individuals and society. It is precisely because terror is a *subjective* experience and that people have such variable 'thresholds' of fear that it is nonsense for terrorists to claim to predict the effects of terrorism upon behaviour. Andreski has aptly described terrorism

as a peculiar kind of tyranny in which 'no observance of commands – no matter how punctilious – on the part of the prospective victims can ensure their safety'.[66]

(3) Terrorism implicitly denies recognition of all rules and conventions of war. It refuses to distinguish between combatants and non-combatants and recognises no humanitarian constraints or obligations to prisoners or to the wounded. All lives, including those of women and children, are considered expendable for the cause. No one is innocent: therefore any victims of terrorism, even the Puerto Rican pilgrims who happened to be in the airport lounge in Lod when the Japanese Red Army attacked the passengers, are claimed by the terrorists to be guilty by association with the 'Zionist imperialist enemy'.

(4) The terrorists' rejection of all moral constraints is also reflected in particularly hideous and barbarous cruelties and weapons. In the recent Provisional I.R.A. bombing campaign in London the bombs contained ball-bearings and coach-bolts to cause maximum deaths and injuries to bystanders. Even in the more rural-based and primitively armed terrorist movements of recent African and Asian history hideous barbarities such as the disembowelment or dismembering of victims have been practised. However, although terroristic violence does not require an advanced industrial or urban base there is no doubt that modern explosives technology and firearms have enormously increased the terrorists' capacity for mass slaughter and destruction.

(5) Politically motivated terrorism is generally justified by its perpetrators on one or more of the following grounds; (i) any means are justified to realise an allegedly transcendental end (in Weber's terms, 'value-rational' grounds); (ii) closely linked to (i) is the claim that extreme violence is an intrinsically beneficial, regenerative, cathartic and ennobling deed regardless of other consequences; (iii) terrorism can be shown to have 'worked' in the past, and is held to be either the 'sole remaining' or 'best available' method of achieving success (in Weber's terms 'instrumental-rational' grounds); (iv) the morality of the just vengeance or 'an eye for an eye and a tooth for a tooth'; and (v) the theory of the lesser evil: greater evils will befall us or our nation if we do not adopt terror against our enemies.

I have defined political terrorism as the systematic use of murder and destruction, and the threat of murder and destruction, to terrorise individuals, groups, communities or governments into conceding to the terrorists' political aims. I have argued that terroristic violence is characterised by its indiscriminateness, inhumanity, arbitrariness and barbarity. It is quite clear that, in the sense that I have defined it, terrorism is an evaluative concept: it is only meaningful to perceive certain behaviour as terroristic if our conceptions of normalcy incorporate the idea of a peaceful order under the rule of law, free from terror and fear. If we view violence in the manner of Sartre and Fanon as positively desirable and 'liberative' we will not of course regard terrorism as a social and political problem. Ideologists of violence may even seek to establish a 'revolutionary' society in which extreme violence becomes more than the midwife of change, a Kafkaesque world in which terror is the 'order of the day'.[67] Like all other evaluative political concepts terrorism should therefore be used with great care. Individuals and groups should only be designated terrorist on the basis of clear historical evidence that they can be held responsible for a deliberate campaign to terrorise. It soon becomes clear to the conscientious student of terrorism, firstly, that this clearly authenticated evidence is often unavailable, and, secondly, that many of those designated 'terrorists' actually expend a considerable proportion of their energies on other modes of violence and struggle apart from planning and executing acts of terroristic violence. Hence it is important to see terrorism as part of a continuum of modes of violence. Sometimes, though by no means invariably, terrorism is concentrated in the initial stages of a revolutionary struggle. Commonly there is a division of labour within the broad coalition of the revolutionary or national liberation movement. Often only small factions specialise in terrorism. Frequently relations between the terrorists and their fellow insurgents worsen to the point of internecine war. It is very dangerous to assume that all terrorist acts committed in the name of revolution have the revolutionary movement's endorsement.

I have attempted to highlight the difficulties and pitfalls of using the concept of political terrorism, and have argued that we should deploy it with clarity, consistency and a constant concern for substantiation from historical evidence. As I have suggested elsewhere, however, the slipperiness and complexity of the concept by no means justify our dropping it altogether. To fall into the nominalist trap of claiming that terrorism does not exist but is merely a 'boo' word for 'freedom fighter' is simply to close one's eyes to whole ugly areas of historical and psychological reality.

I would hope that my conceptual analysis of terrorism, which I have summarised briefly above, is an aid towards introducing greater precision and rigour than has hitherto been customary in this field. Nevertheless terrorism, even on my narrow definition, is an extremely general concept and we need to construct more precise concepts with clear definitional attributes in order to facilitate orderly gathering and classification of information and a more discriminating analysis. In my work I have found it useful to employ a basic typology of terrorism (see Table 3). I propose to use the term *epiphenomenal terror* to denote those random but often extremely deadly acts of large-scale terror which occur in the course of major outbreaks of intra-specific violence such as international and civil wars and mass insurrection. Unlike systematic campaigns of terrorism such acts of terror essentially occur as an unintended consequence of the depradations and devastation of war and mass violence. Where individuals or groups are found to have deliberately committed terrorism and atrocities in war we would term them war criminals. I distinguish three main types of politically motivated systematic terrorism: (i) *repressive terrorism*, which is used most commonly but not exclusively by states to suppress, put down or constrain certain groups or individuals; (ii) *sub-revolutionary terrorism*, which is employed for a variety of purposes short of revolutionary seizure of power such as coercion or intimidation, vengeance or 'punishment'; and (iii) *revolutionary terrorism*, which has the long-term objective of bringing about political revolution, i.e. a fundamental change in the power structure, and often, in addition, fundamental changes in the socio-economic order. (There has been protracted dispute about the definition of political revolution, but I find myself persuaded by those theorists such as Chalmers Johnson and Peter Calvert[68] who have emphasised that violent change is the universal hallmark of political revolution.) In the present study I am concerned almost exclusively with the use of revolutionary and sub-revolutionary terrorism by non-governmental groups.

Urban guerrilla warfare is often confused with terrorism, probably because these phenomena have so frequently been combined in recent revolutionary and national liberation movement struggles. Nevertheless many practitioners and guerrilla war leaders

Table 3

*A basic typology of political terror and terrorism*

| Type | Aims | Characteristics |
| --- | --- | --- |
| Sub-revolutionary | Political motives short of fundamental revolutionary change: for example, to coerce governments into changes of policy or law, removal or 'punishment' of officials, political warfare with rival groups | Typically committed by small groups, though individuals may act alone; highly unpredictable; often difficult to distinguish from psychopathological and criminal violence |
| Revolutionary | Revolution, or to achieve tactical revolutionary objectives | Always a group phenomenon, however tiny the group, with a leadership and an ideology or programme, however crude. Develops alternative institutional structures. The organisation of violence and terrorism is typically undertaken by specialist conspiratorial and para-military organs within the revolutionary movement |
| Repressive | Suppressing or restraining groups, individuals or forms of behaviour deemed to be undesirable by the repressor, or | Often highly sanguinary, developing into mass terror. Typically a specialist terror *apparat*, the secret police, is developed to perform this task, |

| | | | though it often involves other organs such as the ruling party and the army. Its archetypal technique is torture. In the totalitarian ideological régime terror, fear and mutual suspicion can become all-pervasive and all-consuming, and may become the vehicle of the leader's paranoia |
| | simply arbitrarily chosen for 'liquidation' | | |
| Epiphenomenal | No specific aim: a by-product of large-scale intra-specific violence | | Random rather than deliberately planned and organised: occurs in the context of highly sanguinary struggles in which systematic terrorism may be an accompanying element |

and theorists have been very clear about the distinction and some
have warned against terrorism on the grounds that it can alienate
potential support for the insurgents, provoke a backlash, tighten
repression, and only hinder the 'real' revolution. For example,
Guevara believed terrorism to be 'a measure that is generally indiscriminate and ineffective in its results, since it often makes victims
of innocent people and destroys a large number of lives that would
be valuable to the revolution'.[69] And, echoing Lenin's view,
Guevara also argued that terrorism can turn a people against a
revolutionary movement and provoke police repression hindering
the revolutionary movement and its communication with the
masses.[70] Debray, on the other hand, accords it a positive but sub-
sidiary role: 'Of course city terrorism cannot assume any decisive
role, and it entails certain dangers of a political order. But if it is
subordinate to the fundamental struggle, the struggle in the countryside, it has, from the military point of view, a strategic value; it
immobilizes thousands of enemy soldiers . . . in unrewarding tasks of
protection.'[71] Marighela lists terrorism as one of many weapons
open to the revolutionary. He defines it as 'an action usually involving the placement of a bomb or fire explosion of great destructive power. . . It is an action the urban guerrilla must execute with
the greatest cold bloodedness, calmness and decision.'[72] It is quite
clear that he does not equate terrorism with urban guerrilla warfare
in general, though he insists that it is 'an arm the revolutionary can
never relinquish'.[73]

I wish to argue the case here that urban guerrilla warfare has a far
higher 'terrorism potential' than any other mode of unconventional
war. It is possible to see more clearly why this should be so if one
analyses and compares the strategic and tactical aims, uses, methods
and effectiveness of political terrorism and urban guerrilla war.

The long-term aims of political terrorism are dependent upon the
terrorists' ideology which may be anything from neo-fascism and
racism to neo-Marxism and anarchism. Only the nihilist terrorist
groups appear to lack any positive conception of a future ideal society. Instead of seeking utopia the true nihilist follows Nechayev in
dedicating himself entirely to 'destroying this whole vile order'.
Observers sometimes find it difficult to take the long-term
revolutionary aims of some groups seriously. It is true, as one French
writer has said, that 'terrorism is the weapon of the weak pretending
to be strong'. And there is something absurd about the professed

objective of a tiny terrorist group such as the Japanese United Red Army which claims it is working for 'world revolution'. Yet it is precisely their fanatical devotion to ideals that helps to explain the persistence, determination and resilience of these contemporary secret brotherhoods of terror. Some of them at least appear to commit their acts of terror in the manner of the ancient Assassin sect, almost as a sacramental duty.[74] However, the utopias of all contemporary revolutionary terrorists are secular: they want their liberation and justice on earth not in heaven, and they want it now. Common to all revolutionary terrorists is the major strategic objective of smashing the existing régime and seizing power in the name of the revolution. Few of them admit to any doubts as to whether terrorism is either legitimate or effective as a means to this end.

The short-term objectives and tactical uses of political terrorism seem at once more comprehensible and practicable. First and foremost is the aim of gaining publicity for the movement and its cause. Modern developments in the mass media such as the development of television and communications satellites have brought almost instantaneous world-wide publicity for acts of terrorism. Terrorists are so ardent in their desire for access to the media that they have sometimes attempted to set up their own broadcasting, or have demanded, like the F.L.Q. in 1970, that they should have their manifesto broadcast as a condition for releasing their kidnap victims. A kind of competition for the headlines ensues in which only the most sensational outrages tend to capture the big headlines. Another important point about media publicity is that it can be denied or suppressed by authoritarian régimes. Hence, for terrorists waging war against autocracy it is foreign media, and, through them, foreign governments and international opinion, which are the major targets for propaganda of the deed.

Another common objective is to inspire and mobilise followers or potential sympathisers into emulating the terrorists, or into greater militancy. Terrorism can also be employed, as can urban guerrilla warfare, 'to convert the political crisis into armed struggle by the people against the military powers'. It may also help to tempt the government and security forces into heavy-handed over-reaction and thus push people into support of the terrorists who can pose as a self-defence organisation. Terrorism has frequently been used to poison and polarise inter-communal relations and to destroy all middle-ground reconciliatory political elements – this has been particularly evident in conflicts in Ireland, Cyprus and Algeria, for example. Some short-term tactical objectives are a function of the terrorist group's struggle to maintain itself and to acquire vital resources: the use of terror to gain ransoms and weapons, to release colleagues from gaol, to destroy particularly dangerous opponents, to punish alleged informers, and to maintain secrecy and absolute obedience.

Thus far we have identified some of the tactical aims of terrorism when employed in isolation from other forms of revolutionary warfare. As Debray realised, however, terrorism may give useful tactical support to guerrilla operations by creating diversions and tying down large numbers of security forces in costly counter-terrorist activity. Moreover, under certain conditions, a sustained campaign of terrorist attrition can assist the wider revolutionary struggle by sapping the will of the government and security forces to uphold the law, by undermining public confidence in the government and its capacity to protect the lives and property of citizens, and by helping to create a general climate of fear and collapse. Certainly history shows that terrorism has been more effective as an auxiliary weapon in revolutionist and national liberationist struggles. There are only a few examples of terrorism being decisive as the principal weapon: in bringing about Britain's withdrawal from Palestine; causing British withdrawal from the Canal Zone base; and in driving the British to withdraw from Cyprus and later from Aden. One would have to add that in the case of Palestine the terrorism did not help to achieve a lasting and peaceful solution in the area. And in the case of Cyprus EOKA has come nowhere near achieving its professed long-term aims.

Urban guerrillas generally share many of the long-term aims and tactical objectives of political terrorists but it must be admitted that as a principal means of struggle this mode of warfare has been unsuccessful. Such warfare is a form of unconventional war waged in urban or suburban areas for political objectives. It is not seen, even by its most enthusiastic theoreticians, as adequate by itself for bringing victory in revolutionary or internal war. Historically it has generally been waged by movements employing a variety of modes of unconventional war including rural guerrilla warfare, psychological warfare and political terrorism. Overall strategic objectives are laid down by the political leadership of the insurgent movement, therefore, rather than by the urban guerrilla fighters themselves.

Contrary to the claims of the numerous writers who attribute the invention of urban guerrilla war to the Brazilian theorist Carlos Marighela in the 1960s, this mode of war is by no means new. It was experienced, for example, in the 1848 revolutions, in Paris in 1871, in the Dublin Easter Rising of 1916, the German Spartacist Revolution in 1918, the Spanish Civil War, and in resistance against the Nazis in occupied Europe in 1939–45. As a mode of guerrilla war it clearly came into its own with the invention of light, portable, automatic weapons which could reap full advantage from the vantage points and fields of fire afforded by the urban landscape. However, with the possible exception of the Tupamaros in Montevideo (1970–72), no urban guerrilla campaign by itself has sufficed to bring a change of political régime. (And even in the case of Uruguay the consequence was not a pro-Tupamaros régime but a repressive authoritarian government.)

It is not really surprising, therefore, that urban guerrilla warfare has nowhere entirely replaced rural-based struggle. It certainly has not rendered rural guerrillas obsolete. We can easily understand why this should be so. There are the impressive examples of the successes of rural-based struggle in China, Vietnam and Cuba which excite envy and emulation among other Third World revolutionaries. Nor should we overlook the fact that in many African and Asian countries a mere 15 to 20 per cent of the population live in cities. Therefore he who would conquer the country must conquer the countryside.

Urban guerrilla war has, moreover, serious inherent disadvantages compared to rural struggle. It lacks the space for manoeuvre (and the cover) of inaccessible and desolate countryside. Urban guerrillas cannot utilise the hiding places, training grounds and potential base areas of the wild. Rural-based guerrillas have the enormous advantages of being able to harass the enemy's lines of communication while living off the land and building up support and military strength in the peasant areas. Peasantry also constitute a potentially more sympathetic 'sea' for the guerrilla 'fish' than the city dwellers. Peasants in remote areas generally have a traditional distrust of city-based authority and harbour many smouldering grievances. Cities constitute more mixed, volatile and unreliable bases for raising popular support. Except in well-defined ghetto areas, the population is far less homogeneous, and indeed even in the poorest countries the cities contain concentrations of middle-class and business groups who have a major stake in the stability of the régime and will tend to support the security forces.

Given these grave inherent weaknesses in the position of the urban guerrilla one must ask why there has been an extensive shift in Latin America, North America, Western Europe and even in South Asia and the Middle East to city-based guerrilla struggle. One major factor has obviously been the rapid urbanisation of these regions. In some Latin American countries well over half of the population are city dwellers. In countries like Brazil and Argentina it would be naïve romanticism for the revolutionary to pin his hopes on the success of a Guevara-style rural-based *foco*. Indeed it is partly disillusion with purely rural-based strategies in Venezuela, Colombia, Argentina and elsewhere that has driven many revolutionaries to develop the use of urban guerrilla tactics. Another factor has been the logistic, financial and ideological support given by the Soviet Communists, Cuba and other régimes to urban guerrilla movements. Urban movements have also proved able to exploit the growing ghettos and shanty town areas of modern cities as recruiting grounds for activists and supporters. As Fanon predicted, it is among the lumpenproletariat, the marginals and unemployed of the big cities, that Third World 'revolutionary consciousness' finds a fruitful soil. In such conditions those struggling to survive are aroused to envy and anger by the affluence of the wealthy classes the other side of the tracks. A sense of deprivation and injustice festers easily into the kind of latent aggression that can be so readily canalised into violence by the urban guerrilla movement. Also readily available in the cities are the necessary technical and practical requirements for guerrilla activity and the kinds of professionalism and skills — ideological, technological and practical — that are invaluable to the revolutionary movement.

Contemporary urban guerrilla war theorists have made much of the potential assets of the city environment which the urban guerrilla can exploit. (As Professor Walter Laqueur has pointed out[75] such ideas are not really all that new. Johannes Most, the German socialist, developed them very fully in this *Revolutionäre Kriegwissenschaft* and in his articles in *Freiheit* in the 1880s.) Nevertheless most modern urban guerrilla theorists seem to accept that urban-based struggle is not adequate in itself to bring about revolution. Like Carlos Marighela, they see urban struggle as simply part of a wider revolutionary conflict involving hypermobile guerrilla war, rural and urban, in concert with psychological warfare and political struggle. Marighela viewed purely urban-based guerrilla war as simply the primary phase of a larger and wider struggle. In the second phase:

> From the urban front we shall go on to direct armed struggle against the *latifúndio* through rural guerrilla war. With the alliance of the proletariat, peasantry, and students in a decentralized and mobile guerrilla war, we shall extend our activities in all directions through the interior of Brazil and finally create a revolutionary army of national liberation to match the conventional army of military dictatorship.[76]

I claimed earlier that urban guerrilla war had a higher terrorism potential than any other form of unconventional warfare. It becomes clearer why this should be so when one analyses the urban guerrillas' strategic and tactical objectives and methods in relation to their resources and inherent handicaps.

Like the political terrorist the urban guerrilla is frequently engaged in trying to 'militarise' the political struggle and to get the people to blame the government for their discontents and to turn against the régime. But waging armed struggle effectively in the cities demands an adequate supply of dedicated and well-trained volunteers. A certain minimal strength of men and weapons is necessary to initiate the tactical struggle which is supposed to bring in new recruits to form fresh small armed groups and to replace losses. We have already noted that the urban guerrilla is forced to operate in a largely hostile environment. He may face numerous extremely ruthless, capable security forces with superior weaponry, communications and mobility. Suppose his hiding places, 'safe houses', or weapons caches are betrayed? Given such grave reverses the urban guerrilla has less room for manoeuvre than his rural comrade. He has nowhere to run. Faced with heavy losses through police or army action, or with failure to mobilise popular support, or with successful police infiltration of his groups, it is perhaps inevitable that the urban guerrilla will look to terrorism as a weapon of last resort. Certainly Johannes Most and Carlos Marighela would have agreed that the urban guerrilla must never relinquish this weapon, though Most would have gone much further than Marighela in his enthusiasm for terroristic violence for he actually prescribed acts of mass slaughter in public places.

Yet there is also another important factor, in addition to their inherent weakness and desperation, which helps to explain the urban guerrillas' high terrorism potential. It is of the very essence of urban guerrilla war that it involves the use of hit-and-run offensive warfare (ambushes, surprise attacks, etc.) in a theatre of operations with a high population density. It is almost impossible in any protracted urban guerrilla battle to avoid causing the death or injury of the innocent civilian population. Bystanders are bound to be caught in the crossfire. The more desperate and vulnerable the guerrilla group the more they will be ready to use non-combatant civilians as a shield. They may hope that casualties will be caused by, or blamed upon, the security forces, and that this will play into the guerrillas' hands. In any event they are likely to become inured to terroristic violence and to accept terrorism as a useful, even invaluable and justifiable weapon. It is but a small step from this to acceptance of terrorism as an everyday necessity and a way of life. It does not take many people, or indeed much expense or explosives, to conduct a terror bombing campaign. Hence even if the major guerrilla war never gets off the ground, even if the masses inexplicably fail to rise, the fanatical revolutionary can take some small comfort from the continuation of death and destruction in the name of revolution or liberation. Terrorism becomes for them the fig leaf for their revolutionary virtue, a theatre of revolutionary deeds that can be glamourised and romaticised to help the weak actually *believe* they are strong and that the revolution is on the way. Terrorism may become more than a profession: for some it becomes a drug, an addiction to murder in the name of 'liberation' and 'justice' which is in reality no more than a sublimate for the urge to rebel.

In sum I have argued that urban guerrilla warfare's high potential for terroristic violence derives both from the weakness and desperation of the urban guerrilla and from the stategic and tactical imperatives and vulnerabilities of guerrilla war in an urban environment.

# XIII
# TERRORISM AND CRIMINALITY

It is precisely because terrorists, by definition, follow a systematic policy of terror, that their acts are analogous to crimes. The very notion of crime, even in the most primitive legal systems, implies the moral responsibility of individuals for their actions and hence for any violation of the legal code. We cannot make a general rule that terrorists are to be exempted from criminal responsibility unless we are either prepared to plead their irresponsibility on grounds of insanity or are willing to allow the whole moral and legal order to be undermined by deferring to the terrorist. In most legal systems the typical acts of terrorist groups (such as bombings, murders, kidnapping, wounding and blackmail) constitute serious criminal offences under the prevailing codes. Without exception murder is punishable under the legal codes of all states. As terrorism involves systematic cold-blooded murder it is particularly repugnant to the Judaeo—Christian tradition and to all societies which are deeply infused with humane values.

It is still widely held that the divine injunction against murder (the Sixth Commandment) is an absolute imperative which allows only four special cases of exception: (i) murder committed in the course of a just war on behalf of one's country (a pacifist would, of course, object to this exception on conscientious grounds); (ii) judicial execution in punishment for the crimes of murder or treason (a principled abolitionist would deny this ground); (iii) murder committed in the course of a just rebellion against tyrannical rule or foreign conquest; and (iv) in self-defence against violent attack. Clearly there is a world of difference between justification for specific acts of murder and justification for a systematic policy of indiscriminate murder as a means to a political end. Even if the terrorists claim, as they commonly do, that they are waging a just war or a just rebellion in terms of the classical criteria laid down by theologians and moral philosophers, they do not thereby succeed in providing ethical justification for their deliberate choice of systematic and indiscriminate murder as their sole or principal means of struggle. It would be a logical absurdity to try to justify terrorism in terms of an ethic founded on the sanctity of individual human life.

Hence terrorists claim to act according to a higher 'revolutionary morality' which transvalues everything in terms of the revolutionary struggle.

This terrorist revolutionary morality takes many different forms and is informed by a confusing and often self-contradictory collection of self-justificatory beliefs, myths and propaganda, which I intend to discuss in greater detail. The point I wish to establish here, however, is that if we attach any meaning and value to our Western Judaeo–Christian, liberal and humanist values, and the ethical and legal systems that have been shaped by this tradition, we must logically recognise the criminal nature of terrorism. Terrorism is more than simply a manifestation of psychopathology, and more than a symptom of social discontent, oppression and injustice – though it may be both of these things as well. It is also a moral crime, a crime against humanity, an attack not only on our security, our rule of law, and the safety of the state, but on civilised society itself.

The terrorist speaks a different language of justification, and for him the arguments from ethical and humanitarian principle are dismissed as sentimental and bourgeois irrelevancies. Defiantly and proudly they place themselves outside and 'above' the law. Hence, as we shall observe later, the apparently close bonds between terrorists and bandits (whom Bakunin regarded as the natural and original revolutionaries). Hence also the intimate organisational, financial and logistic links between terrorist movements and criminal sub-cultures.

Yet there remains a significant difference between them in that the terrorist, unlike the criminal, insists on the revolutionary legitimacy and historical necessity and significance of his acts. If captured and brought to trial the terrorist thus typically refuses to recognise the legitimacy and legality of the courts: in his eyes the judiciary is simply the contemptible creature of an irredeemably rotten order. There can thus be no meaningful dialogue between them. As we shall observe terrorists generally claim that their own acts dispense justice and punishment according to a higher law of revolution: terrorists claim to extirpate the crimes of the state.

Revolutionary terrorists make war on legality and hence their 'criminality' is an essential part of their self-definition. They regard the law and its agents as both symbol and embodiment of the 'oppressions' and 'injustices' they wish to remove. Echoing Kropotkin they would claim 'everything is good for us which falls outside legality'. Yet the awesome consequences of this nihilistic rejection of all ethical and legal constraints are that the professional terrorists become totally corrupted and criminalised by their obsessive absorption in assassination, massacre and destruction. Terrorism tends to brutalise those involved in its planning and perpetration. A cult of bombs and guns is created and headstrong youths can become so hooked on the life of terrorist murder that they perform their tasks in a kind of sacrificial ecstacy. It must be recognised that just as there are war crimes and war criminals guilty of crimes against humanity, there are also revolution crimes against humanity. Revolutionary terrorists are those who choose to devote themselves to the macabre specialisms of revolutionary criminality. Bakunin understood perhaps better than anybody the self-corrupting and criminalising effects of professional terrorism on the personality of the terrorist conspirator. In a letter to Alfred Talandier, Bakunin vividly describes the case of Nechayev, whose ruthlessness and deceit he suffered for some years. Describing Nechayev's terrorist secret society he wrote:

> Truth, mutual trust, serious and strict solidarity exists only amongst a dozen or so individuals who form the *sanctus sanctorum* of the society. All the others must serve as blind tools, exploitable material in the hands of these dozen men with real solidarity. It is allowed and even ordered to trick them, compromise them, rob them and even destroy them if need be; they are fodder for conspiracy. . . . The sympathies of lukewarm people who are devoted only in part to the revolutionary cause and who, besides this cause, have other human interests such as love, friendship, the family, social relationships — these sympathies he does not consider sufficiently justifiable, and in the name of the cause he has to take possession of your whole being without your knowledge. To this end he will spy on you and try to gain possession of all your secrets.[77]

Bakunin also clearly appreciated the implications of this self-corruption for the revolutionary movement. By depending on educating his followers to cheat, lie, spy and denounce, Nechayev was relying, as Bakunin pointed out, 'much more on the external hobbles with which you have bound them, than on their inner courage'.[78] And he is quick to see the dangerous implications of this system for the revolutionary cause: 'It follows that should circumstances change, should they realize that the terror of the state is stronger than the fear which you inspire, they would (educated by you) become excellent state servants and spies.'[79] Thus the inherently criminalising effects of terrorist conspiracy upon the personalities of revolutionaries may and frequently do, threaten the very survival of the cause. And yet the more dependent the terrorist secret society becomes upon intimidation, blackmail and trickery to coerce and control its own members, the more difficult it becomes for its members to break free of the circle of criminality, mutual suspicion and deception.

# PART II
# INTERNAL TERRORISM AND THE LIBERAL STATE

'The framing of a future, in some indeterminate time, may, when it is done in a certain way, be very effective . . . this happens when the anticipations of the future take the form of those myths, which enclose with them, all the strongest inclinations of a people, of a party or of a class, inclinations which recur to the mind with the insistence of the instincts . . . and which give an aspect of complete reality to the hopes of immediate action by which . . . men can reform their desires, passions and mental activity . . . what the myths contain in the way of details which will actually form part of the history of the future is of small importance: it is even possible that nothing which they contain will ever come to pass.'

Georges Sorel, *Reflections on Violence*

'Representative institutions necessarily depend for permanence upon the readiness of the people to fight for them in case of their being endangered. If too little valued for this, they seldom obtain a footing at all, and if they do, are almost sure to be overthrown, as soon as the head of the government, or any party leader who can muster force for a *coup de main*, is willing to run some small risk for absolute power.'

John Stuart Mill, *Representative Government*

# XIV
# THE PHILOSOPHY OF TERROR

The obscenities and stones hurled against liberal democratic institutions at the height of the student revolt in the late 1960s by the spoiled children of Western affluence and privilege dramatically shattered the illusion that the sole forces remaining to challenge liberal democracy in the West were fascism and communism. By the mid-1960s fascism appeared a totally discredited and defeated movement within Western liberal states, while communism was viewed rather more seriously, as an external threat in the shape of the Warsaw Pact and expanding Soviet military power. Liberal observers of the politics of France and Italy, which both have traditionally large communist votes, noted the extent to which indigenous communist parties and trade union movements could be tamed by the discrete pressures of *embourgeoisement* and privatisation of workers, and by the parliamentarisation of parties. But the street and campus battles of the student revolt disclosed the fanaticism of new, small, but strident minority movements fundamentally hostile to liberal values and politics. A veritable zoo of conflicting sects and factions covering the whole spectrum of neo-Marxists and Third World revolutionism and anarchism sprang up in the heart of Western Academia. And although these groups commonly identified with Third World revolutionary heroes such as Mao, Ho Chi Minh and Guevara, their true intellectual mentors were figures such as Herbert Marcuse and Jean-Paul Sartre, embittered and ageing iconoclasts of the left who would never have been able to enjoy their freedom to spin fresh revolutionary doctrines and myths anywhere else but within the liberal societies they so profoundly despise.

The most elaborate and systematic attempt to create a philosophy, or perhaps more accurately, an ideology, of terror and violence is that of Jean-Paul Sartre. Sartre is significant because he quite explicitly takes an extreme position concerning violence, and he makes a determined attempt to work through the implications of this for both the individual and society. It would be dangerous to assume that Sartre is in any way a representative figure. It is difficult to gauge both the degree to which he has influenced, and the extent to which he has been moulded by, contemporary neo-Marxist and existentialist thinkers. Certainly there are close affinities, for example with both the Frankfurt School and the 'situationists' as well as more obvious links. However, I am not concerned so much here with intellectual pedigree. Sartre is important as both the most radical intellectual proponent of violence and terror, and as one of the leading, and most intransigent, antagonists of liberal values and the liberal state. His *Critique de la raison dialectique* (1960) provides the most dramatic antithesis to the contemporary liberal view of the state and society. It is therefore worth examining his ideas closely not merely because he is an influential exemplar of apologia for violence and terror, but also because he dares to seek to give philosophical respectability to the notion that terror, far from being a cancer of the body politic, is indeed its very lifeblood.

Sartre, in his major theoretical work on violence and terror,[1] attempts to fuse elements of bleak existentialism and Marxian dialectic. He develops a social doctrine which is diametrically opposed to the humane optimism of liberalism. For Sartre the true motive force of history is scarcity: each man is an enemy to every other because each is a dangerous rival in the struggle against scarcity. It is for this reason, he claims, that evil is irremediable and must be made the basis of our ethics. It is important to recognise the implications of Sartre's theory for its influence, often in vulgarised forms, has permeated many revolutionist and terrorist ideologies that have grown within liberal societies.

The state of nature portrayed in *Critique* is infinitely bleaker than that of Hobbes. The world we live in, comprising the world of Nature and Praxis (the artefacts and productions of Man), is seen as essentially indifferent to Man's well-being. This world, which Sartre terms the world of the *Practico-inert*, is seen almost as an antagonist, at times mocking man by the failure of his inventions, and the folly of struggles and actions that actually worsen his position in the struggle against scarcity. And in this struggle every other individual is viewed as the *Other*, a cruel and rapacious antagonist, at once predator and prey: 'Nothing indeed — neither wild beasts nor microbes — could be more terrible for man than this intelligent, flesh-eating, cruel species, which knows how to follow and outwit the human intelligence *and of which the aim is precisely the destruction of man*' (my italics)[2] In Sartre's state of nature no element of altruism or love exists: the individual man is seen not simply as lusting and fighting for power after power, but as a *destroyer* impelled to murder his fellow men. Man in a state of nature thus only shares the negative reciprocity of mutual and deadly antagonism.

Sartre argues that this negative reciprocity is 'dialectically' negated by the social collaboration between neighbours which man finds is essential to overcome scarcity. He terms the form of social structure which man creates to collaborate for collective purposes the *group*. Sartre differentiates the group from the *series* which is a random gathering or clustering of people defined merely by their mutual proximity. Thus a working class may be nothing more than a series of series, a mere category, something less even than Marx's conception of 'a class in itself'. But if a working class becomes committed to a common objective or end, such as revolutionary socialism, it becomes a 'pledged group', something closer to Marx's 'class for itself'. *Le Serment* (the pledge) is the commitment that actually gives birth to the group. Sartre plainly sees it as an almost sacramental act which is binding on the members because it carries the explicit implication that violent sanctions will be invoked against any who break their pledge, or betray, or desert the group.

Thus for Sartre the pledged group is created not from a rational and freely given contract or covenant but from fear, and it is the rule of 'Terror' over every member of the group by all their fellow-members that keeps the pledge enforced and sustains the group. It is only the constant presence of violence and terror, argues Sartre, that prevents the group from dissolving into mere seriality. In this strangely dark and melodramatic vision of the world there are no such things as love or loyalty or fraternity for their own sake: all social relationships are governed by the violence of the terror that negates violence. As Maurice Cranston has observed, for Sartre: 'Terror in fact is fraternity. For Terror is the guarantee that my neighbour will stay my brother; it binds my neighbour to me by the threat of the violence it will use against him if he dares to be "unbrotherly".'[3]

Terror is at the centre of Sartre's political philosophy: it is the very cement of the State which is the most important form of political organisation. Like Hobbes, Sartre assumes that the pledge of obedience to the state totally subordinates the individual to the authority of the sovereign. And because the sovereign thenceforward represents the will of the subjects, the pledged subject, by obeying the sovereign's command, obeys himself. The ultimate paradox of Sartre's terroristic philosophy is that the state's exercise of terror becomes the condition of freedom. His bizarre conclusion is that those who are pledged to the state and have thus totally given themselves to its ends can only be 'truly free' when they are obeying the commands of the state which rules them by terror. What could be further from the liberal conception of the state as a means of security, peace, individual liberty and happiness?

Sartre's vision of the world is unrelievedly misanthropic. In a revealing phrase in Les Mots (1964) he once confessed that he 'became apprenticed to violence and discovered my ugliness. . . '. And indeed his obsession with evil and violence seems to have led him to reduce all human relationships to antagonism, mutual cruelty and torment. Each person is constantly engaged, even when in the most intimate relations with others, in a form of psychological warfare, defending themselves against being objectified as a thing in the world and thus losing their freedom, while at the same time constantly attempting to reduce others to objects. It is almost as if Sartre wishes to people the whole world with the most unpleasant characters in his novels. Unselfish love, trust, innocence, harmony, friendship and co-operation freely given – all these are missing from his view of human life and feeling.

Literary and philosophical critics have, of course, frequently taken Sartre to task on the grounds of his grossly distorted vision of humanity. Yet few political philosophers, with the outstanding exception of Raymond Aron,[4] have clearly identified the dangerous political implications of Sartre's doctrine of man and his dialectical theory of violence. Perhaps the most serious and culpable aspect is his glorification and romanticisation of violence and cruelty. He is not merely content to describe the bestialisation of man: he goes out of his way to accord violence and terror the heroic role in human affairs. Terror is elevated into the engine of progress and freedom. It is my belief that Sartre's political thought is much closer to Sorel than to Marx. Like Sorel he is entranced with the emotive power of revolutionary myth as a means of triggering violent conflict. The details of the future revolutionary society are deliberately left vague.

Sartre's salvation myth is that the workers of the world will unite in a universal violent revolutionary struggle, that they will succeed in overthrowing all the forces of 'capitalist-imperialism', that scarcity will be finally eliminated, and a new socialist man created. Sorel's chosen myth was the general strike by the proletariat leading to the smashing of the bourgeois state and rule by a new élite of worker-revolutionary heroes. Both myths are entirely vague and millenarian in character. But as Sorel candidly admitted: '...what the myths contain in the way of details which will actually form part of the history of the future is of small importance: it is even possible that nothing which they contain will ever come to pass.'[5]

There is, surely, a Sorelian, even fascist tone in Sartre's own exhaltation of action and violence for its own sake, and his callous disregard for the victims and for the social consequences of violence. Sartre's polemical writings often come near to engaging in a kind of pornography of violence and brutalisation. Again and again he hammers the point that violence must be answered by violence and that violence is cathartic and cleansing: 'it is man recreating himself', he writes. In the same notorious passage he claims:

> When the peasant takes a gun in his hands, the old myths grow dim and the prohibitions are one by one forgotten. The rebel's weapon is proof of his humanity. For in the first days of the revolt you must kill: to shoot down a European is to kill two birds with one stone, to destroy an oppressor and the man he oppresses at the same time: there remain a dead man, and a free man...[6]

Is it a mixture of self-hatred and hatred for his fellow men or his nausea at the European society which nurtured him that leads him to 'objectify' (to use his own terms) fellow Europeans into *things* to be killed? In the crude world of Sartre's pornography of violence anyone who gets in the way of Sartre's favoured causes is consigned to the practico-inert.

To a liberal mind Sartre's terroristic philosophy is an extraordinarily baffling phenomenon, a mountain of words and sometimes resplendent concepts and categories with absolutely nothing behind them. It is so difficult for the liberal to understand how Sartre and those revolutionary intellectuals who claim to follow his ideas could actually come to believe that such a philosophy has anything to do with the real world. (A similar difficulty, one should add, arises with the esoteric theories of Marcuse, the Frankfurt school and the 'situationists'.) How can one really believe that all relationships between individuals inevitably take the form of unrelenting antagonism? Surely empirical observation confirms that there are many primary and secondary groups, political associations and interest groups in existence that do not rule either by terror or by threat of terror. It is surely significant that the only historical examples of groups conforming precisely to Sartre's model of the pledged group ruled by terror are the terroristic secret societies from the Assassins to Narodnaya Volya, and the Baader–Meinhof gang. Is it seriously suggested that the oath-taking and internal coercive terror characteristic of these terrorist groups are also elements in organisations like the Friends of the Earth, NALGO or the Labour Party? The pledged group concept is plainly hopelessly inadequate to encompass the manifold and rich variety of the structures of collective action.

Sartre comes closer than any other modern figure to creating a positive ideology of terror. As Arendt, Aron[7] and others point out this distances him considerably from classical Marxist views of violence. For Marx viewed violence not as an end in itself, but as a necessary means for achieving ultimate victory for the proletariat. Violence would be the necessary midwife of revolution, Marx believed, because the bourgeoisie would never finally give up its power without a fight. But he clearly envisaged this as being a once-for-all physical struggle, bloody but short-lived, a final assault on the capitalist bastille. Sartre transvalues and glorifies violence and terror as ends in themselves, and sees violence as a constant duty and self-fulfilment for the oppressed. At the heart of Marx's morally infused doctrine of man is his view that man 'recreates himself' through productive labour, through which he attains a sense of class identity, solidarity and revolutionary consciousness. But Sartrian man cannot achieve revolutionary consciousness or even self-respect unless he liberates himself through acts of violence. Sartre insists that as long as scarcity rules the human condition evil is irremediable, and he founds his whole ethic on the *necessity of evil*.

It is true that the *Critique* expresses a distant hope that the world proletariat will create the ultimate pledged group, a world socialist revolutionary movement which will finally be able to overcome scarcity thus rendering violence redundant. Yet there is no real basis in this bleak and misanthropic political philosophy for such a hope. Sartre's ideology of terror offers no escape, no real alternative to the grim cycle of violence and counter-violence. Any killing or cruelty committed in the name of the revolution is its own justification: the end justifies the means, the means justify the end; terrorism becomes an addiction, an obsession, a way of life, and the act of murder a sacramental duty. Every ideology stereotypes its chosen enemies and scapegoats and mobilises hatred and violence against them. Such campaigns of dehumanisation have invariably preceded the great waves of persecution, massacre, enslavement and genocide that have characterised the ideological terror of the twentieth century. Sartre's achievement, if one can use such a term in this context, has been to create an ideology of limitless and unmitigated terror. *All* are to be parties to murder and all are potential victims. In the diabolically perverted logic of this philosophy all human life is regarded as expendable in the 'dialectical necessity' of realising the Brotherhood of Man. Hatred replaces love, and terror becomes the only true fraternity.

It should be absolutely clear that this philosophy of terror is in fundamental contradiction to the values of a liberal community identified earlier in my discussion of the liberal state. Liberal theorists do not regard man as being inherently incapable of altruism, unselfish love, trust and peaceful co-operation. The capacity of free-will and the gifts of reason and language, liberals argue, enable man to establish some shared humane values to serve as a basis for rational purposes and peaceful social organisation. Liberal theorists, as we have noted, have never accepted that it is either necessary or desirable or even practicable for men to be ruled for any length of time by *force majeure*. Instead they emphasise that any political régime needs some element of popular legitimacy, consent and collaboration if it is to be stable and effective. In liberal discourse the concept of authority implies generally recognised rights, powers and responsibilities, consistently and clearly defined and limited in legal–constitutional terms. The whole thrust of classical liberalism was directed at establishing a government of laws in place of arbitrary and despotic power, and at establishing social peace. And this movement was swiftly followed and reinforced by the pressure of liberal democracy bringing popular participation, representation and a far greater degree of public accountability (and hence of government responsiveness) to public demands and expectations. It is precisely because they are based on popular consent and legitimacy that the very existence of liberal democratic states is so galling to ideologues of terror. For they offer living proof, despite their difficulties and shortcomings, that not all states govern by violence and terror.

One would naturally expect anarchist and neo-Marxist theorists and apologists for terror to share Sartre's cynical contempt for the liberal state. In their eyes the apparatus of government is merely the instrument for the bourgeoisie's exploitative and oppressive rule, and all its claims to democratic legitimacy are sneeringly dismissed. Revolutionary intellectuals such as the Strasbourg 'situationist' group and Marcuse have resorted to elaborate arguments explaining why democratic free elections, party systems and representation are a gigantic fraud, a conspiracy to dupe the masses. They argue that the industrial working class of the Western industrial societies has been bought off or else been irredeemably corrupted by 'capitalist—imperialist' forces. Instead they look elsewhere for their revolutionary vanguard. The lumpenproletariat, the students, the Third World revolutionary movements, or a coalition of all these elements, have all been canvassed as the future flag-bearers of the 'real' revolution. They make no attempt to disguise their profound contempt and hatred for the 'embourgeoisement' and 'reactionary attitudes' of the masses in the Western liberal democracies. Small wonder that they have no compunction about them being slaughtered for the revolution. In their eyes no one is innocent. They share the embittered anti-Americanism and anti-Europeanism which is such a recurrent theme in the writings of Sartre and Fanon.

Terrorist philosophies and ideologies clearly pose a frontal attack on liberal values and principles. Terrorism is essentially an instrument or political weapon developed by revolutionaries in the womb of autocracy. It is generally employed by small conspiratorial secret societies organised in crudely paramilitary structures lacking any mechanisms of internal democracy and employing terror to control and discipline their own members. Terrorist groups within liberal democracies despise democratic procedures and electoral tests of public support and legitimacy. They represent only themselves (or rather their own high-commands or directorates) and yet they seek to exercise a peculiar kind of tyranny over the communities in which they operate, and over elected governments, judiciaries and social and economic institutions.

Frequently terrorist propagandists point to the fact that the governments and security forces have themselves employed violence and terror, for example, in international and colonial wars. It is certainly true that there are few liberal states that could claim to be totally innocent of such charges. Of course there is an important distinction (which terrorists do not recognise) between force as legitimate coercion by the state, and violence. But just because an act is authorised by the government of a state or one of its agencies it is not necessarily made legitimate. If the action is a clear violation of moral laws we must properly regard it as violence albeit carried out in the state's name. It may be in practice very difficult indeed to discover the person or persons responsible, or even to ascertain whether there was a deliberate decision to use illegitimate coercion, for in large and complex institutions such as governments, armies and colonial bureaucracies, a long and rigorous inquiry may fail to establish the truth. But it would be stupid to deny, for example, that acts of murder, torture and intimidation have been committed by forces and agencies of liberal states. (Though it should also be borne in mind that legislative and judicial investigations and processes can be and are frequently brought to bear in these cases.)

Terrorists like to argue that as all states, including even liberal ones professing humane principles, commit acts of terror and violence, then it is permissible for terrorists to do the same. They are not persuaded by the traditional Christian objection that 'two wrongs do not make a right'. Typically they argue that extreme ruthlessness and violence are essential if one is to win the struggle for power and that they too are compelled to fight 'with the gloves off'. They dismiss talk of humanitarian considerations and rules of war as either a trick by their enemies or as so much sentimental rubbish.

It is perhaps not sufficiently widely realised that political terrorism within liberal democracies poses a fundamental philosophical and ideological attack on humane liberal values and morality. Feliks Gross has rightly stressed[8] that every terrorist campaign that is launched in liberal democratic states entails an intensive propaganda warfare stage directed at defamation of liberal values and institutions and character assassination of leaders. The history of terrorism in liberal states totally disproves Hannah Arendt's claim that violence is speechless.[9] However crude or callow their ideology and the content of their propaganda all terrorist campaigns are characterised by frenetic pamphleteering, journalism, and every available use of media. Some groups have set up their own radio stations, others have tried to use hostages to blackmail governments into according them television or radio time for their manifestos to be read. Nor should we forget the more traditional means. In Northern Ireland tub-thumping sermons, speeches, even songs and poems, have all been used as vehicles for propaganda for paramilitary groups.

Every terrorist group in a liberal democratic setting tries to make maximum use of the freedoms of speech and the press which prevail. Terrorists are only too well aware that their really crucial requirement is large and growing public support. Only when they have a solid constituency of public support can they hope to become a more effective political force. The characteristic terrorist organ for waging this form of propaganda and political warfare is a political party wing which can if necessary continue to operate 'legally' if and when, as frequently happens, the paramilitary movement is proscribed under emergency regulations. I believe that these ideological and propaganda war aspects of terrorism are extremely important, and I shall be returning to them later in the analysis.

# XV
# THE TERRORIST THREAT TO
# LIBERAL SOCIETIES

It has been shown that terrorism constitutes a direct repudiation of liberal and humane values and principles, and that terroristic ideology is inevitably and constantly deployed in a struggle to defame and discredit liberal democracy. It is an important, sometimes over-riding, terrorist aim to undermine the political will, confidence and morale of liberal governments and citizens so that they are made more vulnerable to political and social collapse. A second major terrorist political stratagem is the attempt to push the liberal state into authoritarianism, and hence into denying its constitutionalism, into dropping all humane restraints and checks on power, and ultimately into becoming a paramilitary or police state, a mirror image of the terrorism it is supposed to be defeating. Carlos

Marighela's ideas of militarising the situation[10] by trapping the authorities into brutal repression and over-reaction which then alienates the public and drives them into tacit or active collaboration with the terrorists have been widely employed and refined by others. Certainly liberals who neglect the political and ideological warfare dimensions of terrorism do so at their peril. Every action, every response by a liberal democratic régime faced with political terrorist campaigns, should therefore be considered not only for its purely military and physical implications but also for its wider political and socio-psychological consequences for the liberal state. For terrorism thrives and trades on the graver mistakes and misjudgements of the government authorities and security forces, powerful parties and groups within society. Indeed by a whole series of such mistakes liberal democracy can bring itself to the very brink of disintegration without the terrorists having to win any decisive military victory.

Political terrorism is thus, *par excellence*, a weapon of psychological warfare. Its theorists and skilled proponents hope to achieve a climate of fear, panic, disorientation and capitulation out of all proportion to the actual military strength and numerical support of the terrorist movement. And the terrorists judge their own 'success' or 'failure' primarily in terms of political, psychological and propaganda impact rather than purely by the traditional military criteria of deaths and damage caused.

These considerations are important not only in assessing the strategy and tactics of terrorists, which we will be considering more closely later, but also in trying to answer a more basic question: does internal political terrorism constitute a clear and present danger to the security and internal stability of the liberal democratic state? For if we fall into the error of exaggerating the military capabilities and ambitions of terrorists and underestimating the strengths and advantages of democratic governments and their security forces actively combating them, we are in danger of helping terrorist propaganda. A great deal of terrorist effort is devoted to creating an impression of growing and ultimately invincible strength, ubiquity and cleverness. In addition there is a risk of the government being pushed into over-reaction and ill-judged and counter-productive measures. On the other hand there are circumstances where the greater dangers appear to lie in government weakness, vacillation and under-reaction. It will then be important to communicate the indicators and signals portending a more serious escalation of strife to the authorities, and every effort must be made to mobilise government and public to take urgent and tough measures to deal with the terrorism. In summary one can say that an exaggerated assessment of the threat posed by a particular terrorist campaign is always likely to help the terrorists more than the government, and may indeed give the former a considerable propaganda advantage. Realistic, accurate and frequent assessments of terrorist strength and potential, however unpalatable their conclusions, must continually be made available to government and security chiefs in order to guide anti-terrorist policy.

Whereas it may well be possible to engage in trend analysis and prediction over the range of international and transnational terrorism, internal terrorist dangers can only be properly and thoroughly assessed in relation to the unique context of the campaign concerned. There are clearly three major categories of variable that need to be considered in any such analysis: (i) *the nature of the terrorist movement concerned* – ideology, strategic aims, tactical objectives, size and social base, weaponry and financial resources, leadership, discipline, technical and organisational competence, and internal and external allies; (ii) *the condition of the target state and/or community* – internal stability, form of government, degree of popular support for government, strength of popular will to resist terrorism, competence of leadership at various levels of administration, economic and military resources and capabilities; and (iii) *the influence of the international environment* – the nature and degree of influence or direct or indirect intervention by external states in the conflict, opposition or support of foreign-based ideological, ethnic or exile groups for parties to the conflict, influence of terrorist pressure and propaganda on international opinion and on international organisations, the influence of international opinion and organisations on the course of the terrorist conflict, indirect effects of other international crises and involvements on the target state and its military, diplomatic and economic capabilities.

The third category of variables is extremely important, as revolutionary theorists themselves have been the first to argue. In the modern world a 'pure' case of internal terrorism is really inconceivable. Even where the theatre of operations is narrowly restricted, and the terrorists' resources limited, there are almost invariably foreign sympathisers, arms suppliers, ideological allies and neighbouring powers concerned about any adverse change in the local balance of power, exercising some degree of influence, however discreet. There is no necessary contradiction in the conclusion that the outcome of certain internal terrorist struggles may be ultimately determined by the particular conjunction of international relations imposing itself on local conditions.

However in the specific case of terrorism within Western liberal democracies one is dealing with states which are for the most part relatively stable, enjoy a high degree of international as well as domestic legitimacy, and are sufficiently capable, economically and militarily, of defending their sovereignty. Hence in the case of domestic terrorist problems such states have less to fear from direct foreign military intervention. In these states internal factors, particularly the degree of popular support enjoyed by the terrorist movement and the responsiveness and effectiveness of national counter-measures and operations, tend to be far more important.

By far the most important of these internal factors is the degree of popular support and sympathy enjoyed by the terrorist movement. Tiny intellectual cells of neo-Marxist revolutionaries may confidently expect sections of the masses to rise in their support. Anarchist idealists may dream of mobilising public opinion through daring acts of propaganda of the deed, or hope that their gestures of revolt will act as a catalyst for the destruction of the state. Yet for all their cloudy rhetoric in the name of the 'international working class', such movements have signally failed to capture the leadership of large sections of the masses in any Western state. Attempts by groups such as the Angry Brigade in Britain, the Red Army Fraction in West Germany and the Weathermen in the United States to build even a small base of support among the workers proved ludicrously ineffectual. To the man or woman at the factory gate the abstract jargon of these visitors from another planet seemed to signify only the negation of common sense, an irrelevant and naïve utopianism. For example, the West German figures of estimated membership of Communist, Maoist, Anarchist and New Left organisations in that country over the past three years (see Table 4) show that even in 1974, when terrorist incidents in West Germany reached a peak (see Table 5) the total membership of the New Left, Anarchist and Maoist groups was well below 20,000.

The revolution has so far stubbornly refused to dawn for the ideologues of the far left. By comparison movements whose cause is

Table 4

*Membership of extremist organisations in the Federal Republic of Germany, 1973–5*

| Organisation | 1973 Number | Members | 1974 Number | Members | 1975 Number | Members |
|---|---|---|---|---|---|---|
| Orthodox Communist and pro-communist | 110 | 98,000 | 113 | 117,000 | 105 | 119,000 |
| Maoist | 61 | 12,000 | 65 | 13,000 | 64 | 15,000 |
| Anarchist | 32 | 500 | 24 | 500 | 26 | 500 |
| Others of the New Left | 104 | 5,000 | 90 | 4,500 | 74 | 4,500 |
| Total | 317 | 116,500 | 302 | 136,200 | 279 | 140,200 |
| minus 'several memberships' | | 87,000 | | 102,000 | | 105,000 |

Table 5
*Acts of political violence in the F.R.G., 1973–5*

| Acts of terrorism | 1973 | 1974 | 1975 |
|---|---|---|---|
| Murder | 6 | 5 | 5 |
| Kidnapping | – | – | 2 |
| Bombs | 19 | 37 | 21 |
| Arson | 42 | 57 | 13 |
| Robbery | 3 | 5 | 5 |
| Other acts of violence | 494 | 752 | 427 |

ethnic autonomy or separatism constitute a potentially infinitely greater threat where they arise within the boundaries of existing liberal states. Movements claiming to represent clearly defined ethnic identities, such as the French Canadian Québecois, have a ready-made mass constituency which will certainly become a potent political force if and when it succeeds in uniting the whole of the ethnic minority group against other groups and the central government. This potency is further increased in cases where there are multiple sources of social cleavage reinforcing the ethnic divide, as for example in the cases of Quebec and Northern Ireland where historical tradition reinforces the feelings of separate identity.

Terrorist wings or groups within these wider political autonomist and separatist movements therefore boldly claim symbolically, if not actually, to represent the will of the *ethnie*, or minority involved in social conflict. They have naturally been greatly attracted to emulating the models and style of anti-colonial and Third World liberation struggles. For example, admiration for the Cuban Revolution is a recurrent theme in the polemics of Vallières, Gagnon and other terrorist ideologues of the F.L.Q. And Provisional I.R.A. leaders look eagerly at the history of EOKA and F.L.N. terrorism oblivious of the glaring dissimilarities between these and their own situations. Yet if terrorists *believe* they are fighting a classic-style national liberation war this structures their whole perception of their role in society and gives them an exalted sense of historical mission. They find it easy to stereotype as brutal colonial oppressors a liberal democratic government which in fact enjoys wide support and electoral endorsement, in some cases including the backing of a larger number of their own minority group than they themselves can command! The very certainty of their illusions makes them all the readier for desperate action.

Yet perhaps the most fascinating feature of the link between violence and this nationalist syndrome is the extraordinary volatility and fragility of conceptions of national identity. National allegiances and loyalties should never be taken entirely for granted. Who would have imagined that the small band of dreamers who staged the Dublin Easter Rising, in the face of the apathy or plain hostility of the mass of their country, would succeed only three years later in revolutionising the whole paradigm of Irish political identity for the Republican cause? Violence can act as a dramatic revelation and catalyst not only for the destruction of an established régime, but also the forging of a new political community. There is always the slender hope that an ironic twist of history will fulfil the prophecies of false consciousness.

A prudent liberal democratic government will never lightly dismiss or overlook a campaign of terrorism or rebellion which claims to act in the name of a whole nation or people. Why are the dangers inherent in this form of terrorism so much more acute? Most obviously, such a movement may grow in strength and support so that it is able to put in question not merely the principles of national identity and régime legitimacy and allegiance, but even their very survival. Second, it threatens to undermine and even destroy public order by rejecting the bases and procedures of law and justice, and by militarising inter-factional struggle for control of the state. Third, if sustained over months or even years it will tend to broaden out into full-scale civil war. Fourth, the effects of protracted civil strife on the economic and social life of the community are crippling and severely damaging to the viability of the state. Businesses, property and machinery are destroyed, production has to be at least temporarily stopped or drastically reduced, there is a flight of investment, unemployment worsens, and there is a growing fear of total economic collapse. Community relations become poisoned by suspicion, mistrust, feud, violence and a climate of hatred and vengeance. Political co-operation begins to crack up and moderate parliamentary politicians lose ground in favour of extremist and paramilitary leaders. Normal processes of law can no longer function effectively; courts, judges, witnesses and juries are intimidated, and the police find themselves unable to secure the vital minimum of public co-operation to enable them to prevent serious breaches of the law, or to secure the conviction of offenders. The security forces find they are increasingly confronted by a wall of non-co-operation or open hostility from large sections of the population, and thus their work of gathering intelligence for security purposes, which is a vital prerequisite of effective anti-terrorist operations, is rendered infinitely more difficult. Additionally, protracted terrorism has the effect of compelling the authorities to divert considerable resources to their security forces to enable them to cope with the growing burdens of internal defence.[11] Nor must we overlook the potentially destabilising consequences of severe terrorist campaigns on international relations, a problem which we shall be considering in more detail in Part III.

It is therefore grossly inadequate to attempt to gauge the seriousness of the challenge of terrorism purely in terms of fatalities caused. American observers frequently point out that the average annual rate of deaths connected with terrorism in Northern Ireland since 1969 (about 200 per year average) is small compared with the average annual homicide rate in a large U.S. city like Chicago (about 1000 per year average). Yet the case of Northern Ireland vividly reveals the misleading nature of such comparisons. In the first place the crime rate in Ulster as a whole was somewhat below the norm for the rest of the United Kingdom before the commencement of the 'troubles' in 1968. And Britain has in any case always had markedly lower crime rates (and murder rates in particular) than the United States. Hence the 'deaths caused by political violence' in Northern Ireland, 1969–76 (recorded in Table 6) represent not only a tragic waste of human life but also a traumatic shock to the previously relatively peaceful and close-knit communities of this small province (population approximately $1\frac{1}{2}$ million). To get a truer picture of the impact of these fatalities on the province it is worth projecting the equivalent proportional death toll in the total populations of the United States or Great Britain. Assuming that the U.S. population is 138 times that of Ulster, and that the population of Great Britain is approximately 35 times as large as Ulster's the cumulative death toll in Ulster since 1969 is equivalent to almost 232,668 deaths in the United States and over 59,010 in Great Britain. These are truly horrifying figures which indicate something of the intensity and bloodiness of this protracted internal war in Northern Ireland. Despite the declaration of the so-called truce by the Provisional I.R.A. in February 1975, the deaths from political violence have continued to show a steep rise in 1976. The monthly figures for the period January to September 1976 (see Table 7) indicated that the total of fatalities for the year would be the highest since 1972, when 467 people died.

And even these stark figures cannot really convey the extent of the agony of shock and suffering caused to the population of the Province as a whole. Many of the deaths have resulted from acts of cold-blooded random terror. Hundreds of innocent civilians — men, women and children — have been murdered by bombings and shootings. Over 250 British soldiers and over 150 policemen have been killed. Nor should one forget the thousands who have been maimed and injured. Between 1968 and September 1976 there have been over 12,000 injuries to civilians. As Richard Rose has commented (in early 1976): 'Since the Troubles commenced ... more than one Ulsterman in every hundred has been killed or

Table 6

*Deaths by political violence in Northern Ireland 1969–76*

|  | Northern Ireland | | Great Britain* (equivalent annual) | United States† (equivalent annual) |
|  | Annual | Cumulative total | | |
|---|---|---|---|---|
| 1969 | 13 | 13 | 455 | 1,794 |
| 1970 | 25 | 38 | 875 | 3,450 |
| 1971 | 173 | 211 | 6,055 | 23,874 |
| 1972 | 467 | 678 | 16,345 | 64,446 |
| 1973 | 250 | 928 | 8,750 | 34,500 |
| 1974 | 216 | 1,144 | 7,560 | 29,808 |
| 1975 | 247 | 1,391 | 8,645 | 34,085 |
| 1976 | 295 | 1,686 | 10,325 | 40,710 |
| Totals |  |  | 59,010 | 232,668 |

* Assuming deaths in proportion to British population, 35 times that of Northern Ireland.
† Assuming deaths in proportion to U.S. population, 138 times that of Northern Ireland.
*Source*    Northern Ireland data: R.U.C. Press Office, Belfast.

wounded by political violence. Given the size of extended family networks in the Province, this means that nearly one family in every six has had a father, a son, a nephew or an aunt killed or injured in the Troubles.'[12]

In addition we must take into account the destruction of homes and business premises caused by terrorist bombs and arson. Hundreds of thousands of pounds worth of damage has been inflicted every month of the 'troubles'. The economy of the province has been hit not only by the effects of recession but also by the ruinous consequences of terrorism in disrupting normal business activity and driving out investment. The annual subsidy from the British government is estimated to be running at over £600 million, and over £135 million has been paid out in compensation for damage to property in the province since 1969.

Moreover while it is true that the British Army's 'low-intensity operations' have been remarkably effective in preventing an escalation from terrorism to full-scale civil war, the damage caused by political violence to the social and political fabric of the Province should not be underestimated. Over seven long years of shootings and bombings and sectarian violence have inevitably undermined the will and basis for political co-operation both between and within the two communities. Political fragmentation and polarisation have

Table 7

*Monthly deaths connected with terrorism in Northern Ireland, Jan.–Sept. 1976*

| Month | R.U.C. | R.U.C. 'R' | Army | U.D.R. | Civilians | Total |
|-------|--------|-----------|------|--------|-----------|-------|
| January | 2 | 1 | 1 | 1 | 42 | 47 |
| February | 2 | 1 | 0 | 1 | 23 | 27 |
| March | 0 | 0 | 4 | 0 | 13 | 17 |
| April | 0 | 1 | 0 | 5 | 14 | 20 |
| May | 3 | 3 | 0 | 0 | 20 | 26 |
| June | 1 | 1 | 1 | 0 | 34 | 37 |
| July | 1 | 0 | 2 | 1 | 24 | 28 |
| August | 1 | 0 | 2 | 0 | 17 | 20 |
| September | 1 | 0 | 0 | 0 | 11 | 12 |
| | | | | Cumulative total | | 234 |

weakened the position of pragmatic moderates in search of peaceful negotiation and compromise. Moderates searching for some form of power-sharing government to replace the dismantled Stormont system have found their task made far more difficult as the hardliners, acting in close cahoots with the paramilitary leaders, have entrenched maximalist positions. Confidence and morale among moderates has been further weakened by their suspicion of direct 'talks' and 'deals' between terrorist organisations and the British administration.

Still more widely diffused and potentially more dangerous have been the effects of intensifying hatred and suspicion on relations between the Catholic and Protestant communities. A whole generation of children has been born into a culture of bitter sectarian conflict. Paramilitarisation of youth has only served to reinforce the traditionally divisive effects of an education system rigidly segregated on religious lines. Movements of local populations out of vulnerable 'mixed' or 'dividing line' housing areas into the greater security of their own Protestant or Catholic territories provide both clear evidence and reinforcement of the poisoned and embittered state of inter-community relations.

The brave efforts of the Peace movement have to be seen against the whole intractable and terrible background of the present situation in the Province. While the deeply moving Peace campaign has been attracting growing support both in Ireland and abroad, terrorist murder has continued to take its toll (see Table 7). For the unpleasant fact is that it does not take more than a small handful of fanatical people, dedicated to violence and destruction, to keep a terrorist campaign going. The Provisional I.R.A. appear oblivious of the fact that they lack any legitimacy in the eyes of the people they claim to be 'liberating'. In their blinkered ideology they see themselves waging an anti-colonial war of 'national liberation' against the wicked British oppressor and conveniently ignore the fact that the Protestant two-thirds of the population of Northern Ireland are adamantly opposed to a united Ireland on any terms. Paramilitaries on both extremes appear determined to continue shooting and bombing each other to glory, and to use violence against all those, even members of the Peace movement, who dare to get in their way.

Hence however hard politicians and community and church leaders work to establish a peaceful community, and to find a viable political solution, tough security measures are going to be absolutely essential to deal with the men of violence. There is not the slightest chance of any effective constitutional government in Ulster being able to work properly unless law and order is restored and maintained. There is a naïve assumption in some circles that all that the British Northern Ireland Secretary and Cabinet need to do is to facilitate the agreement of Ulster politicians to a suitable formula or constitutional package, and presto!, the troops can be brought out. But, of course, whatever constitutional arrangements are ultimately agreed they are going to be bitterly rejected and fought by at least one of the paramilitary extremist movements on the ground that the purity of their maximalist principles has been betrayed. Rebellions do not generally just fade away. They have to be put down ruthlessly and effectively if normal life and business are to be restored. In a society where, as Richard Rose has vividly shown, [13] government with complete consensus is unattainable, government authority grounded on something less than consensus will have to be imposed and backed by determined bipartisan support at Westminster. Those who will a political settlement in Ireland must will means of iron to effect it.

The case of the strife in Northern Ireland, the longest and bloodiest campaign of terrorism waged within any modern liberal democracy with the exception of Israel in modern times, vividly demonstrates the problems posed by political terrorism in its severe form. Terrorism in the province has brought the country at times perilously close to complete civil war and anarchy. It has vitiated attempts at constitutional reform and progress through the politics of compromise and reconciliation. And it has sown inter-communal hatred, bitterness and blood feud. Nor is that all. Clearly the safety and well-being of the rest of the United Kingdom are also intimately affected by developments in Ulster. The United Kingdom government is the legally responsible body charged with the tasks of protecting life and property and law and order in the troubled Province. Britain provides some £600 million per year in subsidy to support its debilitated economy, in addition meeting the heavy cost of deploying British Army units in aid to the civil power. Moreover, bearing in mind the large Irish Catholic and Protestant communities settled in mainland cities such as Liverpool, Glasgow and Manchester, there can be little doubt that if a full-scale civil war broke out in Ireland it would spill over into British cities.

It is of course true that Britain's financial and military burden in Northern Ireland is a heavy one. In the context of recent swingeing cuts in defence expenditure it is worrying that we have had to cut back force levels in B.A.O.R. commitment so drastically to help service our responsibilities in Ulster. But what are the alternatives? Valiant efforts have been made to strengthen the R.U.C. and the police reserves in Ulster in order to reduce dependence on the army but it is an extremely difficult long-term task to create a force that enjoys confidence, authority and effectiveness among two warring communities, and the police force is by no means ready to manage without the army's presence. There is much wild talk advocating complete withdrawal of British forces. Yet this would undoubtedly make a bad problem much worse. The terrorist organisations of both warring communities would undoubtedly move in fast to fill the vacuum left by the retreating British. A civil war would ensue, and within the resulting terrorist enclaves, whether orange or green, foreign elements hostile to the interests of the United Kingdom, such as the Soviet K.G.B., would be tempted to interfere and establish alliances and bases with the belligerent movements. Britain's abrogation of her responsibilities in Ulster, and her ensuing withdrawal would be worse than the disease. Moreover it would be tantamount to an open invitation to other domestic and international terrorist groups to feed on the carcass of British sovereignty. Furthermore if a major civil war ensued it would certainly spread over the border and draw Irish forces and factions into the fray. In any 'doomsday scenario' of a conflict of this seriousness developing in Ireland the strong possibility of intervention by a United Nations or regional peacekeeping force must also be taken into account.

Thus we see that the situation in Northern Ireland graphically demonstrates both the intractability and potential gravity of prolonged terrorism in a liberal democratic state. It raises, in a particularly acute form, the problems of identifying and implementing the appropriate response and counter-measures by governments and societies under attack. Some of these problems are considered more fully later.

## XVI
## THE ROOTS OF TERRORISM

Having established that internal terrorism constitutes a potentially grave problem for liberal democracy, one is driven to try to gain an understanding of its underlying causes. Attempts have been made to link the onset of political terrorism to particular socio-economic conditions or to psychopathology, but they have been singularly unsuccessful. It is true that political terrorism is a minority activity, but only a tiny proportion of those captured and convicted for terrorist offences have been found to be either psychotic or acutely deprived either in absolute or relative terms. Indeed much of the politically motivated terrorism in liberal democracies for the past decade has been committed by the spoilt children of affluence. The Baader–Meinhof gang, the Weathermen, the Japanese United Red Army and the Angry Brigade in Britain have all mainly comprised young people from comfortably-off middle class homes and with the 'advantages' of higher education. What chance would a mere poverty-stricken revolutionary have of retaining the massive retinue of legal advisers placed at the disposal of Ulrike Meinhof and her colleagues?

Nor does the case of the I.R.A. make such theories any more convincing. For although the Officials and Provisionals in the North are among the small number of modern terrorist movements with large working-class elements in their following, these movements have been spectacularly unsuccessful in mobilising real bases of mass support among the poor either in the North, or in those areas of the Republic where absolute levels of poverty and deprivation are much higher than anywhere else in the British Isles.

If it is argued that political terrorism is a function, or at least a symptom, of marginality and deprivation in an affluent society, why is the incidence of terrorism so much lower in the United States, Canada and Australasia than in Europe and Latin America? On the other hand, if it is seriously argued that political terrorism is a response to high levels of absolute poverty or deprivation, why is it that the annual rate of terrorist incidents in Western Europe far outstrips that of India or of the least developed Afro-Asian countries?

There *is* a much more powerful tool for understanding the roots of political terrorism, though it has been sorely neglected until recently. We can attempt to identify and explore the political motivations of terrorists and to relate them to particular ideologies, régimes, conflicts and strategic and tactical conditions. This approach affords us by far the richest insights into the dynamics of terrorism within liberal democratic societies with which the present work is primarily concerned.

Whatever their ideological colouration, terrorists in democratic societies are desperate people bitterly opposed to the prevailing régime, alienated from all liberal democratic values. Yet, by definition, liberal societies contain overwhelming majorities in favour of liberal institutions and values. Knowing as he does that the liberal democratic government enjoys such universal support and legitimacy the fanatical dissident may give up all hope of gaining influence or political power by peaceful and legitimate means such as electoral struggle — if ever, indeed, he had such hopes — and may consider instead various violent alternative roads to power, including political terrorism. Hence the paradox that a growing popular consensus on the legitimacy of liberal democratic government renders a desperate internal challenge by minorities most fanatically opposed to it more probable.

The rational and well-informed terrorist knows full well that in taking on the liberal state he is likely to be at the dangerous end of an asymmetrical conflict. But if he has given up all hope of any other vehicle of fundamental change — such as the liberal state's defeat or assimilation at the hands of a rival state, or a total economic collapse or a mass insurrection — he may well conclude that terrorism is the weapon of last resort. As we shall shortly observe, in the discussion on terrorist strategy and tactics, the advantages are by no means all on the side of the liberal democratic state in this asymmetrical conflict. However, the point to be made here is that the odds are stacked heavily against the terrorists in any well-ordered relatively stable liberal state. And the very vulnerability and isolation of the terrorist will tend to be intensified as the vast majority of citizens rally and close ranks to protect themselves, their community and the constitutional order which they regard as legitimate. Hence, unless the liberal state's authorities grossly mishandle the situation, public hostility to the terrorists will tend to increase in proportion to the visibility of the terrorist campaign. As the public is roused to outrage and fury by terrorist attacks on life and property, the situation may well rebound upon the terrorist. They become still more marginal, hunted and desperate creatures more often than not flung into heavy dependence upon the criminal underworld or on foreign states for aid, succour and sanctuary.

One of the consequences of the terrorists' relative marginality in the liberal state is that it becomes far easier for the terrorist movement to terrorise the terrorist, to keep tabs on his or her movements and to control and discipline members. Because the bulk of the population support the authorities in their fight to defeat terrorists, the terrorist cannot melt away into the 'background' easily. And once he or she has been 'blooded' in a terrorist attack or venture it becomes easy for the terrorist movement to hold them by threatening to betray them to the authorities: thus the mechanism for terrorist control of the group by means of blackmail and intimidation is all too effective.

Inevitably many who get caught up in the network of terrorist organisations become involved accidentally by virtue of criminal expertise or coercive exploitation by the terrorists. Some are bought. More than a few may be attracted by promises of power or the vicarious sense of power and excitement entailed in any underground organisation. Many more are trapped into collaboration by weakness and fear. Many of the pathetic creatures employed as bomb planters by terrorist 'retailers' fall into this category. However none of these sources of motivation can explain the genuine fanatics, the leaders and the militant activists who sustain both the terrorist movement and its propaganda and political warfare. We must take into account their ideological obsession and fanaticism which is the sustaining passion that drives them to strive to reap tactical gains, especially publicity, for their causes.

It is these aspects of terrorist ideology, and the use of terrorism to control and sustain terrorist movements that are discussed in the following chapter.

## XVII
## TERRORIST IDEOLOGIES AND
## BELIEFS

The lack of any generally agreed and adequate scientific theory of the causes of revolutionary terrorism is too well known to require emphasis. Few have bettered Feliks Gross' checklist[14] of antecedent conditions for terrorism: a sense of oppression or a state of anomie and the availability of a terroristic organisation, leadership and ideology. I would argue that we can usefully add: the diffusion of knowledge concerning terrorist 'successes', methods and technologies which facilitates emulation; the existence of a tradition of terrorism; and the intensification of hatred and the desire for vengeance which characterises communal violence.

General theories of violence are remarkably unhelpful for the study of terrorism. If we examine, for example, the psychological theories of the frustration-aggression and relative deprivation schools we will discover that they build up very sophisticated models of relative deprivation, from which many different socio-political implications can be derived. The difficulty is that whatever relationships between expectations and capabilities are posited the theory only provides a basis for correlating them to manifestations of 'frustration-aggression' in general. The theory cannot explain why, in similar socio-economic and political conditions, some groups resort to terrorism while others manifest other forms of violence or aggressive behaviour. As Durkheim shrewdly observed: 'the psychological factor is too general to predetermine the course of social phenomena. Since it does not call for one social form rather than another, it cannot explain any of them.'[15]

Most social scientific attempts at theory of terrorism suffer from a fatal flaw: they neglect the role and influence of terrorist ideologies and beliefs in inspiring and guiding revolutionary terrorist organisations and in nourishing hatred and violence.

Understanding terrorism is an historical and philosophical, as well as scientific, task. We should not lose sight of the individual values and goals which themselves determine and inform consciously willed social and political action. All too often social scientists regard ideology in vulgar Marxist fashion as a mere reflection or product of the prevailing socio-economic conditions. This neglect is in part a consequence of the influence of Marxism's mechanistic conceptions of ideology as false consciousness and as the legitimation of the ruling class. Marxist and mechanistic sociological theory has generally overlooked the crucial role of ideology in providing for the ageless human need for a meaning to existence. The insights of other social theorists such as de Tocqueville, Sorel and Mannheim, who saw that ideologies and social myths could constitute surrogate religions and guides to conduct, have tended to be overlooked.

It is an extremely difficult task to delineate the ideological development and background of contemporary revolutionary terrorism. A thorough study would necessitate what R. G. Collingwood terms the 'mental re-enactment' of terrorist thought in each tiny terrorist group. All that is possible here is to identify some of their ideologies' dominant features and self-images. There are three major contemporary strands in revolutionary terrorist ideology; (i) 'classical' anarchism and nihilism; (ii) Third World revolutionism; and (iii) New Left ideologies of violence. These elements are frequently combined and are often fused with Marxist, Marxist–Leninist and Nationalist doctrines.

However, the first point to clarify is that revolutionary terrorism is officially rejected by Marxist–Leninist and Maoist parties. They believe that the revolution cannot be made by the subjective act of will of revolutionaries: it must await the correct objective socio-economic conditions.. Moreover, they regard individual revolutionary terrorism as being counter-productive. At best it is seen as misguided romanticism risking valuable lives of potential revolutionaries. At worst it is charged with hindering the real revolution by provoking police repression and hindering the work of the party among the workers. Despite this official stance, however, the Soviet leadership has clearly taken due note of the growth and potential influence of New Left and Third World revolutionary terrorist groups since the early 1960s. They have expanded their repertoire of opportunist tactics to include assistance and indirect financial and logistic support to groups as ideologically diverse as the Provisional I.R.A., the Baader–Meinhof and the P.L.O. Presumably they hope to benefit from the disruptive effects of terrorist operations within non-communist states. The pattern here is clearly opportunist 'proxy' terrorism rather than real ideological affinity.

The anarchist and nihilist strands in terrorist ideology are still strong today as can be seen in the propaganda of groups such as the Baader–Meinhof and Black Cross in Germany and the Weathermen and the S.L.A. in America. There was a strong tradition of physical violence in anarchism going back to Bakunin, Nechayev and Malatesta which declared war on the state and on all forms of government and legality. Some anarchist leaders, such as Kropotkin and Ferrer developed elaborate projects for an anarchist form of society. Others, of course, favoured purely peaceful methods of anarchist education and cultural influence to bring about liberation. The nihilists, of whom Nechayev is the most notorious example, emphasised the need to destroy above all else and did not articulate any vision of a post-revolutionary society. In his *Catechism of the Revolutionist* Nechayev proclaimed:

> The revolutionary despises all doctrinairism and has rejected the mundane sciences, leaving them to future generations. He knows of only one science, the science of destruction. To this end, and this end alone, he will study mechanics, physics, chemistry, and perhaps medicine. To this end he will study day and night the living science; people, their characters and circumstances... His sole and constant object is the immediate destruction of this vile order.[16]

Several themes in 'classical' anarchist terrorism have an extraordinarily modern ring: the notion that violence is ennobling and cathartic (for example, Bakunin's claim that the passion to destroy is a creative urge); the emphasis on 'propaganda by the deed' as a technique of symbolic protest and publicity; and the hopelessly ambitious efforts to organise an anarchist revolution internationally. Mannheim was, we now know, premature in his claim, forty years ago, that radical anarchism had almost entirely disappeared from the political scene.[17] It has come back to haunt us in new forms! Mannheim considered radical anarchism to be an outstanding example of what he termed the 'Chiliastic utopian mentality'.[18] His ideology–utopia distinction has been generally discarded by contemporary sociologists but his brilliant analysis of what he terms the utopian mentality still has much to teach us about the character of present-day anarchism and revolutionary terrorism:

Their thinking is incapable of correctly diagnosing an existing condition of society. They are not concerned at all with what really exists; rather in their thinking they already seek to change the situation that exists... In the utopian mentality, the collective unconscious, guided by wishful representation and the will to action hides certain aspects of reality. It turns its back on everything which would shake its belief or paralyse its desire to change things.[19]

Mannheim emphasises the features of blindness to the existing order, a tendency to simplify everything and to blur all partial differences, and an obsessively Manichean view of history and society which divides everybody into friends and enemies. Above all he stresses constantly the Chiliastic utopians' need for illusions and for action to hide harsh realities. This characterisation certainly holds for the mentality of revolutionary terrorism. Listen to the F.L.Q. terrorist Vallières on Utopia:

...as soon as you begin to act, the old system hastens to turn you into a public menace and a criminal, so as to be able to bury you alive before your 'idealism' puts Molotov cocktails, dynamite, and rifles into the hands of the workers and the young people who are very receptive to the idea of Utopia, which is all they are waiting for to rise up *en masse* against those who organize, profit from, and defend oppression. For no matter what the ideologists of capitalism, neocapitalism, and imperialism may say about Utopia, it is not a philosopher's utopia: it sums up aspirations which cry out not only to be perceived and understood, but above all to be *realized*. Nor is Utopia the final point, the terminus of human evolution. On the contrary, it is only the point of departure, the beginning, the first stage of the new history which men will embark upon together once they are liberated from their present condition as niggers, as sub-men.[20]

Here we have all the elements of Chiliastic utopianism laid bare. There is the nihilist total rejection of the present 'vile order', the absurd illusion that the workers and youth are waiting to 'rise up *en masse*' at the terrorists' first bomb blast, and the desperate impatience of the cry 'Utopia must be realised *now*'. As Dr André

Lassier, a Montreal psychiatrist, has observed: 'The terrorist is a man who cannot wait. He is in a state of mental urgency'.[21]

Which elements in Third World revolutionist ideology have been most influential in moulding revolutionary terrorist groups' beliefs? I believe the significance of Guevara, Debray and Marighela in this respect has been exaggerated. It is true that all these guerrilla war theorists departed radically from Marxist orthodoxies by stressing the subjective factors in revolutionary struggle. Revolution does not have to wait for the 'ripening' of objective conditions. It can be brought about by violence, by military struggle based on the guerrilla *foco*. In their emphasis on the fusion of political and military leadership in the guerrilla they do have organisational affinities with certain terrorist groups. But it should be noted that none of the Cuban guerrilla theorists advocate terrorism as a principal means of revolutionary struggle. Guevara argues that it is actually counter-productive and Debray allows it only a limited diversionary role. It is true that Marighela does advocate terrorist bombings and arson as valuable methods for the urban guerrilla war, but it has an extremely minor role in his scenario of revolutionary struggle. He envisages a hypermobile urban guerrilla war against the security forces to act as a catalyst and support for a general rural guerrilla conflict. At no point does he advocate acts of indiscriminate terror against the population. Marighela sees a concerted urban and rural guerrilla war as the road to revolutionary power.

Sartre and Fanon are of far greater significance in the development of terrorist thought. Their almost mystical view of violence as an ennobling and as a morally regenerative force has been widely diffused among revolutionary intellectuals. So too has their advocacy and championship of terrorism. Sartre claims that revolutionary violence is 'man re-creating himself'. Is Sartre so blinded by hate that he cannot see the roads to utopia strewn with the bodies of their victims? 'O Liberté! O Liberté! que de crimes on commet en ton nom!'

Let us strip away the masks of terrorist illusions and expose the deathhead of murder beneath. Terrorists are fond of using romantic euphemisms for their murderous crimes. They claim to be revolutionary heroes yet they commit cowardly acts and lack the heroic qualities of humanity and magnanimity. They profess to be revolutionary soldiers yet they attack only by stealth, murder and maim the innocent, and disdain all rules and conventions of war. They claim to bring liberation when in reality they seek power for themselves. Some claim that their violence ennobles them: history shows that it is totally corrupting and ultimately is turned against the revolutionary society itself. They frequently profess that they administer 'revolutionary justice': in truth they make war on all ethics and legality and substitute the whim of their own tyranny.

There is another major factor in addition to the ideologies and beliefs of terrorists which plays a major part in sustaining terrorist organisations and activities. This is the use of terrorism by the group leaders to enforce absolute loyalty and obedience to the secret society. Even minor breaches of discipline can lead to brutal punishments and disfigurement: more serious offences such as informing are punished by death. Frequently the families and friends of terrorists are threatened or become targets if the leader decrees reprisals.

Dostoevsky in his fictional portrait of Nechayev (Verkhovensky in *The Possessed*) shows vivid insight into the way in which the terrorist society begins to devour its own members. He has Stavrogin explain to Verkhovensky:

> Can you count on your fingers the people who can be accepted as members of your circles? All this is just bureaucracy and sentimentality – all this is just so much cement, but there's one thing that is much better – persuade four members of the circle to murder a fifth on the excuse that he is an informer and you'll at once tie them all up in one knot by the blood shed. They'll be your slaves.

Of course the historical Nechayev, with the help of five other terrorist cell members, actually did murder a member of their secret society, Ivanov. German Lopatin gives an account of the murder in a letter to Natalie Herzen:

> I already knew that Ivanov was killed not as a spy but as a man who had changed his opinions and deviated from certain paragraphs of the statutes of the 'Committee' [the terrorist organisation]; but of *what* those deviations consisted I did not know. This is what people who took part in the murder, and some other people, say: Ivanov was well off (perhaps even rich), and had supplied Nechayev with money on more than one occa-

sion. Towards the end he began to have doubts that the money was being put to the right use. One day he said to Nechayev: 'This is the last time I'm giving you any money. You know I am ready to give all I have to the "cause", but here I must lay down two conditions: (1) that the person to whom I am to give the money inspires me with more confidence than you do; (2) that I have some kind of guarantee that the person himself knows where the money is going and is not merely a blind tool in someone else's hands.' They say Nechayev did not take the money but went to Uspensky, Pryzhov and the others, and told them that words like these were a breach of discipline, a failure to observe the paragraph of the statutes which declared that 'the property of members is at the disposal of the "Committee" '; such things, (he said) must be nipped in the bud . . . and so on. . . . I knew that Uspensky had lured Ivanov into the wood on some false pretext, and I had always wondered why, since he was walking right beside him, he did not shoot him in the temple. Why did he need five men? But now I hear in letters that the participants, by their own account, lost their heads to such a degree that they forgot they had weapons on them and began striking Ivanov with stones and their own fists and strangling him with their own hands. Altogether it was a most brutal murder. Ivanov was already dead when Nechayev remembered about his revolver, and to make quite sure he shot the corpse through the head. . .[22]

# XVIII
# VULNERABILITIES OF LIBERAL SOCIETIES

Thus far the analysis has been concentrated upon the terrorist movements and their sustaining ideologies. We must now examine those factors that have tended to enhance the vulnerability of Western liberal states to terrorist attacks.

One obvious but extremely important factor is the inherent civil rights and freedoms of the liberal states which terrorist organisations can exploit. Freedom of movement both between and within liberal states, freedom of association, and freedom from totalitarian style police surveillance and control, are all rightly highly valued by citizens of Western liberal states. Yet they can be all too easily taken advantage of by terrorists. They can slip quickly across frontiers if police interest becomes too close. It is relatively easy to move arms, explosives and personnel to target areas. What chance, by comparison, do terrorist movements have in a state like the Soviet Union where every block of apartments, every street, every place of work, is under close surveillance by the secret police or their army of informers, where private vehicles are a luxury reserved for privileged party officials and professional workers, and where all chemicals, explosives and weaponry are kept under the strict control of the government?

The crucial advantage of a liberal state to the terrorist, however, is the freedom of the media. The terrorist operating within such a society knows that his acts of terrorism will be instantly publicised by the television, radio and Press and that pictures of a really sensational attack or outrage can be relayed round the world with the aid of T.V. communications satellites. By contrast, in China or the Soviet Union, where the régime monopolises control of all media of information, terrorism is robbed of all point or effect because the authorities can ensure that news of any attack is suppressed.

Technological developments have obviously rendered liberal societies more vulnerable to terrorism in a number of ways. Terrorists have been able to exploit the new range of light portable automatic weapons, for example, and the increasingly sophisticated techniques of bomb design and manufacture. But far more important than these trends has been the growing technological interdependence of advanced industrial societies. Modern power plants and computer systems and communications centres afford expensive and attractive targets both because of their key role in urban industrial societies, and because relatively simple acts of sabotage can completely disrupt them. The more sophisticated political terrorists are well aware of the potential tactical advantages of aiming at these jugular veins of modern societies. It would be quite foolish and irresponsible of the authorities to blandly assume that these sensitive nerve points will be regarded as 'off-limits' by terrorists. The terrorists may well find strong arguments, within their own standards of rationality and strategic logic, for causing damage of the most extensive and dangerous proportions, for most terrorists are utterly convinced that any means are justified to realise their transcendental ends.

Two other potential weaknesses of liberal states have already been discussed above. First, there is the almost inevitable fact that there are aggrieved constituencies or minorities within any liberal state providing a promising ground for recruitment and support for an astute revolutionary movement that is ready to champion their causes. Moreover it is always possible for a newly mobilised protest group to outbid the authorities in promises to the aggrieved or alienated, for the rebels do not have the complications of power and responsibility. They do not have the much more difficult task of balancing competing claims and demands, and of having to say 'no'. Second, liberal democratic states, if they are to remain such, are bound to respect fundamental civil liberties and to govern within very clear judicial and constitutional restraints. This makes it inherently more difficult for government to act decisively and ruthlessly against insurgents. It is infinitely more difficult to counter terrorism and urban guerrilla war when one is forced to operate at mid-levels of coerciveness, and even governments and security forces of long-established states have to learn the difficult art of combating internal insurgency *de novo* if they have previously enjoyed long periods of internal peace. I shall be examining in greater detail some of the problems involved in government response, and highlighting some of the more dangerous forms of ineptitude in this field, in a later section.

A less obvious yet difficult problem for the liberal state is the covert subversive activities of hostile foreign states and foreign-based groups. The very openness and vigour of liberal societies is both a standing temptation and an offence in the eyes of those, such as the Communist Party leadership of the Soviet Union, dedicated to destroying Western 'capitalist imperialism'. Part of the vast resources of the K.G.B. is undoubtedly devoted to fostering and aiding terrorist groups operating in Western societies. There is evidence that they are prepared to provide indirect and covert support even to groups with which they have little in common ideologically, presumably on the ground that any disruption and damage sown in Western states will have the effect of hastening the 'collapse of capitalism'.[23] Still more serious problems ensue from this 'permeability' of the liberal state when a number of foreign states mount or support rival terrorist groups operating within the same state. For instance, the civil war that wracked Lebanon in 1975–6 was fuelled by interventions from all directions, with Syrian, Iraqi, Israeli and Libyan involvements of various kinds. It is in fact extremely difficult for a constitutionalist liberal state to prevent such flagrant interventions against its internal sovereignty unless it is prepared to take war emergency measures, to close frontiers and to rigidly restrict and control the movements of foreigners and its own population. And even then it is much easier to prevent or monitor the movement of personnel than it is to stop the supply of cash and arms from outside sources.

In addition to these grave potential points of weakness, the liberal democratic state suffers from yet another more deep-rooted and intangible source of vulnerability which is not generally recognised. Liberal states are *par excellence* civilian as well as being civil societies. Except in times of wars of national defence it is customary for civilians with little or no knowledge of war and strategy to predominate in all policy and decision-making. But internal terrorism is after all a particularly barbaric form of unconventional war. To combat it effectively democratic leaders may therefore need to have some of the classic military virtues. For technical military knowledge and tactical advice they can, of course, call on their military and security chiefs. But political leaders and decision-makers may need to make tough and unpleasant decisions to safeguard the security of state and citizens. It is no good having people at the top who are so squeamish about the use of force, so soft and conscience-torn about killing or locking up terrorists, that they are paralysed into inaction. Fighting terrorism, as many families in Britain know to their heavy cost, requires both moral and physical courage of a high order.

The murder of Mr Ross McWhirter is tragic evidence that private citizens who speak out bravely are as much in the terrorists' line of fire as politicians and diplomats. And in a terrorist campaign it is not only soldiers and policemen and public servants who are under attack; the general public is very much in the front line. The moral courage of all citizens in a liberal democracy is put to severe test by prolonged acts of terrorism. In such circumstances the patriotic ethic of loyal service to one's country and allegiance to the constitution must be the basis of public resistance to the petty tyranny of terror. In the final analysis terrorists are engaged in a test of will with the democratic community and its leaders. If the people are not prepared to back their leaders in standing firm against blackmail and intimidation, if a growing number are simply concerned to 'pass the buck' or to seek a quiet life at any price, then the moral will to victory is thereby appreciably diminished. Hence, in so far as most Western liberal democratic societies have recently experienced a serious weakening of the ethic of authority, discipline and political obligation, we must recognise a more subtle and dangerous long-term vulnerability than any we have previously mentioned.

# XIX
# TERRORIST STRATEGY AND TACTICS

I now wish to examine in greater depth terrorist strategy and tactics in the liberal state. It is sometimes claimed that there is a single overarching terrorist strategy,[24] an understanding of which, it is implied, will unlock all doors to a full understanding of the problem. This is absolute nonsense. Terrorists and terrorist movements are as full of rival strategies as a dog of fleas. To begin to analyse them one must first distinguish between their long-term *political* objectives and strategies and their military strategies. The former are naturally determined by their specific ideological alignment which may range from neo-Nazi aims to the ultra-anarchist or nihilist goals of destroying all states and legal systems.

Contemporary British and American commentary on terrorism has tended to assume that it is a characteristic of the ultra-left. But the left has never had a monopoly of extreme violence. The Nazis and fascists invented and refined many terrorist weapons and methods between the 1920s and 1940s, including new and horrifying forms of mass race terror. In many countries today the threat of terrorism from the extreme right is still grave. For example, this is the case in Italy, where the neo-fascist Social Movement and small neo-fascist cells have claimed responsibility for assassinations of left-wing figures as well as for acts of random slaughter through bombing attacks on railways, public buildings and businesses. And in Spain the extreme right has already resorted to bombs in an attempt to halt the movement to democratic constitutional reforms.

Even in Britain, members of ultra-right organisations have been convicted of bomb and arson attacks on immigrants' property. And in the United States a major arms cache belonging to an ultra-right paramilitary organisation has recently been discovered by police.[25] (This propensity of the extreme right for violence is not really so surprising in view of the fact that fascists followed social imperialists in their belief that violence is inherently progressive and valuable. Echoing Sorel, and Marinetti and the Futurist Movement, fascism made a cult of violent action.)

Ideology affects the political strategy of terrorist movements in several very obvious ways. It serves, first of all, to determine the size of the potential social base of support. Nationalist, autonomist and secessionist movements have the advantage of ready-made easily identified constituencies of support to bid for and win over. The more esoteric and doctrinaire revolutionary neo-Marxist groups lacking such social bases may remain permanently isolated and sectarian. But a revolutionary neo-Marxist movement may be able to compensate in another dimension determined largely by its ideology: it will stand more chance of making political headway if it appears to offer a specific and positive programme or manifesto of fundamental reforms. Purely nihilist and anarchist groups labour under the heavy disadvantage of having nothing clear to promise the masses beyond the destruction of what they term the 'bourgeois oppressor state'.

The only real common ground, the *sine qua non*, of all revolutionary terrorists' political strategy is the aim of smashing the existing political system and seizing power in the name of the revolution. But how does terrorism fit in with the revolutionaries' military strategies? We have earlier noted that the track record of terrorism as a weapon for winning political power is pretty abysmal: only in a few cases of independence struggles against the British did it play a decisive role in bringing victory to the rebels. Against liberal democracies its record is even less encouraging for the terrorist: possibly the only case of terrorism playing the major part in smashing a liberal democratic government was in Uruguay in 1972. Yet even there what the Tupamaros' campaign actually helped to bring about was not a neo-Marxist régime of their own choice but a ruthless right-wing authoritarian government.

Of course the past lack of success does not necessarily mean that it is irrational for revolutionaries to utilise terrorism. Some revolutionaries feel that they will be able to prove that it can work, or else that, in any case, it is the only means left to them. Others with more sophisticated strategies plan to deploy terrorism merely in a valuable auxiliary role or as a tactic in a much wider struggle on many fronts. For example, Carlos Marighela, the Brazilian urban guerrilla theorist, envisaged that:

> From the urban front we shall go on to direct armed struggle against the *latifúndio* through rural guerrilla warfare. With the alliance of the proletariat, peasantry and students in a decentralised and mobile guerrilla war, we shall extend our activities in all directions through the interior of Brazil and finally create a revolutionary army of national liberation to match the conventional army of the military dictatorship.[26]

Repeatedly Marighela emphasises that the whole urban struggle must be seen as a *tactical* struggle, and that the decisive struggle militarily will be in the rural area. It will be noticed that his over-all strategy is very close to that of Mao and Giap in that he advocates protracted guerrilla war with decisive military struggle being waged in the countryside. This revolutionary strategy has been most closely followed and applied in Third World countries, but there is clearly no reason to think that revolutionary theorists will not try to adapt the strategy for the purposes of winning power in a Western liberal state. What part might terrorism play in such a strategy? Clearly, as Debray recognised, terrorism could provide a useful diversion, tying down large numbers of government forces in unrewarding tasks of guarding buildings, lines of communication and so forth. Alternatively it may be used as a means of coercing whole districts or groups of officials into submitting to, and collaborating with, the revolutionaries. And in the wake of their military victories the revolutionaries frequently employ terrorism as a means of repression against designated 'enemies of the revolution' in the 'liberated' areas.

A second possible revolutionary strategy is the mass insurrection. It is sometimes assumed that this method had its day in 1917 Russia but is now obsolete. Recent events in Portugal have changed this perception, for it is clear that, in a situation where the armed forces can no longer be relied upon by the authorities, the politics of the streets may still prove decisive in toppling a régime. The more highly urbanised and industrialised the state concerned the greater the potential of mass action by the working class. For again, provided that the armed forces remain neutral or hostile to the government, the industrial workers will find it a relatively simple matter to bring down the government. The major weapon of the workers in such a situation is the withdrawal of their labour. A prolonged and solid general strike can utterly paralyse any liberal democratic régime and enforce major concessions or abject capitulation by the government, as witness the effects of the Ulster Workers' Council strike in 1974 which caused the collapse of the Northern Ireland Executive. Terrorism clearly plays a very minor or negligible role in this particular revolutionary scenario, though of course both individual and mass terrorism may be used by revolutionaries in the course of consolidating a successor régime.

A third possibility (though its usefulness is inevitably confined to those states with inadequate, ineffective or neutralised armed forces) is the armed putsch against the régime leadership and centres of power. This road to power generally involves a considerable element of political assassination and selective terrorism both as a catalyst for rebellion, and to suppress opposition. However, once again terrorism does not really play the decisive part.

There is, however, a revolutionary strategy of more recent origin developed and elaborated by the guerrilla war theorists such as Begin and Marighela. This strategy aims to exploit the asymmetrical nature of the conflict between rebels and régime by inducing the political and moral destruction of the state. There are four major elements in this approach, and in all four the terrorist weapon plays a crucial role. The first element involves what Marighela terms 'the militarization of the political situation'. By confronting the authorities with an armed revolt and frequent attacks and harassment the revolutionaries compel the régime to retaliate militarily, i.e. to deploy considerable numbers of armed police and soldiers to quell the revolt. The second element involves an escalation of terrorism to make repression so costly that the government will prefer to surrender to revolutionary demands. As the situation becomes more heavily militarised so the revolutionaries will attempt to trap the government and security forces into over-reaction. Terrorism is a convenient weapon for the revolutionaries to use in this context. It is almost impossible to prevent acts of terrorism in highly concentrated urban areas. The general population will naturally become alarmed and demand effective protection. Yet effective counter-measures involve the injection of considerably larger numbers of security forces and the adoption of much more intensive body searches, house-to-house searches, and considerable daily interference in the life of the population. The rebels seize on any opportunity to blame the resulting harassment of the population on the government and portray themselves as the defenders of the masses. Thus they aim to polarise opposition to the government and to emerge as a movement of 'self-defence' with mass support and revolutionary legitimacy. A fourth key objective of this approach is to break the will and morale of the government and security forces by sheer superior will to sustain their struggle and to win. Terrorism clearly has a crucial part in this strategy, for the revolutionaries will hope to demonstrate their superior will to survive and to continue bombings and attacks even when all other military 'success' is denied them. In the eyes of the rebels, the very damaging and debilitating short- and long-term effects of the terrorist campaign on the régime and economy offer an attractive bonus. What is more, the financial and logistic support and numbers of personnel required to mount such a terrorist campaign are relatively small and the risks to the terrorists of death or capture are astonishingly slight. It is clear, therefore, that terrorism plays a highly significant part in the strategy of inducing the political and moral collapse of a target régime.

This takes one right to the crux of the nature of political terrorism. It is *par excellence* a technique of psychological and political warfare. Its military effectiveness and value in terms of its capability for inflicting physical damage is relatively marginal. But its potential for sapping the will of a community or target group and for undermining morale is immense. It is the writer's contention that the richest theoretical insights into political terrorism are to be gained from an analysis of terrorism as a distinctive mode of unconventional psychological warfare aimed ultimately at bringing about a climate of fear and collapse in an incumbent régime or target group. Moreover it is a form of clandestine and undeclared warfare, waged without any humanitarian restraints or rules. It is a phenomenon so beyond the ken of 'normal' experience in an ordered liberal democratic society that it tends not only to highly disorientate the general public but also to confuse and confound professional analysts.

Many analysts fall into the error of equating psychological warfare generally, and terrorism in particular, with propaganda. An interesting and influential analysis by Thornton defined terrorism in an internal war situation as 'a symbolic act designed to influence political behaviour by extranormal means, entailing the use or threat of violence'.[27] Yet while one can agree wholeheartedly that propagandising for the insurgent movement is one important possible function of terrorism, the claim that terror and propaganda are both 'tools for creating public support in the pursuit of political ends'[28] is dangerously misleading. For the activity of political *propaganda* among the general public surely implies a positive indoctrination campaign, or 'deliberate efforts for the propagation of a doctrine'.[29] And surely no rational person would attempt to persuade somebody of the truth of a doctrine by blowing them up or shooting them, or even by bombing or murdering their neighbour. Clearly there is a world of difference between a weapon of psychological coercion, the attempt to disorientate or to break resistance, and the techniques of intellectual persuasion. Let us be quite clear that political terrorism falls primarily in the former category. This is not to deny that in the course of deploying terrorism as a weapon of psychological coercion the terrorist is also signalling warnings and threats to the target group or incumbent régime. But the tasks of political propaganda and ideological polemic are far more likely to be effectively performed by the political and propaganda wings almost invariably deployed in support of insurgent movements, and whose significant role we have earlier noted.

In identifying the possible major tactical objectives of terrorism it might, therefore, be useful to start by examining the objective of publicity. Modern terrorists have emulated Bakunin's prescription of 'propaganda of the deed' by seeking to use spectacular acts of terrorism as a dramatic and effective means of publicising both their cause and their movement to specific governments and to world opinion. The principles of propaganda war have been defined as (i) the identification of an appropriate target, (ii) the choice of a particular objective, or message to be conveyed, (iii) the establishing of credibility for the propaganda source, and (iv) the selection of the most appropriate means of communication.[30] Translated into these terms the terrorist by his act of violence is telling the world: 'We are here. Look what we can do. Heed us or there is worse to come.' It is hard to see how such a crude message is 'improved' by the use of bombing, assassination or kidnapping. If you are in the outrage business presumably one kind of outrage is as good as another. Yet certainly there has been an inflation in the cost of violence required to carry an act of terrorism round the world in banner headlines. There is a kind of Gresham's Law of terrorism: 'they who spill the most blood get the biggest headlines.' Certainly committing murders is one way of getting publicity but it is by no means the only way or necessarily the most effective. It may be that the element of violence causes the act to be bad publicity, even among the target group at whom the act is primarily directed. Consider the much more effective and *positive* propaganda value of Martin Luther King's civil rights movement marches — peaceful, yet morally and politically infinitely more powerful than terrorism.

Another propaganda objective of terrorism may be to inspire militancy and emulation among followers or potential followers. Kozo Okamoto, the Japanese terrorist captured and sentenced to life imprisonment for his part in the Lod Airport massacre on 30 May 1972, claimed in his testimony: 'The Arab world lacks spiritual fervour. So we felt that through this attempt we could probably stir up the Arab world.'[31] Among situationist and anarchist terrorist groups there is frequently the aim of using 'propaganda of the deed' to arouse and heighten the popular consciousness of state and capitalist 'oppression'. Closely allied to this is the objective of advertising the movement's strength and capacity for destruction. Yet observers may view such frenetic attempts to establish credibility as evidence of desperation and weakness rather than of strength. Yet we must not overlook the fact that the terrorist organisation badly needs to maintain a high rate of 'successful' operations not only to maintain morale and credibility but also a means of recruiting, 'blooding' and training new members. They have a constant need to create fresh cells and expertise in bomb-making, weaponry, etc. in order to replace groups that have been captured, wounded or rendered inoperable by police surveillance.

Even though terrorists have had extremely limited success in realising strategic aims they have enjoyed spectacular successes in attaining short-term tactical objectives such as: securing the release of imprisoned brother terrorists, obtaining large ransoms with which to finance further operations, procuring weapons and explosives, eliminating dangerous opponents, and creating diversions to take the pressure off guerrilla forces elsewhere. It must also be recognised that terror is widely used as a means of disciplining and 'punishing' members of the terrorist movement, or members of the community which the movement claims to represent politically. Hence much tactical terrorism is repressive or punitive in intent. The classic terrorist organisation consists of a cell structure in which only the terrorist high command knows the identity of all its groups. Within each cell normally only one member is in contact with other unit leaders and with the movement directorate. In such a system intra-group democracy is unworkable and hence the organisation functions on strictly paramilitary lines. Those suspected of betraying the movement, and those who defy orders, are ruthlessly punished. However terrorists can easily overplay this tactic. As Brian Crozier has shrewdly observed: 'Where revolutionaries find it necessary to kill more people on their own side than the enemy, it must be presumed either that their cause is widely opposed or that, at least, it leaves the population indifferent.'[32] One might add that where a population does turn decisively against a terrorist organisation it is possible for the authorities to eliminate the terrorist threat very rapidly.

In summary, it has been argued that terrorism has been in the past of relatively little value in serving revolutionary strategy within liberal democracies. It is a dangerous weapon that often misfires and may actually work against revolutionary purposes by turning the mass of the population against the revolutionaries, or by stimulating the government and security forces into stinging and effective repression. However, terrorism and urban guerrilla methods are still being refined and tested in advanced industrialised liberal societies. It is possible that in the special conditions of socio-economic malaise and acute political divisions terrorism might prove capable of exploiting these weaknesses. By hastening and exacerbating a failure of democratic will and nerve, and by helping to precipitate a political and moral crisis, terrorism could conceivably jeopardise the future of a liberal state.

At the purely tactical level terrorism has already met with considerable successes. It is primarily an offensive rather than a defensive weapon which, in the classic tradition of guerrilla tactics, involves avoiding pitched battles with superior military firepower. Its characteristic *modus operandi* is unwearying hit and run attacks to wear down and demoralise the enemy. In order to carry out these tasks effectively terrorist organisations depend upon adequate leadership, expertise, logistic support, training and operational planning. Again, as is the case in all forms of unconventional war, some degree of popular support and collaboration is a priceless asset to the insurgents. This asset is indeed indispensable to any long-term success for it is only through a widespread network of informers that the terrorists can acquire the essential intelligence to anticipate the moves of their militarily more powerful opponents and to learn when and where to strike at their forces and bases. This mastery of intelligence was the secret of Michael Collins' success in the campaign against the British forces from 1916–21. However, in the vital battle for intelligence, the insurgents do not necessarily possess overwhelming advantage. For modern counter-insurgency forces now invest much skill, special training, experience and money in their own intelligence operations. They take full advantage of any gaps in the terrorists' own internal security system, and systematically infiltrate their own agents into terrorist organisations and circles.

A close study of the nature of terrorist strategy, tactics and techniques would seem to justify Kitson's view that the decisive war against terrorism must be waged in the realm of intelligence and counter-intelligence.[33] It is now time for us to consider more fully the implications for anti-terrorist measures and operations.

# XX
# GENERAL PROBLEMS OF INTERNAL DEFENCE AGAINST TERRORISM

The effects of protracted terrorism are sufficiently destructive and unpleasant to lead one to conclude that prevention is better than cure. Yet unfortunately there are no purely prophylactic measures that can ensure 100 per cent protection of a liberal democratic state against terrorism. Part of the price of a liberal society is that some individuals may begin to use their liberties to plot to radically change or destroy the state by means of violence, including terrorism. It is true that in relatively prosperous and contented society there may not exist any sizable political movement or minority sufficiently alienated to espouse political violence. But as we have noted earlier terrorism does not necessarily need such a launching base of popular support in order to be mounted within a liberal state. A mere *groupscule*, consisting of a handful of ideological fanatics, and attracting certain other psychotic and criminal elements, is quite capable of launching terrorist attacks. Short of instituting a kind of Big Brother police state tyranny how could any government hope to identify and filter out all the possible terrorists in society?

This is a counsel not of despair but of realism. Analysts who claim to have methods capable of totally eliminating terrorism and subversion from society are either not living in this world, or are planning their own tyranny. It is, of course, a fundamental liberal assumption that in a representative democracy governing on the basis of popular consent, government must be dedicated to the good of society and the well-being of its individual members. Liberal democratic government, if it is to serve adequately the welfare of its citizens, must see itself as holding a fiduciary responsibility for meeting ever-changing legitimate popular needs and demands by continual reform and adaptation. This is what the liberal democratic process in a pluralist society is all about.

Yet from time to time, given human fallibility and selfishness, protest and criticism begin to highlight certain injustices and inequalities that have developed within the society and to demand appropriate remedies. When governments and majorities adamantly withold or oppose such reforms then aggrieved minorities may well lose faith and confidence in the democratic system and in peaceful methods of opposition and turn to violence. It follows that by far the most valuable and beneficial prophylaxis available against large-scale internal political violence for the liberal state is a proven and consistent record of effectiveness in responding to pressures for reform. However, it should not be assumed that I am recommending a form of hedonistic utilitarianism solely concerned with maximising economic goods. While it is clearly legitimate and necessary for government to take measures to protect or improve material conditions, employment opportunities, housing and so forth, the most deeply felt grievances and the most passionately demanded reforms often centre on issues of *political* and cultural discrimination, such as unequal treatment of a particular minority or language or discriminatory electoral laws or infringements of constitutional rights.

Yet the key point is that if a government is effective in pursuing the public welfare in this widest sense, and it shows fairness, sensitivity and skill in responding to legitimate demands for reform, there is a much better chance, other things being equal, of avoiding major outbreaks of political violence and internal war. ('Other things being equal' because dramatic unfavourable influences from the external environment, such as outside military intervention by a more powerful state, may supervene.)

We may conclude, therefore, that one of the built-in strengths or advantages of an operative liberal state, under normal circumstances, is that it responds to the demands of minorities and from the population as a whole thus rendering internal violence unnecessary as a vehicle for social change. Hence even in situations where a fanatical hard core of dissidents remain intransigently committed to violence, they will not be able to carry mass support among the population. Interestingly enough this analysis appears to hold up even in the case of contemporary Northern Ireland, where many of the Catholic minority population's grievances concerning, for example, job and housing discrimination, have only recently been met by appropriate government measures. Yet even in Ulster, with its long history of bitter minority grievances, the overwhelming majority of the minority population remain convinced supporters of parliamentary democracy and evolutionary reform. In 1976, seven years after the start of their latest campaign, the men of violence still remained an isolated and beleaguered fringe heartily loathed and condemned by the vast majority of the Catholic population of Ireland.

However, at the same time the Irish case underscores the limitations of prophylactic political and socio-economic reform. For small groups of hard-core fanatics, members of both extremist Loyalist and Republican organisations, appear determined to sustain terrorism and sectarian murders. Prophylaxis certainly helps to keep them isolated, and to prevent mass violence and civil war, but it is not a panacea. It is a grave and dangerous folly to believe that one can 'buy off' terrorists with reforms. For what the terrorist is really after is political power, the destruction of the existing state power and the establishment of a new régime under terrorist control.

Some liberal politicians are so naïve as to believe that they can play Machiavelli's fox to the terrorist wolf by outwitting the terrorists at the conference table. But the historical experience of liberal states that have suffered prolonged terrorist campaigns would suggest that only the lion of superior and resolute force can conquer terrorist movements.

As I have argued elsewhere[34] there is much to be said in favour of adapting the lessons of the 'two-wars' or 'two-front' strategy used so effectively in Malaya for the problems of fighting terrorism and urban guerrilla war in industrialised states. Just as meaningful reforms and some improvement in economic prospects was vital to winning the firm support of the rural Malay population, so is it vital that Western governments should be seen to be doing something to combat the severe deprivation endemic in the slum areas of their major cities. A generous crash programme to revitalise and improve our own inner city areas, for example, is not merely politically expedient: it would be an intrinsically valuable and urgently needed act of social justice and concern. If a liberal democracy ever proves unwilling or totally unable to attend to the most urgent social needs of the mass of the population it signs its own political death warrant. The creation of large alienated groups among the population merely plays into the hands of revolutionaries and terrorists by providing combustible conditions for them to exploit.

Nevertheless there are great dangers and difficulties involved in attempting to harmonise socio-economic and political reform with the other element in the two-war strategy, the security war. One major danger is that the first substantial reforms will set off a revolution in expectations and may create a pace of demands for further improvements that the incumbent régime cannot sustain. De Tocqueville observed, in a famous passage:

> The evils which were endured with patience so long as they were inevitable seem intolerable as soon as a hope can be entertained of escaping from them. The abuses which are removed seem to lay bare those which remain, and to render the sense of them more acute; the evil has decreased, it is true, but the perception of the evil is more keen.[35]

There are two other factors that render the moment of the initiation of reform most hazardous for the stability of a régime. Firstly, the very act of recognising the legitimacy of a particular demand or grievance articulated by one group or minority in society tends to provoke hostile reaction among other traditionally opposed groups who feel their own position is being threatened or undermined thereby. This may unleash full-scale inter-group or inter-communal conflict. Prime Minister Terence O'Neill's courageous attempt to introduce some measures to improve the position of the Catholic minority in Northern Ireland in the late 1960s offers a clear illustration of this reaction. The proposals inflamed the ultra-loyalist Protestants, and the political situation had begun to polarise dangerously by late 1967.

A second major problem arises when reforms or socio-economic measures appear to the general population to have been conceded by the incumbent régime as a direct result of blackmail intimidation by a terrorist movement. It is vitally important that the authorities should avoid any impression of weakness or capitulation in the face of violence and defiance of the law, for such conduct destroys public faith and credit in the government and in its will to uphold the law and protect life and property. It undermines the position of elected political leaders, moderates and conciliatory elements in the population who are trying to work within the norms and processes of constitutional politics. Most dangerous of all it strengthens immeasurably the arrogance of extremists, demagogues and men of violence by giving them an aura of power and respectability. When the paramilitary or extremist groups' boasts of bombing or shooting their way to the conference table and wringing this or that concession out of the government are lent factual justification, support will tend to ebb away from the government and elected leaders, and terrorist propaganda begins to be listened to more attentively by the population. Ordinary people naturally begin to wonder who is running the country and what the next concession is going to be. Terrorists begin to nourish real hopes of a general amnesty, and the laws are held in increasing contempt. Nothing so rapidly undermines the authority and power of a constitutional government as an apparent readiness to treat and bargain with those who have openly abused the constitution.

A fundamental requirement for an effective policy of internal defence is clarity of objectives. Whom or what is one seeking to defend? In the case of an operative liberal democracy the answer must be very clear: one is seeking to protect the *whole community*, their lives, property, resources, social institutions and their legitimate and democratically elected government. In a genuine liberal democracy, neither external nor internal security should remain privileges reserved for a small élite or for the richest or most powerful in the land. If 'law and order' means anything in liberal democratic conditions it involves equal rights and treatment under the law, and equal rights of protection.

It should be clear from what has already been said in Part I of this study that liberal doctrine does not accord state or government unlimited, inalienable and immutable rights over whole populations and territories. Suppose that the people of Northern Ireland, by an overwhelming majority, were to decide that they wished to become either politically independent or united with the rest of Ireland, could any genuine liberal democrat claim that it would be morally right for the United Kingdom government forcibly to resist such a decision? The liberal belief in individual free will and the supreme value of liberty surely implies that large-scale changes in constitutions, political frontiers and allegiances may become morally justified because popularly desired and politically necessary. For liberty in the negative sense of freedom from constraint, which is so essential to the Anglo-American tradition of liberal thought, must inevitably open up the possibilities of truly major and fundamental political and constitutional changes, as well as the prospect of constant small incremental reforms. Thus, inherent in the political dynamic of liberal democracy is constant critical reappraisal of the political context, boundaries, and relationships of the liberal state. One must also bear in mind that, although the guiding liberal principle of international relations must be non-interference, there is constant need to guard against threats to security from aggressive or expansionist states. Moreover there may in certain cases be a moral duty on the liberal state to offer aid and support to popular resistance against foreign tyranny. However the problem of the external relations of the liberal state will be considered more fully in Part III.

We are here primarily concerned with the relationship between internal political change and violence in liberal states. Currently, in the light of separatist linguistic movements in Europe and the Québecois separatists in Canada, we often imagine that all the forces tending towards the modification of contemporary nation-states are centrifugal. But this is to overlook the strong counter-tendencies to centripetalism clearly manifested in Western Europe; the pressures driving towards a greater pooling of elements of state sovereignty to bring faster and more extensive political and economic integration. Contemporary liberal theory and practice constantly explore fresh means of combating, or even of transcending, the political and economic limitations of the nation–state.

It would also be dangerous to over-estimate the popular strength of separatist movements currently active in liberal democratic states. At the time of writing (1976) it is by no means clear that any such movement, whether in the United Kingdom, the European Community as a whole, or in North America, has successfully established a case for independence whether judged in terms of votes cast for separatist parties, referenda or plebiscites. Therefore, although it is essential to allow for the possibility of such radical changes in allegiance it would be premature to predict the fragmentation of liberal democratic states as a result of ethnic cleavages. For the most part, frontiers and national allegiances have remained remarkably stable in liberal states for the past fifty years.

Hence, in terms of dealing with internal political violence, the characteristic model for the liberal democratic state is clearly asymmetrical. Typically it is desperate fringe movements, with tiny or negligible popular support, that have resorted to terrorism against liberal democratic governments possessing high legitimacy. Yet, as we have noted earlier, this imbalance in popular support and legitimacy does not by itself render the terrorists ineffective or harmless: on the contrary insurgents develop special tactics to exploit the situation and to turn their weakness in both political and military terms into political strength. This asymmetrical government–terrorist conflict model obtains in most contemporary Western liberal states. The following outline of counter-terrorist strategy is therefore designed to apply in those kinds of situations.

However a preliminary caution is essential. While there are certain general principles that would appear to apply in most anti-terrorist campaigns in liberal democracies it must be remembered that every terrorist struggle has unique elements and that general principles, measures and tactics designed to counter terrorism need to be considerably qualified and adapted to meet specific situations. In a previous very brief treatment of the subject[36] I have been discomfited to find that, despite my warnings to this effect, the general outline model of the approach has been applied indiscriminately, and even to situations it was never designed to cover. It is important to bear in mind that there is no 'standard', 'normal' or 'predictable' terrorist campaign. They vary enormously in duration, intensity of violence, number of deaths and scale of damage caused, area of operations, and numbers of insurgents involved. Can one seriously imagine that a brief spate of campus bombings by a lunatic fringe revolutionary cell justifies counter-measures of the order called for, say, by the terrorist campaign in Ulster since 1970, where one has seen the situation of a 'contained' or 'suppressed' civil war between terrorist movements, and between the paramilitaries and the security forces?

In what follows, therefore, I shall first deal with the general objectives and principles of counter-terrorist strategy. Following this I shall consider the specific problems and requirements for combating (i) the very low-intensity 'spasm' or brief duration campaign, and (ii) the 'suppressed civil war' or prolonged relatively high-intensity terrorism of the kind experienced in Ulster since 1969.

# XXI
# GENERAL PRINCIPLES OF COUNTER-TERRORIST STRATEGY

The primary objective of counter-terrorist strategy must be the protection and maintenance of liberal democracy and the rule of law. It cannot be sufficiently stressed that this aim over-rides in importance even the objective of eliminating terrorism and political violence as such. Any bloody tyrant can 'solve' the problem of political violence if he is prepared to sacrifice all considerations of humanity, and to trample down all constitutional and judicial rights. The Soviet Union has achieved that kind of internal 'order', if order it be. It has involved turning the Soviet Union into the kind of vast prison house that Solzhenitsyn has unforgettably recorded:

> Throughout the grinding of our souls in the years of the great Nighttime Institution, when our souls are pulverized and our flesh hangs down in tatters like a beggar's rags, we suffer too much and are too immersed in our own pain to rivet with penetrating and far-seeing gaze those pale night executioners who torture us. A surfeit of inner grief floods our eyes. Otherwise what historians of our torturers we would be![37]

Yet that has been one of Solzhenitsyn's most heroic achievements: he is the greatest of all historians of the modern torturers. He has recorded, in encylopaedic detail, the bureaucracy of cruelty, the infinite diabolism of repression developed by a totalitarian police state. Let us make no mistake: with armies of secret police and informers, with constant police surveillance, and with the extinction of fundamental rights and freedoms it takes enormous courage to cling even to the islands of dissent. When a régime is determined to use the full panoply of coercion, persecution and repressive terror from torture and labour camps to the more 'subtle' methods of incarceration in psychiatric hospitals and deportation, it is difficult, if not impossible, for *any* resistance to the régime to take root. And because of the Soviet Union's total control over the media it is almost impossible for Westerners, let alone the rest of the Soviet population, to learn any details of political uprisings. Occasional details of protests and violence in regions such as Georgia and the Ukraine do leak out, which suggests that even a long-established one-party dictatorship with an experienced terror *apparat* cannot totally extinguish the flames of national autonomy movements. It may, by draconian measures, succeed in stamping down protest in one area only to find it springing up elsewhere!

Neither terrorism nor any other mode of revolutionary struggle has much chance, therefore, in a totalitarian state. It does not have a much better chance in an old-fashioned autocracy or a right-wing militarist régime. But no liberal democrat is willing to pay the price of human freedom simply in order to achieve total political obedience or submission. To believe that it is worth snuffing out all individual rights and sacrificing liberal values for the sake of 'order' is to fall into the error of the terrorists themselves, the folly of believing that the end justifies the means.

It must be a cardinal principle of liberal democracies in dealing with problems of civil violence and terrorism, however serious these may be, never to be tempted into using the methods of tyrants and totalitarians. Indiscriminate repression is totally incompatible with the liberal values of humanity, liberty and justice. It is a dangerous illusion to believe one can 'protect' liberal democracy by suspending liberal rights and forms of government. Contemporary history abounds in examples of 'emergency' or 'military' rule carrying countries from democracy to dictatorship with irrevocable ease. What shall it profit a liberal democracy to be delivered from the stress of factional strife only to be cast under the iron heel of despotism?

Even in its most severe crises, therefore, the liberal democracy must seek to remain true to itself, avoiding on the one hand the dangers of sliding into repressive dictatorship, and on the other the evil consequences of inertia, inaction and weakness, in upholding its constitutional authority and preserving law and order. For Solzhenitsyn's argument that the struggle for freedom is indivisible has a far deeper significance than has generally been recognised. It is not simply that the free world as a whole is to an extent morally and politically weakened, and the potential Soviet weight in the overall strategic balance increased, by each takeover by a Marxist–Leninist régime. These are but the outward and visible manifestations of Western weakness of will, ineptitude and lack of unity and purpose. Equally grave are the consequences for betrayals of the cause of liberty, truth and justice of abrogation and cowardice within the liberal democratic states themselves. One kind of betrayal is the deliberate suspension or limitation of civil liberty on grounds of expediency. However hard the going gets in coping with internal terrorism, liberal democratic governments have a primary duty to maintain constitutional government. Hence the suspension of parliamentary democracy, the attempt to rule by emergency decree, abandonment of free elections and all fundamental abridgements of a democratic constitution, must be resisted.

Yet so also must liberal democracy avoid another kind of betrayal, the failure to uphold constitutional authority and the rule of law. If a democratic government caves in to extremist movements and allows them to subvert and openly defy the laws and to set themselves up as virtual rival governments within the state, the liberal democracy will dissolve into an anarchy of competing factions and enclaves. Both dangers are real enough today. India and Bangladesh are a sad reminder of how easily one–party dictatorships can come to power by using the stalking horse of emergency powers, while Lebanon offers tragic witness of a parliamentary democracy almost destroyed by anarchic terrorism and civil war. By late 1976 it was estimated that the collapse of constitutional order in Lebanon had cost over 40,000 lives.

The keynotes of the liberal democratic response to terrorism must be firmness and the determination to uphold constitutional authority and the rule of law. And the political will to do so must be consistently made clear to the citizens and must be translated into effective action. Terrorist propaganda and defamation should be countered by full and clear official statements of the government's objectives, policies and problems. Loyal community leaders, officials and personnel at all levels of government and security forces must be accorded full backing by the civil authorities. Sudden vacillations in security policy should be avoided: they tend to undermine the confidence of public servants, security personnel and the general public and they encourage the terrorists to exploit policy differences and disputes in the government and administration. The government must show that its measures against terrorism are solely directed at quelling the terrorists and their collaborators and at defending society against terrorist attack. A slide into general repression generally indicates that the government is exploiting the crisis situation for the enhancement of its own political powers, or to destroy legitimate political opposition. Moreover, repressive over-reaction plays into the hands of terrorists by giving credence to the claim that liberal democracy is a sham or a chimera, and encouraging terrorists to pose as the defenders of the people.

All aspects of anti-terrorist and security policy and operations should be under the overall control of the civil authorities (that is the democratically elected government) and hence democratically accountable. The government must be seen to be doing all in its power to defend the life and limb of citizens. This is a vital prerequisite for public confidence and co-operation. If it is lacking, private armies and vigilante groups will spring up like a jungle of weeds almost overnight, adding to the general chaos. But the government and its security forces must at all times act within the law. It is vital that normal legal processes be maintained so far as is humanly possible, and that those charged with terrorist offences are brought to trial before properly established courts of law. If the government and security forces flout the law, what right have they to expect that individuals will respect and obey the law? Furthermore, such a betrayal of the authority entrusted to them by the people is likely to undermine or even destroy the basis of democratic legitimacy. The terrorists and their fellow-travellers can make enormous propaganda capital out of violations of the law by members of the security forces and use these as additional justification for their own campaigns. Thus they conveniently divert the public's gaze away from the violations of the law and outrages stemming from their own petty tyranny, and attempt to portray the incumbent authorities as monstrous blood-soaked oppressors.

It might be objected that the principle of operating within the law unduly handicaps the liberal government from undertaking covert intelligence and counter-espionage tasks essential to the security of the state. There are two points to be made about this. First, no one other than a dedicated enemy of the liberal state would advise a liberal state to dispense with its secret service. In the jungle state of contemporary international relations, hostile powers bent on destroying liberal democracies deploy their intelligence and subversion organisation world-wide. It is hard to know whether it is from naïvety or from sinister motives that certain journalists and politicians in Western countries have recently assisted a campaign to discredit the work of Western intelligence agencies. Is it seriously supposed that an act of 'unilateral disarmament' in the intelligence field would lead to the K.G.B. and its satellite organisations from Warsaw to Havana giving up their vast range of covert activities? All who value the defence of liberal democracies know that these defamation campaigns are aimed at crippling a vital arm of Western security.

The second important point about covert operations and secret services is that the experience of many liberal states has shown that it is possible for such agencies within the liberal state to operate firmly within the framework of the law and the constitution. They can be made fully accountable for their operations to the democratically elected government, and through them to the legislature and electorate, despite the fact that most of the information about their actual day-to-day functioning is necessarily secret or under a restricted security classification. The reforms proposed recently by the Church Committee in the United States and approved by Congress, are designed specifically to tighten democratic control and accountability with regard to the U.S. intelligence agencies without damaging their effectiveness as instruments of national security.

The Church hearings inevitably raised a more difficult question, however, which bears heavily on the problem of safeguarding civil rights and liberties within the liberal state. This is the question whether or not the secret intelligence agencies should be empowered to exercise surveillance over their own nationals within their native country. On the face of it, the Church Committee's opposition to such surveillance seems just and reasonable. It is clearly a violation of rights of privacy, and freedoms of opinion, expression and political association which we rightly regard as fundamental in any liberal state. The real danger in allowing such clandestine government operations to proliferate is that the intelligence *apparat* becomes a monster impossible to control. How can one ensure that such organs are not directed against *internal* dissenters or critics of the government? What if they are used to discredit or defeat a rival party *à la* Watergate? Once unleashed in the domestic politics of the liberal state they could corrupt the whole political system. One of the reasons why it is difficult to draw a clear dividing line between interference in domestic politics and legitimate security activities is the practical problem that security services clearly need to observe and report upon the operations of agents of foreign and potentially hostile powers based in, or visiting, liberal democratic states. Hence security surveillance must encompass one's own territory and inevitably a sound intelligence system will bring to light those individuals and groups aiding or collaborating with foreign powers. In addition it is obviously the case that the liberal state's police special branch or intelligence service has a duty to investigate and observe those it suspects of committing serious crimes, whether of a terrorist nature or otherwise. It is only when one or both of these conditions apply that secret service surveillance of one's own citizens may be said to be justified. Any other interference in the affairs of legitimate opposition and protest or dissenting groups would be a totally unwarranted infringement of civil liberties.

Yet another dangerous consequence of a large and ill-controlled secret intelligence and subversion apparatus is that it may end up recruiting assassins and 'dirty tricks' operators for special assignments who later end up organising private terror groups in open defiance of the agency or government that once employed them. A classic instance was the extensive funding and recruitment of Cuban exile groups in the United States, based mainly in South Florida, by the C.I.A. in 1960–61 for covert operations against the Castro régime. Following the Bay of Pigs fiasco in 1961 the exile groups felt betrayed by the U.S. government change in policy towards Cuba and the withdrawal of C.I.A. backing. Many of them were determined to continue the struggle both against the Castro régime and against rival pro-Castro elements based elsewhere.

It is ironic that many of those who have continued the terrorist war in defiance of the C.I.A. were actually trained in small arms and explosives techniques by the Agency. And they have used them with a vengeance ever since. Between Spring 1974 and Autumn 1976 there have been over 100 bombings and shootings in Miami connnected with Cuban exile groups and their internecine warfare, and the F.B.I. has said that it wishes to interview one of the most fanatical Cuban exiles, Dr Orlando Bosch, in connection with the assassination of Allende's former Foreign Minister, Orlando Letelier, by a car bomb in Washington, in September 1976. Bosch was arrested in Venezuela at the end of October 1976, and accused of planning the destruction of a Cuban Airlines plane which crashed shortly after take-off from Barbados, killing seventy-three passengers and crew. It is believed that the plane was destroyed by a bomb planted in the tail. Terrorism is a weapon that can dangerously backfire, and which can get totally out of control. There is no doubt that the U.S. authorities, the C.I.A., and those in the American business community who seek improved relations with Cuba, are deeply embarrassed by the activities of the terrorist monster spawned by the C.I.A. If the U.S. authorities prove unable to stamp out these attacks there is a real danger that they will threaten the continuation of the valuable bilateral U.S.–Cuba hijack pact signed in 1973, and a real risk that a further campaign of terrorism will threaten efforts to restore direct trade between the two countries.

An important advantage, therefore, of insistence that all counter-terrorist measures and operations should be conducted within the law, is that this helps to avoid the danger of creating a kind of 'Caliban' agency which can be turned against the welfare, interests and diplomacy of the liberal democracy itself. Yet another major advantage of working entirely within the law is that this upholds the principle of equality of treatment under the law. If terrorist crimes are dealt with according to precisely known and generally applicable procedures employed in the trial, sentencing and punishment of all criminals, regardless of motivation, then the invidious distinctions accorded by the title 'special status' or 'political prisoner' can be happily dispensed with. For is it right, even on the crudest notions of natural justice, to give a man who is sentenced to imprisonment for murder, but who claims a political motive for his crime, special privileges and favourable treatment

over a man imprisoned for murdering his wife's lover, or a man convicted of committing murder in the course of armed robbery?

Concessions of special status and other privileges to convicted
terrorists tend inevitably to erode general respect for the impartiality
and fairness of the law. They also tend to arouse false hopes of an
amnesty among the terrorist movements, which will naturally place
the demand for an amnesty high among their priorities. Indeed this
demand may provide a considerable source of fervour and determination to even a desperately weakened terrorist group. The
terrorists' objective of getting their 'boys and girls back' becomes
almost more important than the longer-term political aims, and
provides yet another propaganda plank for the terrorist movement.
It should also be noted that the according of special 'political' status
imposes almost intolerable strains on the penal system, which has to
cope with the growing resentment of 'ordinary prisoners' at the
treatment accorded to 'politicals'. Moreover 'special status' leads to
the concentration of members of specific terrorist groupings in
special enclaves within the gaols, and these become virtually self-
administered units modelled on the organisational hierarchy of the
movement outside prison. The prison regimen and attempts at
education and rehabilitation by the prison authorities are completely
vitiated by the indoctrination and training programmes organised
within these gaol 'universities' of terrorism. No doubt it was a consideration of all these factors that led the Gardiner Committee to
recommend the phasing out of special category status in Northern
Ireland gaols, and the British government should be given credit for
its courage and determination in steadily implementing this policy in
1976.

It will be obvious from what has already been said that I am advocating a consistent hard line by liberal democratic states against
terrorism. There is one essential element in the hard line approach
which has attracted particularly heavy criticism, especially from advocates of the soft line approach: this is the hard line principle ruling
out any deals or concessions to terrorists' political demands. A
necessary corollary of the hard line principle is that there should be
no political negotiations or conferences with groups or movements
engaged in, or aiding and supporting terrorism.

Critics object that this position is (i) callous and inhumane in that
it involves sacrificing the lives of innocent persons held hostage by
terrorists and (ii) politically unrealistic in that it excludes the

possibility of making a lasting resolution of the conflict 'stick' through making the men of violence direct parties to an agreement. There is no doubt that any situation involving the lives of innocent hostages necessitates agonising decisions. Moreover in any democratic system there is the added complication that public clamour may force the authorities to concede to even the most insolent of the terrorists' demands for the sake of saving hostages. Even the Israeli government, which has an unmatched record for toughness in the face of terrorist blackmail, was forced, in the face of mounting demands from relatives and Israeli opinion, to consider a deal with terrorists to save hostages at Entebbe. The Palestinian terrorists, who had hijacked an Air France plane near Athens on Sunday 27 June 1976 and flown to Entebbe, threatened to massacre over 100 Israeli hostages unless their demands for the release of large numbers of pro-Palestinian terrorists were met. There is strong evidence that the Ugandan régime was conniving with the terrorists, and that difficulties were put in the way of negotiation with the Israeli authorities. We shall of course never know whether a viable deal could have been made, or whether the terrorists ever seriously intended honouring their side of any bargain, because the Israelis mounted a stunningly bold and successful commando rescue operation on the night of Saturday, 3 July.

Yet suppose that the rescue operation had been militarily or physically impossible? In such an exceptional mass hostage situation the case for making concessions in order to save lives may become overwhelming. But this does not alter the fact that the long-term and political costs of capitulation are very heavy indeed. Wherever humanly possible, therefore, the hard line against any deal or bargain with terrorists should be sustained. The great disadvantage involved in any concession or bargain, which will have to deliver some tangible gain to the terrorists if it is to be effected, is that the terrorists will have set a precedent and established a model for emulation by other groups. Moreover if the terrorist weapon is seen to pay off against a particular government, the authority and credibility of that government is thereby gradually diminished, terrorist groups are tempted into increasingly brazen attempts at blackmail, and there is a dramatic inflation in the ransom price demanded by the terrorists.

It is precisely these longer-term consequences of weakness and capitulation that critics of the hard line tend to ignore. Governments, like revolutionary movements, may have some excuse for failing to forsee the dire effects of concession when they were first struck by the new wave of revolutionary terrorism in the 1960s. But we have had ample opportunity to study these developments and to learn from earlier mistakes. It was Bismarck who once remarked 'Fools say they learn by experience. I prefer to profit by others' experience.' Western governments should all have learnt the lesson by now that weakness and concession in the face of terrorist blackmail in a humane, though often futile, attempt to save the victims of a single attack costs perhaps ten, twenty or a hundred times more deaths and injuries in future attacks.

There is certainly abundant evidence that terrorist movements have rapidly learnt to exploit government weakness and to escalate their demands accordingly in successive operations. Take the case of kidnappings of Western diplomats by Brazilian terrorist groups. On the 4 September 1969 Charles Elbrick, the U.S. Ambassador to Brazil, was kidnapped and his release secured for the ransom of the release of fifteen terrorist movement prisoners. For the release of Ehrenfried von Holleben, the German Ambassador, kidnapped on 11 June 1970, the ransom price paid climbed to forty prisoners. And when the Swiss Ambassador, Giovanni Bucher, was kidnapped on 7 December in the same year, the price paid for his release had escalated dramatically to seventy prisoners.

The U.S. Government has held firmly to a policy of 'no concessions' when faced with the kidnapping of American diplomats, officials and businessmen. This has been especially hard to sustain not only because of pressures from the media and humanitarian pleas but also because the United States has been the front-line target for this kind of attack in almost every part of the world. In the demonology of Marxist revolutionary terrorist groups practically all the world's ills are blamed on to 'Yankee imperialism' and the countless attacks on American persons and property are an index of this ideological hatred and fanaticism. It is, moreover, an impossible task to protect the thousands of Americans working and travelling abroad. Even the United States has not the resources for this, and in many Third World countries political violence is so endemic that it is totally beyond the capacity of local police and security forces adequately to protect or to save lives threatened with capture or murder at the hands of terrorists. The problem of recovering

American hostages is further complicated by difficulties of communication with kidnappers and by the need to deal through intermediaries of the host government who may themselves be diametrically opposed to any negotiation or bargaining with the terrorist group involved. Numerous diplomats, businessmen, missionaries and tourists have disappeared as a result.

But the advantages do not always lie with the terrorist side. The real strength of the no-deals and no-concessions approach has been demonstrated most effectively in a number of recent siege–hostage situations. It used to be thought that such situations presented the authorities with only two stark alternatives: either capitulation to the kidnappers' demands to save hostages' lives or frontal assault on the kidnappers' base in order to catch the terrorists dead or alive at the probable cost of the hostages' lives. In late 1975, a number of Western governments, learning from some useful tactics pioneered by New York city police in criminal kidnappings, proved conclusively that there was a third option for dealing with politically motivated siege situations; standing firm, breaking down the morale and will of the terrorists, and forcing them to surrender peacefully without harm to the hostages. The new techniques were tested by the Irish security authorities during the eighteen-day siege of the kidnappers of Dr Tiede Herrema in October–November 1975. The kidnappers, Eddie Gallagher and Marian Coyle, were fanatical members of the Provisional I.R.A., and their ransom demand for the release of Dr Herrema was the release of three I.R.A. prisoners held by the Irish government: Dugdale, Mallon and Hyland. The Dublin Government made it plain from the outset that they would not give in to blackmail. Later Gallagher reduced his ransom demand to the release of Dugdale. When this was refused he demanded £3 million; again this demand was refused. The Irish army and police were moved up in strength to surround the two-storey council house at Monasterevin, Co. Kildare, where Coyle and Gallagher were holding Dr Herrema prisoner. The latest surveillance techniques, cameras and listening devices were used so that every move and every change in the mood of the kidnappers and the plight of Dr Herrema could be monitored.

The security forces called in several psychologists who were able to advise the police when to put pressure on the kidnappers and when to try to cool the situation. In broad terms they selected periods when the terrorists were relatively relaxed but with low morale to put forward demands for the terrorists to give up, while during periods of high nervousness and tension among the besieged they attempted to reduce tension and soothe the situation with offers of food and clothing. One great advantage of this strategy of patience by the authorities is that while they are applying psychological pressure against the terrorists, the hostage has at least a chance of developing a personal relationship with his captors which might make the hostage's execution less likely. When Gallagher eventually came to realise the hopelessness of his situation, he decided to surrender and allowed Dr Herrema to go unharmed. Similar techniques of firmness and subtle breaking down of the terrorists' resistance were employed successfully by the British police in the Balcombe Street siege involving four Provisional I.R.A. gunmen, in December 1975. And in the same month the Dutch utilised very similar tactics in handling the South Moluccan terrorists' sieges of the Indonesian consulate at Amsterdam and a hijacked Dutch train near Beilen. It is surely hoped that, following these important victories, the authorities concerned will not be faced with a spate of kidnap attempts or mass hostage situations involving these or other terrorists groups. If some political terrorists are rational maximisers, they may have learnt from these experiences that the odds are now heavily stacked against their winning even minor tactical objectives in siege situations.

In the long run, one is forced to conclude, governments have nothing to lose but possibly much to gain from holding firm to the policy of no capitulation, no concessions, and no deals, when confronted with terrorist blackmail.


# XXII
# THE ROLE OF INTELLIGENCE


No liberal democratic government worth the name can afford to tolerate terrorism either within its own frontiers or against its citizens, representatives and interests abroad. It may be quite unrealistic to hope for the total elimination of terrorist violence within free societies because even if the more dangerous politically motivated groups can be defeated by firm and well-planned counter-action there remains the probability that psychopathic individuals and criminal groups will engage in sporadic terrorist attacks. But liberal states must recognise that in seeking to combat politically motivated terrorism, they are fighting groups engaged in a particularly dangerous form of clandestine, undeclared and ruthless unconventional war.

Moreover, as has been argued earlier, it is a mistake to imagine that political terrorists can always be 'bought off' by the introduction of radical political or socio-economic reforms. The hard-core fanatics are not really interested in social amelioration except in so far as they can exploit grievances for political ends. They are primarily interested in weakening and ultimately subverting the political system and seizing power. As one authority has shrewdly observed:

> It is a disheartening fact that even 'good' governments are not necessarily immune to insurrection. For the techniques of revolutionary war . . . are designed to create grievances where none previously existed, to provoke the authorities into unpopular excesses and to cause a breakdown of law and order.[38]

Thus, purely prophylactic measures are not going to be sufficient to stop terrorists, even though they may be very effective in drying up the potential bases of popular support for the terrorist movement. The authorities must be prepared for the eventuality of attacks and campaigns of varying duration and intensity launched by numerically tiny groups which may entirely lack popular sympathy or support.

As we have already observed, mass support is not a prerequisite for launching a terrorist campaign. Indeed the archetypal terrorist organisation is numerically small and based on a structure of cells or firing groups, each consisting of three or four individuals. These generally exercise a fair degree of operational independence and initiative, and are obsessively concerned with the security of their organisation and lines of communication. This cell structure is designed to enhance secrecy, mobility and flexibility while at the same time facilitating tight overall central control by the terrorist directorate. Paramilitary command structures and discipline are fostered to ensure unswerving obedience to the leadership; offenders against the terrorist code are ruthlessly punished, often by death. It is generally the case that only one member of each cell is fully acquainted with the group's links with other echelons and with the terrorist directorate. Experienced terrorists develop sophisticated cover against detection and infiltration. They are adept at hiding in the anonymity of the urban landscape, and at swiftly changing their bases of operations. Terrorists are also constantly engaged in training new 'hit-men', bomb-makers, small-arms specialists and assassins. In a protracted and carefully planned campaign certain individuals and cells in the terrorist movement will be strategically placed as 'sleepers' to be activated as and when required later in the struggle.

These features of terrorist organisations face the security authorities with special problems. The terrorists' small numbers and anonymity make them an extraordinarily difficult quarry for the police in modern cities, while the ready availability of light portable arms and materials required for home-made bombs makes it difficult to track down terrorist lines of supply. Yet once the key members of a cell have been identified it is generally practicable to round up other members. And on the basis of information gleaned from interrogating a relatively small number of key terrorist operatives it is possible to spread the net more effectively around the whole organisation.

A crucial requirement for defeating any political terrorist campaign therefore must be the development of high quality intelligence, for unless the security authorities are fortunate enough to capture a terrorist red-handed at the scene of the crime, it is only by sifting through comprehensive and accurate intelligence data that the police have any hope of locating the terrorists. It is all very well engaging in fine rhetoric about maximising punishment and minimising rewards for terrorists. In order to make such a hard line effective the government and security chiefs need to know a great deal about the groups and individuals that are seeking rewards by terrorism, about their aims, political motivations and alignments, leadership, individual members, logistic and financial resources and organisational structures.

However much tender-hearted liberals quake at the thought it is the vital business of a liberal democratic government to amass as much information as possible about extremist political groups both within and beyond its borders. Many of these political groups openly declare their aim of destroying constitutional democracy. It is surely the clear duty of government to equip itself to defend the constitution from its declared enemies, for it is not only the danger of terrorism that justifies the precautionary gathering of such intelligence: the prime threat to the political system may come from subversion or from planned armed insurgency with foreign support, or from assassination of key political leaders. Can any modern liberal state afford to turn a blind eye to such dangers and deny itself any intelligence concerning those who plan its destruction?

The greatest weakness of modern liberal states in the field of internal defence, as Brian Crozier has percipiently observed,[39] is their 'reluctance or inability to see subversion as a problem until it is too late'. Professor Feliks Gross has emphasised that the development of a terrorist campaign in a liberal democracy is almost invariably preceded by a campaign of defamation and subversive propaganda against the liberal democratic leadership, institutions and values.[40] No intelligence service worth the name should ignore such indicators of possible impending insurgency. However some terrorist groups (for example, the Angry Brigade in Britain and the Armed Proletarian Nuclei in Italy) are too shrewd to reveal even their existence, let alone their aims, prior to their attacks, while others produce propaganda which may be so callow or confused that it does not give the intelligence authorities enough data for them to evaluate the threat. Yet even in the absence of hard political data, there are many other indicators of an impending insurgency such as thefts of arms and explosives and medical supplies, temporary disappearance of known revolutionaries, or meetings with representatives of hostile states or fellow ideological extremists. If the significance of a whole pattern of such developments is missed by the authorities it may well be too late to nip political violence in the bud, for the actual signals of an insurgency or of a full-scale terrorist campaign, such as a 'conference' (council of war?) of revolutionary leaders or a dramatic act of sabotage or assassination, may immediately presage a major escalation of political violence.

The primary objective of an efficient intelligence service must be to prevent any insurgency or terrorism developing beyond the incipient stage. Hence a high quality intelligence service is required *long before the insurgency surfaces*. It is vital, moreover, that such a service should have a national remit — to avoid duplication and rivalry between area police forces — and that it should be firmly under control of the civil authorities, and hence democratically accountable. In normal circumstances in a liberal democratic state the most appropriate body for the tasks of intelligence-gathering, collation, analysis and co-ordination is the police Special Branch or its equivalent: it is normally the case in a liberal state that the police service enjoys at least some degree of public confidence, and co-operation. Moreover the routine police tasks of law enforcement and combating crime at every level of the community give the police service an unrivalled 'bank' of background information from which contact information can be developed.

However, the development of a reliable high quality intelligence service is not easily accomplished. There are serious pitfalls. In the first place, the police may lose confidence and co-operation of certain key sections of the population. This is especially probable where the police has been controlled, administered and staffed predominantly by one ethnic or religious group, and is hence regarded as partisan by rival groups. In such conditions, it often becomes impossible for the police to carry out normal law enforcement functions, let alone develop high standards of criminal investigation and intelligence work. In extreme cases – such as in Ulster in 1969–70 – the police system is faced with almost total breakdown and another agency (in the case of Ulster, the army) has to be brought in to provide the intelligence system as well as exercising the major constabulary function.

The breakdown of normal policing due to political and communal conflict is fortunately a rare occurrence in liberal states. Police and intelligence services are costly to establish and maintain, and their breakdown creates grave internal dangers. But armed forces are even more expensive and no liberal state today can view with equanimity the diversion of large numbers of expensive military personnel, some with very sophisticated technical training, away from their vital external defence role and into what are essentially internal police functions. It is certain that Britain's small professional all-volunteer army cannot afford the manpower, time or special training required for such tasks. And even among the conscript armies of our NATO allies there is not one that can afford to dissipate strength in such extensive internal responsibilities. In the light of the evidence, mounting almost daily, of the continuing growth in Soviet hardware and weapons development and overall level of armaments, it is surely vital that the energies and full strength of NATO forces should be devoted to countering the threats from the

Warsaw Pact and Soviet global expansion. It would therefore logically follow that the primary task of military intelligence in NATO countries should be to reinforce and assist this external defence role.

It is a different matter altogether if the state is faced with the breakdown of civil policing and the total collapse of law and order, either nationally or in a particular region. In such circumstances who can the democratic government call upon to uphold order other than the army? As will be argued later, the army then has an absolutely crucial though unenviable role as a weapon of last resort. It has the duty to restore order in such cases. It is obvious that in a situation such as the Northern Ireland conflict, where the army was called in for just such an emergency, the army has to provide the necessary intelligence system for the restoration and maintenance of order. And for these purposes the army will certainly need to train personnel in intelligence gathering and analysis, and constantly to refine and improve its intelligence techniques. The British Army has an impressive record not only in Northern Ireland but also in many previous internal security operations, in creating a sophisticated intelligence system for countering terrorism and guerrilla war. In many cases this has been done with little or no assistance from the civil police or the administration. In the fields of covert operations and combating all kinds of unconventional war, the British Army has built up a body of intelligence expertise which is an invaluable resource for the state to call upon *in extremis*. But in my view it should be regarded as a special resource to be deployed with extreme parsimony and the greatest reluctance. The tasks of intelligence in an incipient civil or inter-communal war are onerous in the extreme, and the routine work of gathering and building up contact information on terrorists from a mass of background information consumes reserves of time, training and manpower that an army can ill afford. One has only to imagine the effect on British force levels in B.A.O.R. and our overall NATO role if a second Northern Ireland-type situation were to develop, say in Scotland, requiring the army to undertake a similar role in aid of the civil power.

A recurrent problem for the police forces of liberal states is the difficulty of co-ordinating and gathering intelligence on a nationwide basis. This has particularly adverse effects on anti-terrorist operations. For instance, in the United States there is a plethora of legal codes and law enforcement agencies differing widely in resources and methods between cities, counties, states, and federal level. There is no agency at federal level in America with the resources or the constitutional powers to gather and co-ordinate intelligence on a national basis. In Canada, inter-force rivalries have had most damaging repercussions, as shown by the poor relations between the Quebec provincial police and the R.C.M.P. in the October 1970 kidnap crisis. In Britain there have been instances of jealousy and misunderstanding between provincial forces and between these forces and Scotland Yard. And within all police services there is endemic rivalry and tension between the law enforcement and administration sections and investigative and intelligence branches.

There are a number of crucial preconditions for an effective co-ordination of intelligence at national level. The continuing confidence and co-operation of political leaders and the general public must be maintained. Hence it is vital that such agencies are seen to operate within the law and that constitutional safeguards against the abuse of their powers should be seen to be effective. Secondly, there must be close and constant liaison and co-operation with the military and state security services in intelligence matters. Access to the very latest technologies of intelligence gathering, communications and surveillance is essential. A most important need is for centralised intelligence data computerisation which can provide information swiftly for all levels of the security forces. Last but not least among the fundamental intelligence needs is the requirement for closer international co-operation among allied states in the exchange of information on terrorist movements and activities, the involvement of hostile states and transnational or foreign revolutionary movements, and other relevant data for combating political violence. As the charter of INTERPOL precludes the communication of material concerning politically motivated crime, bilateral and regional machinery for international co-operation in this field needs to be more fully developed.

# XXIII
# COUNTERING 'SPASM' TERRORISM

Suppose, however, that the intelligence system fails to observe or to report the indicators and signals of an impending insurgency or terrorist campaign? Or suppose that the elected government fails to act on the intelligence briefings and advice rendered by the security authorities? What should be the response of the liberal state to an ensuing campaign?

Let us first consider the resources and action appropriate to counter what I have earlier described as a 'spasm' terrorist campaign, that is to say, a series of attacks of relatively low intensity and brief duration. Examples would be the bombing campaigns of the tiny fringe ideological groups such as the Weathermen in the United States, the Angry Brigade in Britain, or the Baader–Meinhof gang in the Federal German Republic.

The main burden of containing and defeating terrorism of this kind in liberal democratic states is carried by the police services. Despite some bad mistakes and weaknesses, Western police forces generally have shown commendable speed, energy and determination in adapting their organisation and methods to the intensifying challenge of terrorist violence since the late 1960s. And, partly as a result of their experience in combating I.R.A. terrorism, the British police have been in the vanguard of success in this field. This has had the effect of enhancing the reputation of the police among the general public: in combating terrorism with such courage and skill, the police are after all in the front line of defence of the community as a whole. The general public has the sense to realise that in terrorism *everyone's* safety is at risk. It is left to the hysterical minority of revolutionary propagandists[41] and terrorist fellow-travellers to cry 'police oppression' and 'police state' in a feeble attempt to discredit the police and to portray them as lackeys of some supposed capitalist conspiracy. Sane and fair-minded people look eagerly and gratefully to growing evidence of police effectiveness in securing the capture and conviction of terrorist murderers, for it is ordinary people – men, women and children – who have suffered death, injury and terror in successive terrorist attacks. It is with these innocent victims that the democratic society identifies – the long roll of victims of Northern Ireland bombings and shootings, the children maimed or orphaned, the young people blown up while relaxing in a pub, and the kidnap victims and their families. Faced with such outrages the vast majority of democratic citizens are more than ever convinced that an effective police force is the most valuable friend and guarantor of domestic peace and security.

The anti-terrorist counter-measures appropriate for the police in fighting terrorism are closely analogous to those required for combating other serious crimes of violence. But the tasks involved require a high degree of specialised knowledge and experience combined with tactics, techniques and intelligence resources beyond the scope of the normal criminal investigation departments. Hence all Western police services have developed special anti-terrorist units. The impetus for West German initiatives in this field came from the Baader–Meinhof campaign and the massacre of eleven Israeli athletes at the 1972 Olympics in Munich by Arab terrorists. In cases where the *Lander* police are overstretched, the Federal Border Guard is empowered to intervene. A special 176-man unit of the guard was formed in April 1973 for anti-terrorist functions. It is organised into detachments stationed in the major conurbations, and its members receive thorough training in armed and unarmed combat, terrorist tactics, psychology, etc. Members of this crack unit are also trained in individual specialisms such as marksmanship and explosives. The Federal Criminal Office is now in overall control of police measures against terrorism.

By contrast, the United States has been far less successful in its efforts to establish adequate centralisation and co-ordination of anti-terrorist police measures at federal level. In practice, the Federal Bureau of Investigation (F.B.I.) has the major responsibility for intelligence co-ordination and investigation. Unfortunately it does not have adequate financial or manpower resources for this task. Furthermore, it is continually running into conflict with powerful vested interests of state and city police departments in the more populous states. Its response to these constraints has been to form *ad hoc* investigations into specific terrorist attacks, campaigns and groups. Some progress in establishing a centralised police intelligence centre for the whole country has been made by the Law Enforcement Intelligence Unit (L.E.I.U.), established in 1965. But although it has gathered data on political terrorism, its main priority has been the pooling of information on organised crime rackets. L.E.I.U. is therefore no more than a skeletal framework of what is really required. It is both cause and effect of these inadequacies at federal level that many city and state police departments have formed their own special units to deal with terrorism, such as the Special Weapons and Tactics (SWAT) squads which exist in over 500 police departments. SWAT squads are organised on paramilitary lines and are specially trained and equipped to deal with riots and terrorism. The F.B.I., the armed services and the Secret Service have all contributed to the special training of SWAT squads in the smaller, less well-endowed police departments, and the development of SWAT squads has brought some gains in closer military–police co-operation at local level. However there is real cause for concern not only in the unevenness of provision in this field across the United States but also in the proliferation of units which are inadequately trained and directed.[42] A more successful American innovation has been the New York Police Department's Hostage Negotiating Team, formed in 1972. This unit of seventy sharpshooters and detective–negotiators has pioneered techniques of kidnap siege and negotiation which have provided invaluable lessons for other forces.

Terrorism has presented especially grave problems for the Italian police, who have had to combat large-scale terrorist violence from extreme right-wing and neo-fascist groups such as the *Avanguardia Nazionale* and *Ordine Nuovo*, as well as from left-wing extremists. The murder of the head of the police anti-terrorist section in Rome in December 1976 is dramatic evidence that the problem is still acute. An anti-terrorist central inspectorate was set up at the Ministry of the Interior in May 1974 as a result of the authorities' concern and the lack of confidence in the ability of the Special Branch, Secret Service, the *Carabinieri*, the *Guardia di Pubblica Sicurezza* (GPS), and the *Guardia di Finanza*, to cope with the situation. The anti-terrorist inspectorate has been valuable in co-ordinating the activities of the three separate police forces and the Secret Service in anti-terrorist operations, and is under the direct supervision of the Minister of Interior.

In Britain the police have set up several special units to fight terrorism, and these have apparently co-operated very efficiently and met with a high degree of success. The Metropolitan Police's special Bomb Squad carried out the main burden of combating the I.R.A. mainland bombing campaign between 1974 and 1976. In February 1976 this squad was reorganised into the Anti-Terrorist

Squad with a somewhat wider remit, a measure advocated by the present writer in 1974. The new squad has a strength of approximately 150, and can call upon the Technical Support Branch which possesses the latest expertise in surveillance and monitoring devices and communications technologies. (It was this branch that was called in to assist the Irish police during the Herrema siege in October 1975.) Also playing an important part is the Metropolitan Police Special Patrol Group (S.P.G.) formed in 1965. It is over 200 strong, equipped to move rapidly to reinforce any police operation throughout the country, reputed to be able to muster in less than an hour, and trained to give saturation cover to a concentrated area. It consists of an élite uniformed force of volunteers, half of whom are trained in the use of Smith and Wesson 0.38 revolvers, issued when the group faces armed terrorists or bandits. (Armed members of the S.P.G. are pictured on the cover of this book, where they are shown covering their colleagues approaching the I.R.A. kidnappers besieged in Balcombe Street in December 1975. This operation resulted in the surrender of the four gunmen and the release of the two hostages, Mr and Mrs Matthews, unharmed. The Bomb Squad, the S.P.G. and the Technical Support Branch were the main police units involved.) Other units concerned with anti-terrorist operations are: Scotland Yard's specialist firearms squad, D 11, which can provide élite marksmen; the Diplomatic Protection Group (formed 1974) which protects foreign embassies and missions in London, and about one-third of whom are armed; the Special Branch Personal Protection Squad providing bodyguards for Ministers and V.I.P. visitors; the Royalty Protection Group; the Police Bomb Squads recruited mainly from Special Branch and C.I.D., and mainly designed to track down bomb-makers, supplies of explosives, and to detect patterns in bombing incidents; and Police Bomb Disposal Squads based in major cities and mainly recruited from, or trained by, the army.[43]

However it is not enough that the police should be properly trained and organised for countering terrorism. It is also vitally important that the units concerned should be adequately armed, and that they should be thoroughly trained in marksmanship, weaponry and tactics. Of course it is very difficult for many politicians and the general public in Britain, steeped in the ethos of an unarmed police, to accept the need for special armed police units, and for modern weaponry and weapon-training to be made available in the police.

But it is simply no good pushing police and guns out of sight and pretending there is no problem. Faced with increasing probabilities of confronting armed terrorists, protracted sieges, assassination bids and other terrorist activity it would be suicidal to expect the police to try to cope unarmed. Nevertheless there are serious tactical problems involved. Traditionally, policemen in Britain have been trained to use minimal force. Whereas the soldier's instincts and training tell him to destroy 'the enemy' without hesitation or qualm, the policeman is traditionally supposed to protect the public from the criminal and to effect the arrest of the criminal in order to bring him to trial before a court of law. There is little doubt that this traditional 'constabulary' ethic will serve no useful purpose in confrontations with heavily armed terrorist groups. Many terrorists are armed with more sophisticated weapons and with greater firepower than the police can range against them. The terrorists may on occasion possess weapons with an enormous destructive capability which constitute a grave threat to the lives of the public the police are trying to protect. For instance, terrorists have been found to possess hand-held heat-seeking surface to air missiles on the perimeters of several international airports. The Federal German Republic police believe that the terrorist groups attempting to release the Baader–Meinhof gang from gaol in Stuttgart had acquired quantities of mustard gas. Recent reports suggest that phials of the nerve gas Tabun, developed by the Nazis in the Second World War, may have fallen into the hands of terrorist groups. [44] Quite apart from the more unusual weapons of destruction, terrorists frequently threaten to cause large-scale loss of life and destruction by bombings and arson. Under English law a police officer is entitled to use 'such force as is reasonable in the circumstances'. Surely, therefore, when faced with such threats to the public, the police are justified in shooting the terrorists, and shooting to kill. One senior police arms training commander summed up the position thus: 'If a criminal is killed when we shoot we must be justified in our actions. Otherwise we must not shoot at all. . . There can be no question of trying to wing or wound. The results are too uncertain and the danger of death too great.' [45]

Yet there are still enormous problems of judgement involved. How can the police officer be so confident that the person in his sights is guilty of terrorist activity or any other serious crime? Suppose there is a case of mistaken identity? If the police officer cannot prove justifiable homicide must he face conviction for murder? Must officers always wait for the suspects to fire first? There are no easy answers to these onerous questions.

Other difficult problems arise from the real dangers of innocent members of the public being caught in the cross-fire of a police shoot-out with terrorists. One of the weapons recommended for police use is the L39A1 sniper's rifle which is fitted with the Rank image-intensifier night sight. This weapon is potentially of great value to police marksmen because of the astonishingly effective night sight, especially as 90 per cent of armed confrontations with police occur during the hours of darkness. But the L39A1, like many other modern weapons, is extremely high powered; its bullets can penetrate through concrete buildings, and its ricochets can travel 1000 yards. For the police this makes it an extremely dangerous weapon, for it further endangers the lives of the public. Police targets are often surrounded by, or in close proximity to, innocent civilians whose lives the police are supposed to protect. For these reasons enormous care has to be taken over choice of appropriate police weapons, and even greater care has to be taken in instructing, ensuring the strictest control over their use. There must be no 'cowboys and indians' attitudes among the armed police. Training procedures must be designed to go beyond good marksmanship and attempt to ensure that all armed police have the necessary personal qualities to handle weapons: self-discipline, stability and the elusive qualities of calm and common sense in a crisis. Among the weapons now favoured in British police units are the Parker–Hale .222 high velocity rifle, which is less prone to 'over-penetration', the Smith and Wesson .38 revolver, and the 10.38 revolver (four-inch barrel) with greater punch at longer range. The great advantages of pistols for police use are that they are easy to conceal and light to carry. However, the new American 180 laser sub-machine-gun should prove an invaluable anti-terrorist weapon. It has a laser beam sight which renders marksmanship skills unnecessary, and the laser beam itself can be used to scare the terrorist into surrender without a shot being fired, or to dazzle the terrorist and thus prevent return of fire. Anti-terrorist squads must have the best available weapons training, and the government and security chiefs must continually review the position to ensure that these exacting standards are being met.

One continuing problem for the police which has obvious implications for their capacity to deal with protracted terrorist campaigns is that of manpower. In England and Wales as a whole the police services were 9.1 per cent below established strength on 30 November 1975. This was an improvement on 1974 when the overall deficiency was 12.2 per cent.[46] Nevertheless a shortfall of only 9.1 per cent represents 10,701 vacancies, and these are deficiencies in an establishment strength which many experts believe is already too low in Britain's major cities, especially in London where there is still a grave manpower crisis.[47] Moreover although the police, almost alone among the public services, were permitted to recruit up to authorised establishment in late 1976, there have been potentially damaging cuts in civilian support staff and technical services. If the police are to be expected to perform their extraordinarily difficult, sensitive and often dangerous work with deteriorating financial provision for support services, then it would be wise for the government to ensure that they are compensated by appropriately higher levels of pay and better working conditions, even if they have to treat the police as a 'special case' in order to do so. After all the miners have in the past been treated as a special case on grounds of physical danger and arduous conditions. And the police, unlike the miners, are forbidden to strike or to affiliate to the T.U.C. Police morale is an invaluable commodity and could be all too easily undermined by petty meanness. A recent perceptive study of the police in Britain states: 'The first need today is to give the police proper political priority, not merely in the provision of sufficient pay to attract enough recruits of the right calibre, but in the introduction of measures that will reduce external pressures.'[48]

One useful means of reducing external pressures and simultaneously mobilising citizens for the defence of the community is to enrol larger numbers of able-bodied men and women into the police reserve. The only circumstances when such expansion of police reserves might be unwise would be in a serious inter-communal conflict where one or more of the warring communities attempted to take over the reserve police units and their weaponry as a private army of semi-legalised vigilantes. Such exploitation would do more harm than good in the battle for law and order. However these conditions certainly do not apply in mainland Britain where the vast majority of citizens is totally loyal to the constitution. One is aware that these auxiliaries are treated with some disdain by the professionals, and that there is considerable resistance in some quarters to extending the police reserve. Nevertheless when so many of our major city police forces are below efficient strength a large injection of police reserve manpower could considerably ease the situation. It would have an obvious benefit for the effective conduct of anti-terrorist operations. Full-time and specialist-trained officers would be freed from more routine duties and more time and manpower could be devoted to combating terrorist crime. Moreover there is no reason why police reserves could not adequately perform many of the extra duties of patrols, searches and vehicle checks that may be necessitated by a terrorist emergency. The writer strongly recommends that measures to increase the police reserve be given urgent consideration.

Another valuable way of mobilising public assistance against terrorism is through a concerted programme of public information and education on the recognition of bombs and terrorist weapons, the procedure to be adopted when a suspicious object is sighted, the kind of information that might be valuable to the police, the fastest method of communication with the anti-terrorist squad, and so forth with a much greater use of television, radio and public advertisement to convey this essential information. There is a rich fund of experience from Ulster and elsewhere concerning the most effective methods of mobilising the public behind an anti-terrorist campaign. The security authorities should also take care to brief special groups such as property-owners in areas under attack and businessmen concerning the particular terrorist hazards that they are most likely to confront, and to give special advice on appropriate counter-measures. It is to be hoped that the police in British cities have already held such consultations with owners of premises and places of entertainment frequented by the general public. The police should also make a regular practice of informing regional hospital authorities of the kind of emergency situations that are likely to arise through terrorist attacks. This programme of public education and mobilisation is just as vital to the task of saving lives as the formulation of contingency plans for military and police action.

One general aim of such measures should be to make the public far more security conscious. Members of the public must be constantly vigilant for suspicious objects or activities in the environs of buildings, for signs of tampering with vehicles, and for unattended bags and parcels. Gunsmiths and commercial suppliers of chemicals and explosives should, as a matter of routine, check that their customers are *bona fide*. Any irregular transactions or unaccountable losses should be immediately reported to the police. The public will have to be the eyes and ears of the security forces. Indeed, without the fullest public co-operation special preventive measures against terrorism are bound to fail. Take, for example, the matter of storage of detonators and explosive substances for industrial purposes. If the government were to bring in a new act imposing severe penalties for failing to keep explosive stores fully secure, it would achieve nothing if the actual workers and managers involved in their industrial use still failed to observe the minimal rules of security. Police are generally only called in when there is an explosives or weapons theft, i.e. when it is probably too late. Truly preventive action against terrorism demands the fullest co-operation of every member of the public.

# XXIV
# ARMY'S ROLE IN COMBATING 'SPASM' TERRORISM

Though it is right and proper that the police should carry the main responsibility for dealing with spasmodic terrorist attacks, the army also has an important 'firefighting' and back-up role. When Sir Robert Mark, in his last year as Metropolitan Police Commissioner, referred in a speech in Leicester to circumstances when the assistance of the army might be necessary to fight terrorists,[49] he was merely stating what was already common knowledge to those acquainted with defence and security policy. The predictable outcry from the National Council for Civil Liberties[50] and ultra-left M.P.s revealed either staggering naïvety or a peculiar zeal to save the lives of terrorists at the expense of the lives and safety of the public. It is sheer common sense that the army should be prepared to render what is known officially as Military Aid to the Civil Power (M.A.C.P.) in the event of any threat to security which the police are inadequately equipped to deal with. And no government, or its police and security chiefs, could sleep easily in their beds, without the secure knowledge that they could call in the army in such circumstances. It is nonsense to pretend that this entails some sinister plot to end civil liberties. The M.A.C.P. role of the army is firmly and completely under the control of the civil authorities, and it is designed to be terminated as rapidly as possible, that is to say as soon as the level of violence falls sufficiently to enable the civil police to take over and the army units to be withdrawn.

Clearly there are a number of circumstances in which even the best equipped and best trained police anti-terrorist squad will not possess the necessary firepower, equipment, special military skills, or tactical mobility to deal with armed terrorist insurgents. One of the most likely scenarios is the capture of an embassy or a key installation by a terrorist group armed with submachine guns or mortars. There is no Chief Constable in the country who would hesitate to request the Home Office and the Ministry of Defence for the use of troops when faced with this form of attack. Joint police–army contingency plans for anti-terrorist operations are an obvious necessity, for example, to counter terrorist aircraft hijackers who may be heavily armed and may threaten to destroy aircraft on the ground or to occupy airport buildings. Army assistance was obviously justifiable for the serious threat posed by Palestinian terrorists believed to be planning a SAM–7 missile attack on a plane at Heathrow Airport in January 1974. Fortunately this attack did not take place, but this and the successive army–police joint exercises at Heathrow in June, July and September 1974 certainly provided valuable practice for countering the more serious terrorist attacks with really effective forces – so-called Stage II operations. The army's role in such operations must be to provide superior firepower and essential military skills plus the defensive armour to minimise loss of life among both the general public and the security forces. An interesting use of the army in this kind of role, from which many lessons were drawn, was at Stansted Airport in January 1975, when a British Airways jet was hijacked en route from Manchester to London. Special Air Service units (S.A.S.) were rapidly deployed to Stansted, and the lone hijacker (who, it transpired, was not politically motivated) eventually surrendered after negotiations.

The S.A.S. provides the army's élite anti-terrorist unit, drawn from 22 S.A.S. Regiment, and on constant three-minute standby. There are also facilities for calling in other specialist army units such as Army Bomb Disposal teams as well as units of conventional infantry if required. The army units have the vital tactical mobility and range to counter terrorist attacks in remoter parts of Britain or in British waters. For instance one of the army's responsibilities would be to counter terrorist attacks on British oil rigs and pipelines, and the S.A.S. have helicopters and Hercules air transports on permanent standby in the event of such attacks.

In sum, there are clearly certain types of armed terrorist threat which it would be totally unreasonable to expect the police alone to deal with. It would be sheer folly for any liberal state faced with modern terrorism to forego the option of military aid to the civil power. For this reason, therefore, if for no other, government must ensure that there is the closest possible intelligence co-ordination, liaison, contingency planning and tactical co-operation between police and army at every level.

What are the alternatives to M.A.C.P. in case of serious armed terrorist threat? None are likely to be attractive to British ministers, parliamentarians or the general public. We have already rightly ruled out capitulation to the terrorists. We cannot allow the terrorists to massacre members of the general public and lightly armed civil police. The possibility of establishing a 'third force' of totally militarised police to deal with political terrorism and violence is sometimes discussed as a possibility for Britain. But the difficulties and internal criticisms aroused by the use of similar forces, such as the *Compagnies Républicaines de Sécurité* (CRS) in France, do not inspire emulation. There are serious political and psychological disadvantages to having a permanent 'third force' of this type. Ordinary members of the public might come to look upon a fully militarised force with mistrust, if not with fear, and the excellent relationship of trust, confidence and co-operation which the British uniformed police have built up so successfully would be placed at risk. Perhaps the worst danger is that a government might make the mistake of relying on such a 'third force' to break up industrial protests or to interfere in industrial disputes, for this would totally destroy the police reputation for political neutrality and impartiality as guardians of the law. It is my firm conviction that these objections cannot be adequately answered by proponents of the 'third force' idea. Finally I remain unconvinced that such a force would be *militarily* effective against the most serious forms of terrorist attack of the kind discussed above, a type of threat which I believe only the army is professionally qualified to meet.

# XXV
## COUNTERING INCIPIENT CIVIL WAR

We must now consider the much more serious and daunting problems posed for liberal democratic governments by severe, prolonged and widespread campaigns marked by higher intensities of violence, which I have earlier described as incipient or suppressed civil wars. The current conflict in Northern Ireland, spilling over occasionally into the Republic and into mainland Britain, falls into this category. In this kind of conflict the civil police and the authorities are quite unable to contain the escalating level of inter-communal or political violence. In such a situation it is only by committing the army that the government has any hope of containing the conflict and preventing a full-scale urban guerrilla war, and ultimately a general bloodbath.

It must be a cardinal principle never to commit the army to take over overall responsibility for the tasks of restoring and maintaining public order unless it is absolutely beyond doubt that the civil police can no longer cope. This situation may be forced upon a government extremely rapidly when the police system in a particular region or locality completely breaks down for any reason. This may often be due to sectarian or inter-communal conflict and the collapse of confidence of one part of the community in the police. Thus, for example, by 1969, the then Home Secretary Mr Callaghan and his cabinet colleagues, had virtually no alternative but to commit troops to Northern Ireland.

There are very strong reasons why governments of liberal states should only employ troops for internal security purposes with the very greatest reluctance, and why they should seek to withdraw them at the earliest opportunity. First, in any conflict of this scale it may be assumed that the belligerent faction or factions enjoy at least some support or sympathy in sections of the general population. Hence an unnecessarily high military profile may merely serve to escalate the level of violence by polarising pro- and anti-government elements in the community. Second, internal security duties under the strict limits imposed in a constitutionalist liberal democratic system conflict fundamentally in many respects with the professional instincts, traditions and ethos of the military. The soldier's main task is seen as the identification and destruction of the enemy. In internal security duties it is often extremely difficult to know who or where the enemy are, for friends and enemies all look the same. Moreover according to the constabulary ethic, the prime objective is not to kill lawbreakers, but to apprehend them and secure their conviction before a court of law. There is a constant risk that a repressive over-reaction or a minor error of judgement by the military may trigger further civil violence. Internal security duties inevitably impose considerable strain on the soldiers who are made well aware of the hostility of certain sections of the community towards them. A further danger is that the civil power may become over-dependent upon the army's presence, and there may be a consequent lack of urgency in preparing the civil police for gradually resuming the internal security responsibility. On the other hand, governments may become lulled into a false sense of security by the skilful peacekeeping of professional troops and rush into premature troop withdrawals only to find that the police are unable to hold the line. Last but not least there is the important strategic consideration that we have already noted above: prolonged internal security duties absorb considerable manpower and involve diverting highly trained military technicians from their vital external defence role.

A government in full knowledge of these factors that commits its armed forces to taking over the internal security role in a whole city or province does so because it has no option. The army is needed because the government faces the threat of a full-scale insurgency or civil war. Unfortunately the civil authorities are often unable to appreciate the full implications of this threat *in military terms*. They sometimes try to pretend that if the army could only function like a substitute police force, all would be well and the security situation would somehow automatically rectify itself. The British Army in Northern Ireland has unfortunately all too often suffered at the hands of government ministers and officials labouring under such illusions.

When troops are really needed in a liberal state to restore and maintain law and order by definition the conditions of normal policing do not obtain. The very fabric of the state and the life, safety and property of its citizens are under armed attack by ruthless and fanatical opponents. When a state of internal war exists it is no earthly good trying to keep a low profile, or restraining the soldiers from pursuing and defeating the insurgents. What on earth is the good of attempting to defeat ruthless armed insurgents, fanatically determined to destroy the state, strictly according to Queensberry rules which are not even acknowledged by the enemy? There is only one sensible objective for an army engaged in internal war, and this is to root out and defeat the enemy, to destroy the insurgent movement as a military and political force so that the constitution and laws can be restored and upheld.

The major lesson of recent urban guerrilla campaigns around the world is that they can and have been defeated by efficient armies provided that the troops are not made to fight with their hands tied behind their backs. A powerful demonstration of effective military tactics to defeat an urban guerrilla war is provided by the record of the Israeli Army in Gaza strip, 1970–71, when they were permitted to use draconian measures to combat widespread and escalating Arab terrorism in Gaza in that period. Moreover it acted quickly. 'If it were done t'were best it were done quickly': this should be a motto for all governments seeking to defeat urban guerrilla insurrection. The Israelis used a combination of extensive body and house searches, curfews, and preventive detention of terrorist suspects. Furthermore they achieved major rehousing of Arab refugees in newly built housing projects, designed in blocks and sealed off. Even more draconian was their procedure of dynamiting houses (emptied of their occupants) as a reprisal for harbouring terrorists. Punishments for terrorism or for aiding and abetting Arab guerrillas were severe. Store-owners, for example, were punished for closing stores in the face of terrorist threats. Part of the overall Israeli strategy included extending generous incentives for Arab refugees to move to jobs in the West Bank region. By late 1971 the Israelis had managed to reduce the terrorist incident level in Gaza to three per month.

It would of course be foolish to make any simplistic comparisons between urban guerrilla warfare in the Gaza Strip area and the conflict in Northern Ireland. Terrorism is a common thread in both, and Israel is undoubtedly as much a parliamentary democracy as Britain. However Israel is a state which is surrounded by irreconcilable enemies. Since its inception the state has been under siege from terrorism and guerrilla war both within and from outside its borders. Furthermore the Israelis are an occupying power in Gaza, and the Arab population of the territory do not enjoy full rights or power. Nor were the Israelis exposed to the spotlight of national or international television coverage of their counter-measures. The ruthless Israeli methods, whatever their efficacy in Gaza, would be considered impracticable for the British security forces in a province regarded as an integral part of the United Kingdom, because they involve such a sharp departure from the liberal democratic norms and traditions of the British political culture.

The fact remains that the strong political reluctance to allow the British Army to go over to the offensive against the terrorists in Ulster has cost us dearly. The conflict has been dragging on for over seven years without any real end in sight. Total deaths caused by political violence in the Province in 1976 (295) were the highest since 1972, and there was no prospect of respite beyond a brief Christmas truce by the Provisional I.R.A. The economic difficulties have considerably worsened, with unemployment running at 10 per cent, the worst since 1939. As Mr Brian Faulkner has warned: 'That is not just a social disaster, it is also dangerous in the explosive atmosphere of Northern Ireland.'[51] This is a particularly serious feature of the situation because it is now well attested that a measure of economic prosperity is required to ensure a hostile environment for urban guerrilla war.

The British Army has achieved a truly impressive record in countering revolutionary war and major terrorist outbreaks around the world since 1945. British soldiers have shown enormous skill, courage and patience in carrying out these tasks, and their loyalty in carrying out instructions from the civil government has never been put in question. The army is steeped in the democratic ethos. It is doubtful whether any other army in the world could have performed the internal security role in Northern Ireland with such humanity, restraint and effectiveness. It is therefore particularly galling that the civil authorities have prevented the army from deploying its two greatest strengths in countering insurgency; its field intelligence, and its professionalism and flair in offensive operations. There is no doubt whatever that the army could inflict total military defeat on the Provisional I.R.A. if they were given the freedom to do so.

In 1972 and 1973 the army chiefs in Northern Ireland clearly recognised that they could not defeat the Provisionals simply by acting as 'substitute policemen' giving effect to the ordinary law. The Provisional I.R.A. had in effect declared war on the government and the whole system of law, and by terrorism and intimidation they had rendered normal policing in certain areas (the so-called 'no-go' areas) impossible. Moreover, by intimidating witnesses and juries and terrorising whole districts, they had succeeded in causing a breakdown of the normal procedures of the law. The army was charged with restoring order, but political constraints ruled out the use of martial law, i.e. the complete takeover of the machinery of civil government for the period of an emergency. Hence the British government adopted the only sensible alternative: the use of special powers legislation for the emergency to give the army and the civil authorities the necessary teeth to suppress the insurgents. This middle course involves maintaining the independence of the civil power, while at the same time establishing special army–government co-operation at all levels.

By means of operations such as 'Motorman' the army was swiftly able to end the 'no-go' areas; the 1973 Northern Ireland (Emergency Provisons) Act enabled the army, by late 1974, to get on top of the security situation in Ulster. The 1973 special powers gave them *carte blanche* to enter any premises at any time and to question anybody at any time for up to four hours. By late 1974 the army intelligence system had built up an impressive bank of detailed intelligence on over 40 per cent of the population of the Province. These details were fed into the centralised master intelligence computer based at Lisburn Army Headquarters. A vast amount of this intelligence was gathered by means of 'P-tests', whereby people would be asked at random for personal details concerning every detail of their families, friends, occupation and religious and political affiliations and involvements. In addition random close searches of houses were undertaken, 'head-checks' were conducted to scrutinise all occupants of a house, and extensive open and covert photographic surveillance was utilised. This massive intelligence effort paid enormous dividends in 1974. In that year 71,914 houses were searched, 1260 guns and 26,120 lb. of explosives were found. The Provisionals' main explosives experts were inside Long Kesh and the Belfast Brigade of the Provisionals was denuded of leadership by the arrest of three leading officers in September 1974. By December 1974 the Belfast Brigade was in such weak shape that it comprised only fifteen or so active bombers and marksmen, mostly boys aged between fourteen and seventeen. Internment had begun literally to throttle the I.R.A.'s organisation on the ground *because the army's intelligence had become so accurate that it had been able to identify the terrorists. The I.R.A.'s main force of bombers was, by November 1974, either interned or imprisoned.* Overwhelming evidence that the army had beaten the Provisional I.R.A. to its knees by December 1974 is provided by the figures of bombings and shootings for the month: bombings were down to fewer than one a day and shootings to an average of five per day (three per day involving the army and therefore indicating at least a strong likelihood of contact with the enemy). These figures for terrorist incidents were *the lowest in Northern Ireland since 1970.*

With benefit of hindsight it is now possible to see that the army had practically beaten the Provisional I.R.A. by December 1974. Hence the Provos' Christmas truce, and their so-called 'cease-fire', proffered in January 1975, were declared from a position of desperate weakness: they had been decimated as a military force and they urgently needed time to lick their wounds, recruit and train new members, await the release of their key men from internment, and regroup. There is absolutely no evidence of a sincere desire for peace on the part of the I.R.A. Nor is it clear what possible basis could exist for agreement or compromise between the terrorists and the government. The Provisionals' main demands, including total British withdrawal from Northern Ireland and a general amnesty for all convicted terrorists, are fundamentally opposed to the policy agreed by both major political parties in Britain.

It is difficult to escape the conclusion that the so-called I.R.A. 'cease-fire', in which more civilians have died than ever before in Northern Ireland in the past year, was bought at the cost of a fatal degree of appeasement by the British government. It is too early for us to be able to learn what secret deals and agreements may have been entered into as a result of talks between Provisional leaders and government officials, but at least three restraints have been imposed by the government which in my considered judgement constitute a fatal crippling of the army's counter-terrorist capability in Ulster. Indeed these self-imposed handicaps are so grave that one is led to wonder whether the British government really wants to see the Provisional I.R.A. defeated in Northern Ireland.

The first crippling handicap is the restraint imposed on army intelligence-gathering activities. Since the 'cease-fire' the army has been ordered not to carry out 'P-tests', i.e. not to question people at random for personal details. They have been forbidden to arrest people as I.R.A. suspects unless they are absolutely certain they have enough evidence to satisfy a normal law court. In order to search occupied houses patrols have first to seek permission from Brigade H.Q. in Northern Ireland. Photographing crowds or individuals openly has also been forbidden, and 'head-checks' on occupants of houses have been discontinued. The combined effect of these constraints has been to reduce the amount of vital intelligence data gleaned from screening and questioning that can be passed on to army headquarters. Without this effective intelligence back-up the security forces cannot possibly hope to contain the large-scale terrorism that exists in Northern Ireland.

The second major obstacle to successful anti-terrorist operations in Northern Ireland has been the ending of internment. By the end of 1975 Mr Merlyn Rees, then Secretary of State for Northern Ireland, had carried out his declared intention of releasing all internees. But as fast as they were released they were returning to active service with the I.R.A. units that had been so depleted by army and police success in 1974. The army estimates that up to 70 per cent of released internees became reinvolved.[52] It is all very well saying that detention-without-trial is too draconian a measure to use in a liberal democratic society, and that because some people do not like it we must not resort to this device, but the plain fact is that normal liberal democratic government and the rule of law have not been *able* to function in Ulster properly for the last seven years because they have been under direct attack not only from the I.R.A. but also from a multiplicity of 'Loyalist' assassination squads and private armies such as the Ulster Volunteer Force (U.V.F.), the Ulster Freedom Fighters (U.F.F.) and the Protestant Action Force.[53] There are long terrorist traditions in both Protestant and Catholic communities. Where evil men are determined to disrupt the law, and render normal judicial processes unworkable through intimidating and killing witnesses, the government has surely a duty to invoke special powers to protect the community, restore order, and re-establish the rule of law. In a situation such as that obtaining currently in Ulster I cannot accept that the abandonment of internment was other than an act of incredible folly, a self-inflicted wound on the part of the civil authorities. It is an affront that men and women known by the police, the army and the community at large to be terrorist leaders and assassins are allowed to walk the streets of Northern Ireland in broad daylight.[54]

The third serious handicap imposed by the civil authorities on the army in Northern Ireland is one that afflicts the army's offensive capability in confrontation with armed terrorists. It is often forgotten by those who have neither visited Northern Ireland nor studied the situation closely, that the army has frequently been called upon to fight pitched battles with terrorists both in urban and rural areas. Indeed the conflict between the security forces and the Provisional I.R.A. in certain areas, such as the countryside of South Armagh, has resembled traditional guerrilla war more than terrorism proper. Yet in this guerrilla war the army's flexibility has been limited not only as a result of inadequate manpower and the skilful campaign waged by one of the most ably-led I.R.A. units in Ulster, but also by a government constraint on the army's use of their firepower.

This constraint is the 'yellow card' instructions issued to soldiers laying down the precise circumstances when they are permitted to open fire. The 'yellow card' can only have been drawn up by a civil servant, not a soldier. It is based on the entirely illusory assumption that the army in Northern Ireland should function strictly as a constabulary in khaki, not as a military force: yet constables cannot defeat well-armed, well-funded and well-trained terrorists and guerrillas! The yellow card – appropriate only in colour! – lays down absolutely that the soldier may only shoot someone actually in the act of killing or causing serious injury to another, or who is immediately about to do so. The card is clearly based on the constabulary ethic of minimal reasonable force in self-defence, in defence of another, or in prevention of a serious crime. For an army engaged in a shooting war it is absolutely suicidal, for it gives the shooting initiative to the enemy. The army always has to wait for the enemy to strike first, and thus has to stay on the defensive. It is at least partly as a result of this handicap that so many British soldiers have been lost in the war in South Armagh, with very few terrorists killed in return. (In late 1975, for example, there had been forty-nine soldiers killed in the South Armagh area with no recorded I.R.A. losses.) Anyone who doubts whether this constraint does really hurt should study the numerous cases of prosecutions of soldiers in Northern Ireland. It results in soldiers being deprived of all confidence in their legal position and protection. To beat the Provisional I.R.A. the army needs to be able to give its men clear military objectives, a properly defined remit of responsibilities, and the complete backing of the government for a campaign to kill and defeat the terrorists.

And finally, perhaps the most important requirement for winning the battle against terrorism in Northern Ireland is that the government should be clear about its political objectives. There is a great deal of nonsense talked about the search for a 'political solution' or some grandiose settlement 'agreed by the people of all communities' in the Province. As Professor Rose and others have pointed out time and again such hopes are completely unrealistic. The *best* one can hope for is that one might find a mode of devolved government in the Province which has at least the tacit consent or co-operation of a majority of the Protestant population and a sizeable proportion of the Catholics. Ironically it was again in 1974 that the government came closest to achieving this minimal viable framework for government. This took the form of the Northern Ireland Executive, which resulted from the implementation of the Sunningdale Agreement. There was a great deal going for this innovation. It enjoyed the wholehearted support of the then Prime Minister, Mr Edward Heath, and of his Secretary of State for Northern Ireland, Mr William Whitelaw, a tough and firm minister whose experience and political sensitivity had earned him great respect among all parties to the Ulster problem. Dublin had been fully consulted and was lending full support.

The experiment in power-sharing which ensued – bringing together progressive Unionists under the Chief Executive, Mr Brian Faulkner, and Catholic politicians of the Social Democratic and Labour Party (S.D.L.P.) – was a remarkably brave and promising advance. Ironically it was wrecked not by political terrorism but by a mass strike organised by the Ulster Workers' Council which almost paralysed the Province. It would be naïve to assume that the strike had anything like unanimous support among the Protestant community. Many Protestants were shocked and bitter that direct action of so-called 'Loyalists' should have been allowed by the authorities to destroy the Province's new form of government. Certainly to my personal knowledge, many of the workforce were intimidated into staying away from work by threats from the paramilitary groups. The ultimate tragedy for the British government was that it failed to maintain the Executive at its first major confrontation. One is bound to conclude that there was a certain lack of political will to stand up to the strikers. The army's reluctance to take over the operation of key services was natural enough, but it should have been overriden. Emergency powers should have been used to conscript certain key workers and public utilities for the duration of the Emergency. The leaders of the strike could have been arrested and detained quite legitimately under the existing powers as their avowed aim was not economic but political. They had set out to break the power-sharing Executive, and to do so they were prepared to derogate the Constitution and to resort to widespread intimidation of workers. It is a sad fact that if and when a new viable framework for devolved administration in Northern Ireland does emerge it is likely to very closely resemble the model of Mr Faulkner's administration. Has the British government the will to sustain a renewed attempt at even this modest degree of political advance against the threats of intimidation and terrorism by means of which groups of extremist 'irreconcilables' will inevitably try to destroy it? Slow, painful, political advance and the struggle for order will either go hand in hand or fail separately.

Experience not only in Northern Ireland but in many advanced industrial societies shows that the main danger in times of acute economic and political crisis is likely to stem not from military *coups* but from a polarisation of the community into extremist factions. Each side will tend to paramilitarise, to rely on forming its own private armies to counter the other, for in such crises neither extreme trusts the government to do its job of ensuring both social justice and political order. This was certainly the repeated experience of the Weimar Republic and the French Third Republic between the wars, and in post-1918 Italy. More recently it has been tragically repeated in Lebanon. A careful assessment of the recent political history of Northern Ireland amply confirms the gravity of the dangers which threaten a liberal state which under-reacts to an incipient or full-scale internal war.

Faced by such severe and cumulative dangers there are other emergency measures that can be used to save the state. In discussing special powers any liberal will speak with strong distaste and reluctance. Acton's famous dictum applies with obvious relevance to special powers: all power corrupts, and special powers are especially corruptive. In the light of the infamous uses of emergency decrees in Germany in the 1930s, or in India and Bangladesh in the 1970s, this liberal distaste seems to me to be perfectly justified. Too many cases come to mind of ambitious politicians around the world who have exploited such measures for their own ends, or who would dearly like to do so. Mainly because of these abuses and the real dangers of permanent dictatorship emerging, liberals are right to insist that special powers should only be used if there is a fundamental threat to the political or economic system.

Yet it is certainly possible to imagine circumstances when the use of such powers, however unpleasant, is a lesser evil than the total collapse of democracy that might otherwise occur. The main principles liberals would want to insist upon in the event of any introduction of emergency powers are: (i) that, however bad the crisis might be, the power to grant and to revoke special powers must be reserved to the legislature; (ii) that the constitution as such should *never* be suspended; (iii) that the legislature should remain in session for the whole period of the emergency legislation; and (iv) that specific emergency powers should be granted only for a fixed and limited period. The maximum should be six months, subject to the legislature's right to revoke or renew the special powers should circumstances require. Emergency measures should be clearly and simply drafted, published as widely as possible and administered impartially.

As we have already noted, in regard to Northern Ireland, the special power of detention without trial is one of the most controversial: it clearly does involve an infringement of the principle of *habeas corpus* in respect of terrorist suspects. However, as has been argued above, the normal judicial processes may be rendered inoperable in a serious terrorist emergency. The police may be totally hamstrung in their efforts to get a man who they know to be guilty actually convicted, because of widespread terrorisation and intimidation of witnesses, juries and lawyers. The judges and magistrates have frequently been targets for assassination attempts in Northern Ireland and some of these attempts have succeeded. Under such circumstances, should the authorities allow the terrorist to roam freely in society to continue systematic murder? In a *really severe* terrorist emergency detention is a power that the government cannot afford to discard lightly. However, if detention without trial is used it is essential that it should be subject to automatic periodic review by an impartial judicial tribunal to guard against abuse.

In 1975 the Northern Ireland (Emergency Provisions) (Amendment) Act transferred executive power to order temporary detention from the panel of commissioners who had previously administered it to the Secretary of State for Northern Ireland. The Act laid down a new procedure for detention. The Secretary of State was empowered to make an interim custody order only where it appeared that there were grounds for suspecting a person of the commission or attempted commission of any act of terrorism or directing, organising or training persons for terrorism. Within two weeks of the date of the order the Secretary was to refer the case to an adviser. If this was not done within two weeks the order ceased to have effect. As soon as possible thereafter the detainee was to be served with a written statement on the nature of the terrorist offences of which he or she was suspected. The detainee could then make written representations and ask for a meeting with the adviser. The adviser would report to the Secretary of State as to whether it was necessary for the person to be detained, and the Secretary would make the detention order or direct release accordingly. If a detention order had not been made within seven weeks from the date of the interim custody order, the order ceased to have effect. It is worth spelling out this procedure in detail to indicate that detention was not quite the arbitrary weapon it was sometimes alleged to have been. However, undoubtedly the review procedures required considerable improvement.

The value of detention in a grave emergency is as a crude instrument for reducing the level of violence, and possibly, if it is sustained for a long period, as a deterrent to others. It certainly does not help forward the business of the detection and conviction of terrorists. And it has the most grave disadvantages. Detention without trial is a useful propaganda weapon for the terrorist both among his home community and abroad. And the detention centres themselves become intensive training centres of terrorist ideology, tactics and techniques: as one Senior Army Officer in Northern Ireland put it: 'detention becomes a kind of Staff College for terrorists'.

Of far greater use in the detection, conviction and punishment of terrorists are special powers of arrest without warrant, prolonging the period for which suspects may be held for questioning, and extending police powers of search. We have earlier noted, in the context of discussing terrorism in Northern Ireland, the vital importance of intelligence-gathering for the security forces. Interrogation of suspects is, of course, one of the vital intelligence sources. It is clear that the most valuable powers gained by the British police from the passage of the Prevention of Terrorism (Temporary Provisions) Act, 1974, are those increasing the period for which terrorist suspects can be detained for questioning.

The Prevention of Terrorism Act was not a panic measure. Its main provisions had already been prepared well before the carnage of the Birmingham pub bombings of 21 November 1974, in which twenty civilians were killed and 180 injured. And it was right and necessary that the government had such legislation ready, because the war in Ulster had already spilled over into the mainland over the previous eighteen months. Indeed before the Bill was introduced into Parliament nearly 700 people had been injured by I.R.A. bombs in Britain. On a single day in March 1973 nearly 250 people had been injured and one killed in two bomb attacks at the Old Bailey and Great Scotland Yard. In 1974 there had been attacks at the National Defence College, Latimer, and on a coach on the M62 in February, at the Tower of London in July, at Guildford in October, and at Woolwich in November. But it was the Birmingham pub bombings that finally convinced public opinion, M.P.s and the government that emergency measures were necessary to try to prevent the spread of this barbarism.

The Act introduced by Mr Roy Jenkins provides a valuable example of the kinds of special powers that can be used effectively to protect a society under severe terrorist attack, without simultaneously suspending the constitution or destroying civil liberty. One of its major provisions, the proscription of the I.R.A. as a terrorist organisation, is, arguably, 'more spectacular than effective'.[55] Security experts have long argued that proscription simply tends to drive the target organisation completely underground and makes the tasks of intelligence-gathering and detection more difficult for the police. Nevertheless this move was politically well-judged, for it would have outraged public opinion if the I.R.A. had been permitted to continue to meet, raise funds and recruit support openly in British cities. It was, after all, already a proscribed organisation in Ireland, both north and south of the border. Moreover the stiff penalties for belonging to, or professing to belong to the I.R.A., giving it financial or other support, or arranging or assisting in the arrangement of an I.R.A. meeting, were a useful token of the government's determination to crack down on terrorist organisation. And one positive benefit of proscription is that it deprives the terrorists of the opportunity to march, demonstrate and provoke affrays with rival groups. This helps to free the police from the dreary and time-consuming work of crowd and riot control on the streets, and enables them to concentrate on protecting the general public and catching criminals.

Of proven value to security forces is the power to exclude terrorists by denying them entry to Britain or by deportation. Clause 3 of the 1974 Act 'enables the Secretary of State to make exclusion orders to prevent acts of terrorism, wherever committed, designed to influence public opinion or Government policy with respect to affairs in Northern Ireland'.[56] This enables the authorities to deny entry to (or to deport) any person suspected of terrorist offences, or suspected of entering Britain for the purpose of committing terrorism. Under the Act even U.K. citizens who have lived in Britain for less than twenty years may be expelled across the Irish Sea. As the necessary instrument of this Act, port controls by police and immigration officials have been considerably tightened. Port police have the power to stop, question and search any suspected person. These controls have already yielded much invaluable information to the security authorities. They are paralleled by similar powers of exclusion wielded by the Secretary of State for Northern Ireland under the 1976 Prevention of Terrorism Supplemental Temporary Provisions, Northern Ireland Order 1976. Police, immigration officers and members of the armed forces have the power to examine persons leaving or entering Northern Ireland in order to determine whether they are involved in terrorism and if they should be recommended for exclusion. This applies whether the suspect is a U.K. citizen or not, providing that he or she is not a native of Northern Ireland. An important provision in the 1976 Act is the requirement that any person flying a private aircraft has to obtain police permission before take-off or landing anywhere in the Province unless they use Sydenham or Aldergrove airports. It is, of course, a considerable problem to police these measures. And so far as the smaller fishing ports and remoter rural areas are concerned the authorities must rely on aerial surveillance and patrols by the security forces to observe any illegal entry or exit.

Another very important power for the security forces is that of searching any person suspected of committing, preparing or instigating acts of terrorism. Apart from body searches of suspects, which may yield valuable evidence and intelligence, random searches of premises, and searches for specific equipment and materials utilised for terrorism, such as explosives and transmitters, may be specifically authorised by emergency legislation.

By far the most useful of the powers afforded by the Prevention of Terrorism Act, however, are those under section 7, clauses (1) and (2), dealing with arrest and detention. The police are thereby empowered to arrest without warrant a person whom they 'reasonably suspect' to be (i) a person guilty of a terrorist offence, or (ii) a person concerned in the commission, preparation or instigation of acts of terrorism, or (iii) a person subject to an exclusion order. Moreover in particular cases the Secretary of State has the power to extend the period for which a suspect may be detained for questioning beyond the normal maximum of forty-eight hours. The additional period may not exceed five days, making the maximum period for which a person could be detained without being charged seven days. This power is an invaluable aid to the police, for it is interrogation that saves lives and provides the leads for catching other members of the terrorist organisation. And in the judgement of most intelligence experts forty-eight hours is not long enough for the process of interrogation to yield results. Seven days is generally just long enough for conventional police questioning methods to wear down the suspect's resistance. Frequently the longer period enables the police to use bargaining power. Exceptionally, with the co-operation of the Director of Public Prosecutions, they may be able to offer certain suspects immunity from prosecution in return for everything they know. This method can be particularly effective in cases where suspects are likely to have become enmeshed in terrorist activities more through blackmail and intimidation than political conviction.

One element essential to special powers legislation for any protracted terrorist campaign must be adequate measures to protect public security. For the kind of situation we are discussing is a war situation. (This in my view is the only circumstance that could justify the draconian measures discussed above in a liberal state.) In an internal war terrorists will stop at nothing. One of the tactics which they widely employ is espionage and infiltration of the government and security forces. This technique was brilliantly deployed in Ireland as far back as 1917–21, when Michael Collins managed to acquire agents and informers in every part of the government, police and army bureaucracy. Even the irresponsible leaks or publication of official documents can cause considerable disruption and damage to the government politically and psychologically. This can be well attested by the numerous unaccountable leaks of official documents in Northern Ireland. The Irish government has been by no means immune from this problem either. In September 1974 a confidential appreciation by Dr Conor Cruise O'Brien on Irish Cabinet options in the event of a civil war in Northern Ireland was leaked to the press. The document stated that the Dublin government was doing all in its power to prevent a loyalist majority emerging in the Northern Ireland Convention. A full report appeared in the Belfast *News Letter* and loyalists expressed rage and fury about what they regarded as interference by the 'hostile government' in Dublin in their internal politics. Undoubtedly the disclosure was a useful propaganda weapon for the loyalists and did nothing to help Mr Faulkner and his colleagues. Unfortunately it is very difficult to see what can be done to prevent such disclosures other than by stringent application of the Official Secrets Act and disciplinary codes.

Espionage by terrorists within the administration and security forces can do even more damage. In an attempt to deter such activities, Section 20 of the 1973 Northern Ireland (Emergency Provisions) Act made it an offence to collect information about either the armed forces or the police which was likely to be useful to terrorists. The 1975 Northern Ireland (Emergency Provisions) (Amendment) Bill, Clause 13, extended this provision to cover information about persons holding judicial office, court officers and prison officers.

There are certain other kinds of measures that governments may find valuable if not essential in the longer term to defeat a protracted terrorist war. There is the possibility of concerted action with neighbouring states sharing a common border. This is especially necessary where the terrorists are using the border as an escape route from the security forces within their target state. Hence, the development of many different modes of co-operation between the British and Irish governments affords a useful example of what can be achieved.

There has been, for some time, growing cross-border communication and co-operation between the *Garda* in the Republic and the R.U.C. in the north. For political reasons an extradition agreement covering terrorist offenders between the Republic and the United Kingdom has proved impracticable. But in the past two years a great advance has been made towards closer judicial co-operation with the parallel passage of the Criminal Jurisdiction Bill through the British parliament and the Criminal Justice Amendment Bill in the Dail. The Irish Act now makes it possible for fugitive offenders to be tried in Irish courts for offences committed in Northern Ireland or in mainland Britain. A procedure has been established whereby a court can obtain evidence from witnesses too frightened to travel to give evidence. The British Act affords complementary procedures. It is to be hoped that this valuable example of bilateral co-operation can be followed up by establishing proper full-scale cross-border co-operation between the British and Irish armies. This was still some way from achievement at the time of writing. Further discussion of problems of international, regional and bilateral co-operation against terrorism is included in Part III. The important point to bear in mind in the context of the present discussion of national emergency measures against severe terrorism and internal war is that however firm a particular government's measures may be, and however expert their security forces, the efficacy of tough measures can be gravely weakened or even undermined if a bordering state offers sanctuary to terrorists, is soft in its treatment of terrorist organisations, and witholds security co-operation from a neighbouring state. One could perhaps imagine certain difficulties arising for Britain in Northern Ireland if the Irish Republic were to become taken over by a Marxist–Leninist régime which proceeded to promote I.R.A. terrorism as a form of surrogate war against Britain! We should be thankful for the liberal statesmanship and courage of Mr Cosgrave and his colleagues in the present sad and trying situation.

It is also important to hit hard at terrorist sources of weapons and firearms. One line of attack must be to try to reduce the flow of funds into the terrorist organisation, for provided terrorists have adequate cash there are always arms dealers prepared to sell them all they require. Nor are private arms dealers the only source. Colonel Gaddafi of Libya has eagerly provided supplies of weapons usually obtained orginally from the Soviet Union. And the Soviet K.G.B. has itself, on many occasions, sanctioned the supply of Soviet-made arms to terrorist groups in the West. They are not choosy about the ideological purity of the group concerned. For example, it was clearly with Soviet connivance that a shipment of arms from Czechoslovakia to the Provisional I.R.A. was arranged. This happened to be intercepted at Schiphol Airport in Holland. The interesting point is that these arms were being provided not for the Marxist Official I.R.A. but for their avowed enemies, the Provisionals. It seems clear that the Soviet government decided that the growth of new violent extremist organisations among Western youth which mushroomed in the late 1960s could be usefully exploited to promote internal disruption and turmoil in Western cities.

Yet it is also clear that much of the cash for the I.R.A. has come from other sources. The first main source is expropriations, protection rackets and 'legal' businesses in Northern Ireland itself. Indeed the Provisionals have become so locked in with the criminal community in the Province that terrorism has become more than simply a hobby or a cause for many: it has become the main source of livelihood. A second important source is funds from the American Irish community channelled mainly through NORAID, an I.R.A. front organisation thinly disguised as a charity. Now more and more Americans are realising that donations to the I.R.A. are donations of death and maiming to the innocent of all communities in Ireland, and the flow of funds is likely to dry up. However, in the meantime the U.S. Treasury has shown commendable energy in investigating the accounts of NORAID, which now faces legal action because it has failed to make proper returns detailing its income over the past two years. It is to be hoped that the U.S. government continues to take firm action against those who sponsor murder in Ireland. But the British and Irish governments also need to do far more to explain to the American public, and to international opinion, the real nature of the conflict in Northern Ireland. For the sad fact is that there really are still people abroad who do not realise that there has been an inter-sectarian, inter-communal conflict going on in Northern Ireland. There are even some who have fallen for the I.R.A. propaganda picture of themselves as heroic Robin Hood revolutionaries fighting colonial imperialism on behalf of the shackled and oppressed natives! One of the sadder consequences of the virtual neglect of serious in-depth documentary analysis on television concerning Ulster is that even the population of the rest of the United Kingdom is not as well informed about the history and political—economic background of the conflict as it should be. There is still a big task here for the British and Irish media and governments.

Apart from efforts to starve terrorist movements of funds, governments can also take other measures to regulate the availability of fire-arms and explosives and the sale and distribution of potentially dangerous chemicals. The United States in particular stands in urgent need of a comprehensive system of fire-arms registration, licensing and control similar to that obtaining in Britain and other Western European countries. If the United States ever faces another civil war, which Heaven forbid, it would be potentially the most sanguinary and difficult to contain or to terminate, in large part as a consequence of the practically universal possession of fire-arms. If guns are not available, those who commit acts of violence but who do not have a single-minded desire to murder, are less likely to kill.[57] The only governmental resource for countering the massive illegal build-up of arms is, however, thorough and constant arms searches by the security forces, including the use of naval and air patrols to prevent arms smuggling. Regulations concerning the manufacture, sale and supply of explosives should also be tightly supervised by governments and closely policed. In Britain there is an urgent need for stricter rules concerning the security of explosives: manufacturers of detonators should be required to mark them with a code indicating place and date of manufacture; all industrial users of explosives should be required to account for all detonators passing through their hands; there should be an obligation to report losses of detonators and explosive substances; and, finally, we require a tougher scale of penalties for explosives offences.

Some governments confronted by escalating terrorist campaigns have acted to deny the terrorist organisations the publicity they so ardently seek by banning them from the media. One example is the Irish Republic's 1960 Broadcasting Authority Act, Section 31. The Irish government used this section of the act in 1972 to ban the state radio and television service (RTE) from carrying interviews with Provisional or Official I.R.A. spokesmen and sympathisers. Since October 1976 the ban has been extended to cover interviews or reports of interviews with members of the political wing of the Provisional I.R.A., the Provisional Sinn Fein, or members of any organisation proscribed in Northern Ireland. The Provisional Sinn Fein protests that it is a legalised political party, though unregistered, with twenty-six elected local councillors throughout the Irish Republic, and that it has a legal right to broadcasting time.

The minister who imposed the ban, Dr Conor Cruise O'Brien, stated:

> The propaganda activities of Provisional Sinn Fein in support of the Provisional IRA are in our view a danger to the state... The threat posed by the Provisional IRA in this state is probably clearer now than ever before... It seemed to me that their presentation of their propaganda would suggest to the public that in some way Provisional Sinn Fein was accepted as a legitimate political party. I do not accept it as such. I accept it as the propaganda wing of a criminal organization: a public relations agency for a murder gang.[58]

It is ironic that in Northern Ireland, which is suffering directly from major terrorist violence, no such broadcasting ban exists, and the British media (television, radio and press) which have very wide circulation in Ireland, have frequently carried interviews and reports of interviews with Provisional I.R.A. and Provisional Sinn Fein spokesmen. This is clearly a case of Britain dragging its feet on a most important aspect of anti-terrorist policy. The United Kingdom government is, after all, directly responsible for the Province of Northern Ireland where a bloody internal war has raged for over seven years: that war came home in earnest to the British mainland between 1974 and 1976. It is therefore absurd to pretend that the British government can stand aloof, detaching itself from the problem. In a hot war one does not normally invite the enemy to have broadcasting time on one's state radio and television networks. It is surely crazy to allow spokesmen for terrorists out to destroy the state to enjoy all the advantages of broadcasting their message of hatred and fanaticism and to inspire their small cadre of militants to further outrages. That would not simply be an abuse of liberty: it would be the more irresponsible licence. Yet, under present British broadcasting practice, that is what is allowed to happen!

I believe that it is not undemocratic in the least to ban murderers and apologists for terrorist crimes from the broadcasting services which reach into practically every home. For if there is an ultra-pornography of violence then they are its ultimate representatives. And I do not see that it does any service to our democracies or our cultural and intellectual life to indulge such evil. There is, in my view, nothing to be said in favour of attempts to control or censor the reporting and analysis of terrorist campaigns in the press. The British and Irish daily press has in general shown extraordinary accuracy, fairness, humanity and common sense in covering Northern Ireland. They have not allowed themselves to be used as propagandists for any party or cause in the conflict, and the chances of a responsible British or Irish daily or weekly journal being taken over by a proscribed terrorist organisation as a propaganda vehicle seem so remote as to be hardly worth considering. So far as the terrorists themselves are concerned, experience in many countries shows that it is access to broadcasting that they value most highly for they appreciate its potency, its immediacy and its vast potential audience. Groups as disparate as the F.L.Q., Palestinian terrorists and the Tupamaros have all from time to time attempted to blackmail governments into ordering that their manifestos and demands be broadcast. The press does not really interest the terrorist to the same extent. Many terrorist movements have tried to set up their own clandestine broadcasts. But this is expensive and highly risky for the terrorists unless they are lucky enough to be able to operate from the territory of a sympathetic neighbouring state. It is up to responsible liberal democratic governments to co-operate, so far as they are able, to deny the terrorists this most powerful of all contemporary propaganda weapons.

# PART III
# INTERNATIONAL TERRORISM

'But the revolution does require of the revolutionary class that it should attain its end by all methods at its disposal – if necessary by an armed uprising: if required by terrorism.'

Leon Trotsky, *Terrorism and Communism*

'As soon as men decide that all means are permitted to fight an evil, then their good becomes indistinguishable from the evil that they set out to destroy. The subordination of morals to politics, the reign of terror and the technique of propaganda and psychological aggression can be used by any power or party that is bold enough to abandon moral scruples and plunge into the abyss.'

Christopher Dawson, *The Judgement of Nations*

# XXVI
# INTERNATIONAL AND
# TRANSNATIONAL TERRORISM

The term 'international terrorism' is often used so loosely that it implies only that terrorism is a world-wide problem or that most terrorism has some influence, however marginal and indirect, on international opinion and behaviour. More rigorous standards of definition are required for such tasks as scholarly investigation or legal codification. Even academic publications, however, sometimes betray extreme carelessness in the use of the term. A 'Chronology of Recent Incidents in International Terrorism' presented to a recent conference committed the *faux pas* of including Provisional I.R.A. attacks in London while omitting cross-border terrorist raids in the Middle East.[1] Moreover, progress towards more rigorous definition is a precondition for effective analysis and policy prescription, particularly at the levels of intergovernmental negotiation and political and judicial action. The need is well illustrated by the following item in a report of the Fifth U.N. Congress on Prevention of Crime and Treatment of Offenders, Geneva, September 1975: 'The attention of the participants was focused on the phenomenon of "terrorism" which has no accepted definition in any legal code resulting in real difficulties in considering it in the context of criminal justice processes.'[2]

An attempt has already been made in Part I to distinguish terrorism from other modes of violence. When does an act of extreme violence and coercive intimidation for political ends become international? The most obvious case is that of the state which uses coercive or repressive terror in the process of conducting foreign war, conquest, annexation or colonisation. Second, there is the direct terroristic attack by a faction or movement against the citizens and property of a foreign state: such attacks range from the cross-border raids of the type Israel has experienced almost ceaselessly since 1948 to long-range forays such as the Munich massacre in 1972 or the OPEC Conference hijack of 1975 in Vienna. Next there is the terrorism committed by government, faction or movement operating in their own country of origin or in third countries against foreign citizens, property or means of transport. Terrorist acts can also be accurately designated 'international' if they are committed as the result of connivance, collaboration or alliance between terrorists and the governments, terrorist movements or factions of foreign states. In short, political terrorism becomes international in the strict sense when it is; (i) directed at foreigners or foreign targets; (ii) concerted by the governments or factions of more than one state; or (iii) aimed at influencing the policies of a foreign government.

The definitional debate has become somewhat confused in recent years by the introduction of the term 'transnational terrorism'. And one writer has gone so far as to suggest that terrorism 'becomes transnational when it involves individuals of different nationalities. . .'[3] This seems unnecessary because the term international has never been restricted exclusively to inter-governmental relations as such and is generally used to apply to cultural, economic and other activities and transactions involving citizens of different countries. Other writers have suggested a more specialised use of 'transnational', applying the designation to those terrorists who operate internationally with the express long-term aim of global revolution or of establishing a revolutionary supranational world order. According to this stricter definition transnational terrorist groups clearly constitute a small, though exotic, minority of international terrorists. The vast majority of acts of international terrorism have clearly far more limited objectives, such as national liberation, secession or seizure of power over a specific political régime. Examples of international terrorist movements in the transnational category would be the Bakuninist Anarchist International active in Europe in the 1870s, or the Japanese United Red Army with its professed aim of 'world revolution'. But the Popular Front for the Liberation of Palestine would not be included because its primary declared aim is the liberation of the Palestinian people and the establishment of a secular Marxist Palestinian state: it is to a high degree international in its targets and *modus operandi*, but this does not make it a transnational organisation in the same league with the Bakuninists or the modern anarchists and nihilists.

# XXVII
# FORCE AND VIOLENCE IN
# INTERNATIONAL RELATIONS

In the context of the liberal polity, as I have argued at length earlier, the distinction between force and violence is of the greatest importance. Responsible and limited constitutional government provides a formula by means of which citizens may enjoy the highest degree of individual liberty compatible with security against the violence of tyrannical government, foreign enemies, private persons or groups. But we also noted the agonising dilemmas that may arise in liberal political practice when force and violence become so blurred as to be almost indistinguishable. For example, if the laws of the state require a man to act contrary to his private morality, under what conditions should he place obedience to conscience above obligation to the state? Are there circumstances when, even in a liberal polity, one may be morally justified in resorting to political violence? It was not suggested that there are any easy general answers to such questions.

However if we consider the problem of force and violence in the context of international relations as a whole the moral problems involved are infinitely more complex. For there is no world sovereign authority with the power to make universal law, order, peace and justice. The noble hopes of the liberal internationalists have been sorely disappointed by United Nations experiment. For while idealists looked eagerly for signs of an embryonic world authority emerging from Lake Success, the sickening realities of deepening division into armed camps, the strategic arms race, and continuing ideological and military struggles have dragged the organisation into the Slough of Despond. In the absence of any effective world body with the necessary authority and power to impose peace and order it is, as always, the strongest states or alliances that have determined for themselves when war is necessary and, hence, justified.

In this desert of ruined hopes there remain some miraculous blades of hope. There is the historic but painfully slow progress towards a more comprehensive and effective international law. Yet this remains tenuous and vulnerable because, unlike the positive laws of states, international laws must depend solely on a combination of international consensus, appeals to reciprocal self-interest, and retaliatory sanctions. According to some legal theorists this makes international law more closely analogous to customary law and convention than to law proper. History abounds with examples of states that have defied such rules with impunity. The development of a more elaborate body of international law may in itself be encouraging evidence of greater international co-operation and interdependence. And since the Second World War this development has been vastly reinforced by the movements towards greater international organisation in the economic, technical and scientific spheres. But no realistic statesman pins too many hopes on the grandiose rhetoric of brotherly love or treaties, protocols and agreements, for it is all to easy for statesmen to sign resolutions and treaties to which they have no intention of adhering. And inter-state relations can still shift from toleration to envenomed conflict with astonishing rapidity as a result of revolution, *coup* or other dramatic internal changes.

Internationally liberal theory has to come to terms with these realities. Liberal states inhabit a hostile environment, and the greatest immediate dangers they face stem from the Soviet Union with its explicit world revolutionary aims and rapidly growing offensive military capability.[4] Moreover, liberal democratic states are becoming an increasingly beleaguered minority, as evidenced by their growing isolation and frustration in the U.N. General Assembly. According to a recent survey only 19.6 per cent of the world's population life in free countries.[5] The vast majority live under military régimes or one-party states of one kind or another. It is absolute utopian nonsense to speak as if an international community of shared liberal values already existed. In an unfriendly and dangerous world what alternative have liberal states but to arm themselves for their own protection and to form defensive alliances to try to ensure against Soviet aggression? Only an absolute pacifist would want to deny them the right of self-defence.

# XXVIII
# INTERNATIONAL TERRORISM AND INTERNATIONAL RELATIONS

Any honest survey of violence in contemporary international relations would have to admit that, even in the very shadow of nuclear weapons, internal and international conflict is endemic. Liberal statesmen are already, in this sense, struggling to build peace within a framework of failure. Since the Second World War there have been over 200 internationally significant outbreaks of violence. And although less than 10 per cent of these have been direct military conflicts between two states, a large proportion of the major internal conflicts and revolutionary civil wars has involved considerable covert or indirect foreign intervention. [6]

Hence there has been no diminution of what has been earlier designated (see Part I, pp. 48–57) as epiphenomenal terror, that is the large-scale terror which is an inevitable concomitant to wars and mass insurrections. And it would clearly be dangerously naïve to assume that the preservation of a merely formal peace between the major powers is enough to secure a significant reduction in the degree of epiphenomenal terror. For the Soviet Communist leadership has clearly demonstrated that it believes the pursuit of *détente* and the so-called 'peace-offensive' on the diplomatic front to be entirely compatible with the waging of ideological and armed struggle in furtherance of the world-wide aims of Soviet Marxism—Leninism. Not only have the Soviet leaders never renounced Lenin's injunction that any means are justified to further their world revolutionary aims, they have actually refined and added to their repertoire new and more insidious modes of unconventional war.

In an age of nuclear stalemate the Russian leaders are astute enough to realise that there is no need for them to put at risk all their hard-won economic development by provoking all-out nuclear war. By the selective adoption and covert promotion of a host of 'armed liberation struggles', by subversion and sabotage, and by terrorism, they have been able to nibble away piece after piece of the non-communist world. The new generation of their satellite and client régimes – in Cuba, in Vietnam, in Somalia and now in Angola – is ample testimony to their growing success in techniques of internal subversion and take-over in Third World countries. And unless the Western powers can find an effective counter strategy all their nuclear strength and military technology will not be able to prevent the fall of the non-communist world by a thousand cuts. As Liddell-Hart observed: 'The implied threat of using nuclear weapons to curb guerrillas was as absurd as to talk of using a sledgehammer to ward off a swarm of mosquitoes. The policy did not make sense, and the natural effect was to stimulate and encourage the forms of aggression, by erosion, to which nuclear weapons were an inapplicable counter.'[7]

There are a number of very widespread misconceptions about the nature of unconventional and irregular war in general, and about revolutionary and subrevolutionary terrorism in particular, which need correction. The case of international terrorism is especially appropriate to illustrate the falsity of a number of these assumptions. First, it is a widely held belief that guerrilla struggle is essentially a defensive response to superior military power, that it is always the weapon of the weak. But this is to overlook a significant shift in the strategic environment in favour of indirect means: 'In the past, guerrilla war has been a weapon of the weaker side, and thus primarily defensive, but in the atomic age it may be increasingly developed as a form of aggression suited to exploit a situation of nuclear stalemate. Thus the concept of "cold war" is now out of date, and should be superseded by that of "camouflaged war".'[8] The peculiar aptness of Liddell-Hart's term 'camouflaged war' to terrorism hardly needs emphasis.

Of course it is undeniable that in many cases the guerrilla struggle is an asymmetrical conflict with cumulative advantages accruing to the incumbent régime. This has been true of most, though not all, national liberation wars waged in poor Third World countries. But it is really a question of who is calling the shots. We now have a situation in which the Soviet Union and other communist states and some Arab states have actually initiated, armed and directed struggles in foreign states. We have seen the second most powerful military power in the world waging a kind of proxy war by means of guerrilla movements, terrorism and subversion in many countries. It is clear that where powerful states exploit such methods, and provide the very latest weapons and training for the guerrilla or terrorist operatives, one is confronting a new and dangerous variety of offensive war, 'camouflaged' but deadly enough to its targets.

There is considerable evidence that the Soviet Union has not been content merely to give diplomatic support to national liberation movements for its own purposes. Since 1967 the Russians have reconsidered the potential of the plethora of New Left revolutionist and anarchist movements in Western industrialised states. They have shifted from regarding them solely as ideological heretics to using them in certain circumstances to weaken and disrupt liberal democracies through terrorism and student strife. For example, Soviet encouragement and indirect assistance to the Provisional I.R.A. has taken the form of allowing Soviet arms to be supplied to the terrorists. A large shipment of arms from Czechoslovakia, which must have been cleared by the Russians, was intercepted *en route* to the I.R.A. at Schiphol Airport in Holland in October 1971. There are the numerous supplies of Soviet-made equipment to terrorist movements of almost every ideological hue channelled through Libya, in addition to the massive aid they provide for the P.L.O. Evidence has even come to light of communist willingness to assist the anarchist–nihilist group, the Baader–Meinhof terrorists.[9]

It has been repeatedly suggested[10] that, in this offensive role, international terrorism is a form of 'surrogate war' between movements or states, but this term is dangerously misleading. International terrorist attack is simply a different mode of war, not an alternative to war as such. Indeed it may actually parallel conventional conflict, as in the case of many Palestinian attacks, or the recent war in Lebanon, or it may be designed to act as a catalyst for a wider conflict. A more accurate description of the involvement of states in mounting long-range terrorist attacks in 'enemy' states would be 'proxy war'. International terrorism evinces similar characteristics to those of terroristic acts in the domestic context; arbitrariness, indiscriminateness in effects, non-recognition of any rules or conventions of war, inhumanity and barbaric cruelty. As has been argued earlier, terrorism represents the militarisation of politics. Instead of seeking negotiation, diplomacy and compromise, terrorists see their struggle in zero–sum terms. They will not rest until they have secured final 'victory'. Anything that aids their struggle is good and justified. The world is divided in Manichean terms into friends and enemies. There can be no neutrals: 'you are either for us or against us.'

It is because revolutionary terrorists perceive themselves as being engaged in a zero–sum conflict rather than a 'mixed game of conflict and co-operation'[11] that it is so dangerous to assume that governments can bargain meaningfully with them. The most frequent mistake is to confuse their short-term tactical demands for their strategic objectives. The latter are strictly non-negotiable. Hence the suggestion that terrorists and government have 'a common interest and consequently the possibility of a mutually advantageous outcome'[12] is illusory. The terrorists always have their eyes not merely on a specific confrontation, but on *winning their campaign*. In dealing with terrorists with determined political objectives totally opposed to its own, governments have far more to gain from holding fast and attempting to defeat the terrorists. Deterrence and bargaining will not suffice. Any government weakness encourages further assaults, and any release of terrorists as part of a bargain simply strengthens the terrorist groups staging such assaults.

A second major misconception is that guerrilla and terrorist movements invariably wage war in a noble and just cause. It is so often tacitly assumed that anyone who takes guns and plastic explosives aboard an aircraft to stage a hijack must be a *bona fide* victim of oppression or injustice. This is by no means always the case. A more balanced view has been expressed by General Frank Kitson:

> Many regard subversion as being principally a form of redress used by the down-trodden peoples of the world against their oppressors, and feel, therefore, that there is something immoral about preparing to suppress it. Undoubtedly subversion is sometimes used in this way, and on those occasions those supporting the government find themselves fighting for a bad cause. On the other hand, subversion can also be used by evil men to advance their own interests in which case those fighting it have right on their side. More often, as in other forms of conflict, there is some right and some wrong on both sides. . .[13]

A third common error is to assume that international terrorism is a new invention. There were numerous incidents of international terrorism in the nineteenth century. One of the most famous was the attempt by the Italian patriot, Felice Orsini, to assassinate the Emperor Napoleon III and the Empress Eugenie on 14 January 1858. The Bakuninist International believed it was engaged in a campaign of European dimensions. After the First World War international terrorist attacks were endemic in the new Balkan states and the internecine feuds of the Internal Macedonian Revolutionary Organisation (I.M.R.O.) spilt over into Vienna and Milan. Hence it is nonsense to suppose that international terrorism was invented by Latin American guerrillas in the mid-1960s. However, there *has* been a remarkable increase in the incidence of international terrorism during the past decade.

A recent American study of acts of international and transnational terrorism between 1968 and 1975 [14] records a total of 913 incidents including 375 involving the use of explosives, 137 hijackings of aircraft and other means of transportation, 123 kidnappings, and 48 assassinations. Investigation shows that between 1968 and 1975 approximately 800 people were killed, and over 1,700 injured as the result of acts of international terrorism. The incident rate climbed from below 50 per year in the period 1965–8 to 100 per year in 1969–70 and to 200 per year in 1973. By the end of 1975 the rate had dropped slightly to 175 incidents per annum. Incidence was highest in Western Europe with Latin America and the United States coming second and third respectively. The figure for communist bloc countries is almost zero.

Our next task must be to attempt to discern the underlying causes for this dramatic increase in international terrorism.

# XXIX
# UNDERLYING POLITICAL AND STRATEGIC CAUSES

I believe the most significant underlying causes of the recent upsurge in international terrorism to be political and strategic. As has already been emphasised, international war has increasingly become a less attractive option for states in the nuclear age. There is the grave risk that limited war might involve intervention by one or more nuclear powers with the inevitable consequential dangers of escalation to the nuclear threshold or beyond. And these dangers may be just as real, indeed perhaps more potent, in the case of small or medium-sized non-nuclear powers for they have no deterrent with which to assert any power over their own destiny. Moreover the costs of maintaining large military forces, even of a purely conventional nature, impose their own constraints. Those medium and small powers that have no oil revenues to fall back on are faced with increasing economic strains, acute shortages, deficits and severe economic instability in many cases. Governments struggling simply to meet maintenance costs for their armed forces are unlikely to contemplate with equanimity the far vaster costs of waging war. Bernard Brodie's judgement seems sound: 'We may not be able to predict with high confidence that the outcome of some particular rivalry will be pacific, but we can predict over the longer term a much lesser inclination than in times past to take for granted the periodic recurrence of war, certainly the recurrence of large-scale warfare.'[15]

But the effect of these strategic constraints is likely to be, as suggested above, that violence in the international system will increasingly take the forms of guerrilla warfare and terrorism. And these strategic factors are strongly reinforced by general political trends. Since the end of the main wave of colonial independence struggles in the early 1960s the political frontiers have rigidified. New post-colonial régimes have remained dedicated to maintaining the last inch of their colonial patrimonies, and innumerable new secessionist and autonomist movements have hurled themselves against new and intransigent régimes. Thus the ending of colonial empires has not magically eliminated the legions of the aggrieved and alienated willing to fight 'oppression' and 'injustice' in new guises. Moreover, irredentist minorities are more than ever aware of their relative weakness, politically and militarily. They are no longer able to capture the sympathy and support, from revolutionists and other new states, that had been so freely proffered when they were ruled by European imperialists.

Geoffrey Fairbairn has drawn attention to a particularly weak and desperate minority which leapt into the headlines briefly in September 1970: the Ambonese. Many of these people, who originated from the small island of Ambon, now part of Indonesia, live in refugee camps in Holland. When President Suharto paid a state visit to Holland in September 1970 a group of Ambonese militants seized the Indonesian Embassy in the Hague with the apparent aim of publicising their cause and trying to force the Indonesian President to negotiate the future of Ambon. A similar motivation lay behind the actions of a rather more fanatical group of Moluccans, also exiled in Holland, when they seized the Indonesian consulate in the Hague and hijacked a passenger train at Beilen in

December 1975. Fairbairn's wry comment applies with equal force to the cases of both these desperate minority groups:

> The Indonesian regime now being regarded by the West as a friendly one in South East Asia, the guerrillas had no hope of support from the Western Establishment; and not being able to propagate their cause as 'progressive' or 'revolutionary', they could not obtain that instant recognition of purity of motive accorded by the Western liberal-left to far more squalid movements, the colour of whose cockades have been made more readily obvious to the jaundiced eye.[16]

It could serve as a sad epitaph for many such groups, from the Biafrans to the Kurds. There is an almost infinite number of movements of the aggrieved, the alienated and the desperate. It is reasonable to suppose that some of them, generally those most lacking in any political or military resources, will resort to terrorism. And because many of them have been forced into exile, and because they believe their only hope is to direct the attention of international opinion to their plight, their terrorism is most likely to be conducted internationally.

A second major political factor has been the shift in revolutionary theory away from an interest in strategies of rural guerrilla war *simpliciter*, and from electoral struggle, towards urban guerrilla war and terrorism as major or auxiliary forms of armed struggle. In part this new emphasis was provoked by the dramatic failures of attempted follow-ups to the Cuban guerrilla victory. Rural insurgencies in Venezuela, Argentina and Bolivia suffered grave defeats at the hands of increasingly better-equipped and better-trained government security forces. Furthermore, the revolutionaries came to realise that in heavily urbanised states like Brazil and Argentina, where well over half the population was in the cities, they had to win power in the cities as a condition for seizing state power. The dramatic methods and Robin Hood-style mythology attaching to the urban struggles of Carlos Marighela's urban guerrillas and Raoul Sendic's Tupamaros in Uruguay also had the effect of stimulating emulation.

Moreover, as we have noted earlier, the cities afforded the guerrilla certain attractive advantages over the countryside: superb fields of fire; instantaneous and spectacular publicity; ready access to cash, weapons, vehicles and other material resources; and, last but not least, ready-made recruiting grounds among the *barios* and the *marginais*, the slums and shanty towns that engulf the cities.

It is hardly coincidental that, in the late 1960s, this shift in the ideas of the revolutionaries was paralleled by a new interest in urban guerrilla war and terrorism on the part of the sponsor régimes of revolutionary movements. We have already noted how Moscow's pragmatic application of Leninism increasingly promoted such methods. But they were not alone by any means in providing extensive training schools, cash and weaponry for terrorists. Often the larger terrorist movements set up their own schools. Al Fatah, for example, trained personnel from many other terrorist groups in the deadly arts. The key operatives in the Baader–Meinhof gang, it is worth remembering, were trained at an Al Fatah camp in Jordan. Six weeks later they were busy establishing the Red Army Fraction urban guerrilla in Germany.

The Soviets have also encouraged their client states to share in the tasks of training, financing and assisting terrorist activity. In 1976 Western security services uncovered a widespread North Korean smuggling racket, carried on under the cover of diplomatic immunity, trafficking in drugs, cigarettes and alcohol. Western police believe that some of the proceeds have been used to aid terrorist groups such as the Japanese Red Army, Palestinian groups, and the I.R.A. It is estimated that somewhere in the region of 5,000 terrorists are in training in North Korean camps. Palestinians, Eritreans and Japanese are among their 'graduates'. It is clear that North Korea has provided the meeting point for the otherwise somewhat unlikely alliance between Japanese and Palestinian terrorists. The importance of the role of these 'subversive centres' (as one authority has termed them[17]) in indoctrinating and training terrorist 'hit-men' and explosives and weaponry experts should not be underestimated. It is perhaps not sufficiently well known that the notorious terrorist Carlos 'the Jackal' is only one among hundreds who have been processed through Soviet training schools, and who have received their instruction in assassination, subversion and sabotage under communist auspices.

One of the major underlying political causes of terrorism, however, cannot be placed solely at the door of the Soviet Union or her allies. It is the Palestinian problem. Over 90 per cent of all Western European international terrorist acts since 1967 have been professedly committed by members of Palestinian groups or on behalf of the Palestinian cause. Between November 1947, when the U.N. voted for partition of Palestine, and May 1948 when Britain withdrew, some 300,000 Arabs became refugees. After the proclamation of the state of Israel, over 400,000 further refugees fled into neighbouring Arab states in the course of the fighting. In the U.N.W.R.A. camps and the large Palestinian communities in Jordan and Lebanon hatred and resentment festered among the refugees, and for the first time a distinctively Palestinian 'national consciousness' began to emerge. At first their resentments were directed mainly at the Israelis and at those among the Arab states who seemed unwilling or unable to help them. They awaited eagerly the long-promised successful assault by combined Arab armies to recover their homeland. After the cataclysm of the Six Day War in June 1967 it became clear to the Palestinian political leadership that their position had become desperate. Israel was firmly entrenched in occupation of extensive and strategically valuable territory in Sinai, West Bank, Jerusalem and the Golan Heights. The Arab states' armies were licking their wounds, and Arab leaders had not yet been able to maintain unity or to utilise their full power over oil supplies to realise their political objectives. It was in these desperate circumstances that factions of the Palestinian Liberation Organisation, Al Fatah and the Popular Front for the Liberation of Palestine began to seriously develop international terrorist tactics to augment their traditional methods of guerrilla border raids and conventional attack. This shift to terrorism was intensified after the further disastrous defeat of the *Fedayeen* at the hands of Hussein's forces in Jordan in autumn 1970.

It is by no means clear how the wave of Palestinian terrorist attacks on Western airlines, and random slaughter of civilians, is supposed to have assisted their cause. Western opinion was already well aware of the highly charged nature of the Arab–Israel conflict, for all Western governments had been deeply involved, through the U.N. and bilateral diplomacy, with trying to prevent the succession of Arab–Israel wars which threatened to suck in the super-powers into open conflict. The main impact on international opinion, even on moderate Arab opinion, was revulsion at attacks on the innocent. As Arab rulers became increasingly aware of the fanaticism of the extreme neo-Marxist Palestinian factions that were mainly involved in promoting terrorism they became increasingly apprehensive about assisting the birth of new militant revolutionary state in their own backyard. As for the Soviets, they did not need terrorism to persuade them to give arms and financial support to the P.L.O. They have consistently viewed the P.L.O. as a useful stalking horse for furthering their own strategic and ideological objectives in the Middle East.

From the Western point of view there have recently been several factors tending to mitigate the severity of the threat of Palestinian international terrorism. First, the Arab states managed to salvage a major boost to their morale from the Yom Kippur War of October 1973, even though they suffered a military defeat. For the first time the Arabs were able to inflict heavy losses on Israeli aircraft and tanks. And in the battles on both the Suez and Syrian fronts Arab armies were able to deploy their Soviet-supplied SAMs and S.S.M.s with deadly effect. This stronger Arab military performance has undoubtedly helped to restore morale after the ignominious failures in the 1967 war. It has also served as an ominous warning to the Israelis that their opponents have been able to effectively deploy more sophisticated weaponry, and that the military balance is gradually shifting inexorably against them. Israel has been made cruelly aware of her complete dependence on U.S. military aid and support for her very survival, and, internally, the embittered postmortems among the Israeli military and deepening political divisions about future options provide evidence of growing malaise.

Terrorist attacks on Israel, and on Israeli citizens abroad, have only served to toughen Israeli resistance and political will. On the other hand, the crippling effectiveness of the Arab oil weapon has forced Western governments to take a more accommodating line towards the Arab states generally, and this has included public support for the aims of implementing U.N. Resolution 242 (calling for Israeli withdrawal from occupied territories), and a general commitment to the establishment of a new Palestinian state on the West Bank. Arafat, the P.L.O. leader, has attempted to exploit this new favourable juncture for Arab diplomacy to the full, achieving observer status in a number of U.N. bodies, the formation of a Palestinian 'government-in-exile', recognition by the Arab summit at Rabat of the P.L.O.'s status as legitimate spokesman for the Palestinians, and the ultimate accolade of a hero's welcome at the U.N. General Assembly. Yet in order to cultivate this image of successful diplomacy from a position of moral strength, Arafat and his fellow moderates in the P.L.O. have found it necessary to shake off the terrorist image. Since 1973 they have made numerous forceful denunciations of 'reckless and irresponsible' acts of international terrorism. And, furthermore, as if to add conviction to these claims, the P.L.O. leaders have frequently threatened punishment for hijackers and others who engage in international terrorist activities.[18]

In 1975–6 the Palestinians' diplomatic strategy was still gaining momentum, despite their bitter denunciations of President Sadat and the United States for their role in the conclusion of the 'step-by-step' Sinai agreement in September 1975 between Egypt and Israel. The Palestinian movement itself has suffered both severe setbacks and some encouraging successes of recent months. Its bases in Lebanon have suffered decimation in the civil war, culminating in the massacre at Tel-el-Zaatar. Within the West Bank occupied territories, however, the P.L.O.'s candidates swept the board in recent elections, thus giving real substance for the first time to their claims to be the sole legitimate spokesmen for the aspirations of the Palestinian Arab population. There can be little doubt that if the political and diplomatic efforts of the P.L.O. continue to reap concrete results and appear to presage a successful settlement of their aspirations at Geneva, the incentive for a renewal of large-scale terrorist attacks will continue to be minimal.

Yet it would be premature to predict with any certainty the complete elimination of international terrorism on behalf of the Palestinian cause. For, as we have already noted, the P.L.O. is an extremely loose congeries of competing ideological factions, many of whom are deeply divided over the question of tactics. Militant P.F.L.P. and P.D.F.L.P. groups, and many exiled Palestinians in Europe, Iraq and Syria, are passionately arguing the 'Rejectionist Front' or maximalist position on the Palestinian question. They believe that Arafat and the moderates would be selling out Palestinian interests by accepting anything less than the total elimination of the Israeli state and its replacement by a Marxist Palestinian state. 'Rejectionist Front' leaders attack Arafat for his willingness even to negotiate a settlement with Israel, and they are adamant that the compromise contemplated by the moderates (that is a new state comprising the Gaza strip, West Bank and Jerusalem), is totally unacceptable. The question arises, therefore: if Arafat and the moderates can achieve a Geneva settlement which they believe to be acceptable can we be sure that all the Palestinian Arabs are going to accept it? At the very least one is likely to have a situation, analogous to the I.R.A.'s struggle against the Irish Free State in 1922–3, in which the 'maximalists' engage in a terrorist war against the new régime. And again, quite possibly, because international terrorism is part of their traditional repertoire these tactics would continue to be employed in Europe and elsewhere by extremist Palestinian groups. Yet another potential source of inter-factional feud in the event of the establishment of a new Palestinian state would be the position of those Arabs who continued to live in Galilee and other Arab areas of Israeli-held territory. Would they not begin to demand similar rights to those of their brothers? And might they not use political violence to achieve them?

For the meantime, however, the present policy of the P.L.O. leadership is undoubtedly one of the factors militating against any increase in Palestinian terrorism. Indeed, in combination with improved counter-terrorist measures by governments, airlines and airports it has probably significantly helped its decrease. But we should not be too sanguine: there are many terrorist factions, both Palestinian and non-Palestinian, fanatical and desperate enough to launch a new hijack campaign. And even in major international airports the security arrangements are still full of weaknesses, as was amply demonstrated by the ease with which four Palestinian terrorists boarded an Air France plane in Athens in June 1976, and hijacked it to Entebbe.

# XXX
# VULNERABILITIES: TARGETS, TECHNOLOGY AND TOLERANCE

Nor must we overlook certain features of modern industrial societies, in particular of liberal democracies, which afford essential enabling conditions for international terrorism. These are so obviously relevant that they tend to be recapitulated *ad nauseam* in every academic discussion of terrorism. They will be identified briefly here. The first two are inter-connected: accessibility and vulnerability of targets, and technology. Western 'open' societies have traditionally enjoyed relative freedom of movement across their own national frontiers and within them. Terrorists can exploit this freedom, for example by shifting their bases of operations from state to state. Modern air transport, road and rail communications, enable them to move rapidly to and from their targets. At the same time the complex and costly technological systems of society — power plants, nuclear research centres, airports and aircraft, computers, industries — have themselves become sitting targets for terrorist attack, disruption and sabotage. It would be impossibly expensive to provide all these facilities and resources with round-the-clock police protection. In any case, few industrial processes are proof against determined attempts at sabotage by terrorists infiltrated into the industrial labour force.

Western personnel and plant in Third World countries are also highly vulnerable, especially in areas of endemic terrorism such as Argentina and Brazil, where the local security forces are already overstretched or in some cases totally unable to cope. Citizens of the United States, which is the designated 'bogey-man' of most revolutionary terrorist groups have proved particularly popular targets for international terrorists when they are based for any length of time in Third World countries. But, as Richard Clutterbuck warns[19] politicians and executives abroad must consider themselves in the 'front-line' in the terrorist war.

Technology has also, of course, been exploited by terrorists to increase their own fire-power and capacity for destruction. Increasingly they have managed to obtain supplies of the latest light portable arms, grenades, mines and equipment for the manufacture of bombs. If a group cannot obtain these from a friendly government, there are many private arms dealers who will oblige. Terrorist groups also train their own experts in weapons technology, and, as the recent experience in Ulster has shown, they are often capable of designing bombs with novel anti-handling devices capable of posing a problem for even the most experienced bomb disposal squads. Some terrorist groups have gained possession of hand-held heat-seeking surface to air missiles. Others have somehow obtained small quantities of even more deadly weapons. There is always the real danger, in a period of rapid nuclear proliferation, that a 'crazy state' terrorist group might gain control over a small nuclear weapon, or sabotage a civil nuclear plant or process, to wreak extensive havoc, panic and destruction.

Liberal democratic societies also suffer from two additional vulnerabilities. First, and most important, we have free news media: this means that any group that brings off an act of terrorism can be confident of at least some free publicity, provided it avows responsibility, to draw national and foreign attention to the existence of their movement and their cause. Nevertheless, most of us prefer to put up with this disadvantage rather than sacrifice the freedom of the press. It remains true that total government censorship, of the kind existing in Russia, is a huge disincentive to terrorist groups in such a régime. It robs them of the chance of realising one of the main tactical aims of terrorism – publicity. (Note, however, that this is not enough to render the Soviet system immune from terrorist attack. A desperate dissident group may still manage to evade secret police surveillance for long enough to stage occasional bombings,[20] assassinations or even a hijack. There are clearly other aims which such terrorism might serve, such as, in the case of bombing, trying to wrest concessions from the authorities, or, in the case of hijacking, securing escape from the Soviet Union. In the case of terrorist bomb attack in a large city, of course, even totalitarian press censorship cannot rob the act of all publicity. News of the explosion and casualties and damage caused, will spread rapidly by word of mouth. It may not even be so simple for a totalitarian régime to entirely suppress news of an insurrection in a provincial town or rural area.)[21]

Closely linked with this vulnerable aspect of liberal democracy is the constraint of public opinion. Liberal democratic governments have to carry their publics with them in broad support of their responses to terrorism. Moreover, due to the efforts of free and energetic media, the public generally develops very strong emotions and opinions about the terrorism in the headlines. And, as Richard Clutterbuck has argued: 'The public cannot identify themselves with the thousands who are killed in a battle, but we can and do identify ourselves with the individual hostage . . . this very awareness does strengthen the hand of the terrorist and makes his political violence more effective.'[22] Thus, paradoxically, the humanity and compassion which are part of the moral strength of liberal democracy may also be an achilles heel in the war against terrorism. For the insolent confidence of terrorist attacks is bound to be encouraged if governments are driven by public opinion into putting the lives of hostages before all other considerations.

Yet the psychological vulnerabilities of liberal states are even more complex than this. For while there is public identification with hostages, there is also a sneaking sympathy for the 'revolutionary guerrillas', at any rate until they harm or kill an innocent civilian. The terrorist group will try to portray itself as representative of the oppressed, struggling legitimately and desperately for 'justice'. Among liberal and left opinion in democracies this strikes a responsive chord. If the group's pronouncements and propaganda are cleverly couched in the language of revolutionary socialism and internationalism they may find valuable spokesmen, or at any rate apologists, among influential media commentators and intellectual opinion-leaders on the left.

The more subtle terrorist propaganda does not attempt to polarise itself against democratic opinion as a whole: rather it attempts to profess that the terrorists are appealing to shared values of humanity and justice. Douglas Pike has aptly christened this 'the true genius of revolutionary guerrilla war'. The skilful international terrorist who understands the social psychology of the democratic society in which he happens to operate will make clever use of this technique of using liberal democratic values against the state or the government he claims to be fighting. He will be careful not to identify the people as his enemy. The enemy are 'the corrupt and unjust leaders', the 'Establishment', or the 'ruling class'. The 'true enemy' is portrayed as a powerful and cynical ruling clique waging unjust persecution or war against poor and helpless people. 'Surely', the terrorist implores, 'you are not one of *them*. You must help us in our legitimate campaign for our rights.' The terrorists hope that by means of such insistent propaganda, democratic opinion will be thrown off balance or confused, and the government's political will paralysed or neutralised. At the very least it is likely that elements in government, media and public opinion will be 'softened up' by the drip effect of unremitting propaganda into advocating a concessionary policy towards the terrorists and leniency in punishment.

At their most potent and insidious these effects lead to widespread glamourisation of the terrorists, especially among the bored and impressionable youth of affluent Western societies who long for the excitement of action. We must not overlook the problem that the very openness and accessibility of the media and public opinion in liberal states makes them vulnerable both to terrorist propaganda and to the recruitment of terrorist activists and sympathisers.

Another important factor is the considerable immigration of peoples from developing countries into Western countries in search of jobs and better living standards, which has resulted in the establishment of considerable communities of foreign workers in many Western cities. For example, there are the large Palestinian communities in West Germany and the United States, Turks employed in France and West Germany, large Pakistani and Indian populations in Britain, and many different Indonesian minorities settled in Holland. Clearly these are high risk groups for terrorist infiltration for a number of reasons. Many of the first generation immigrants have good reason, from their own life experiences, to sympathise with the political aims of a specific revolutionary or nationalist movement. Some individual immigrants are quite likely to have been compelled to leave their native country for political reasons. Moreover, these groups often suffer considerable hardship, alienation and resentment as the result of discriminatory treatment in their adopted societies. Many are simply unhappy, disorientated and confused. They offer a 'natural constituency' to which the international terrorist may appeal for sanctuary, funds or direct assistance such as spying or sabotage.

The other major vulnerabilities that international terrorists can exploit are inherent in the condition of international relations. Each state has its own jurisdiction, legal code, judicial procedures and punishments. There are enormous variations among legal systems with regard to recognition and definition of terrorist offences, sentences prescribed for such offences, and policies concerning right of political asylum and extradition. Moreover, as we observed earlier, there are states which actively support and justify terrorism, on ideological and political grounds. They are likely to continue to obstruct or defeat any attempt at a general convention on the extradition and punishment of terrorists — unless they themselves become victims of frequent terrorist attacks, in which case they may understandably decide that the costs imposed by tolerating terrorism outweigh the disadvantages of supporting international measures to suppress it. In the absence of international legal agreement and procedures to deal with crimes of terrorism, the international terrorist can play off one state against another and escape swiftly into zones of safety beyond the reach of law. And, sad to say, there have been many occasions when a Western government has had both the opportunity and the legal basis for bringing a terrorist to trial or extraditing him, and yet has failed to do so for fear of causing political embarrassment or incurring terrorist reprisal attacks.[23] All the efforts made to improve international police co-operation are wasted by these very grave weaknesses of judicial anarchy, confusion and pusillanimity.

# XXXI
# PRECIPITATIVE CAUSES

Thus far attention has been concentrated on broad underlying causes and conducive conditions. We must now consider some of the more specific precipitative causes of the recent major upsurge in international terrorism over the past decade. How did terrorism become a fashion which caught on all over the world? I do not believe that we really understand much about the inner motivations of those who so readily enunciated terrorist techniques. Much more research is needed before we can begin to increase our understanding of the personalities, social and cultural backgrounds and attitudes of terrorists. And it is important that this form of investigation is conducted over a very wide range of terrorist organisations covering as wide a spectrum of nationalities and ideological alignments as possible. We already know enough about terrorist behaviour to discount the crude hypotheses of a 'terrorist personality' or 'phenotype'.[24] Until we have far more data available generalisations about motivation and personality are probably best avoided. It has been suggested that all terrorists have 'tunnel vision', i.e. are totally obsessed with a single goal; that terrorist groups are bound together by the intensity of their hatred against society;[25] or that they have suicidal-schizophrenic tendencies.[26] But none of these hypotheses is proven.

It is perhaps more fruitful to speculate about the more practical triggering causes. How did the terrorists get the idea of a bombing campaign or a kidnapping. Was there a key personality with special influence over the others who put them up to the whole project and bullied and cajoled his colleagues into carrying it out? Are the media the major source of models and techniques, via their detailed reportage, and as constant evidence of the efficacy of terrorism in winning publicity? Certainly there seems to have been something of a 'bandwagon' effect. And no doubt this was encouraged, at the personal level by growing bilateral and multilateral contacts between individual members of extremist movements. As early as 1972 an international conference of revolutionary movements from all over the world, including delegations from the Tupamaros and the Vietcong, was held in Beirut for the purpose of enlisting support for the Palestinian movements.[27] There is little doubt that such gatherings provide excellent opportunities for exchange of ideas on weaponry, tactics and techniques.

Also very important to the terrorists are the tangible rewards of success in attaining certain key tactical objectives. For instance, many movements have succeeded in extorting huge ransoms with relatively small risk to themselves in the process. In Argentina it was reported that the *Ejercito Revolucionario del Pueblo* (E.R.P.) gained a ransom of 14 million dollars for the release of an oil executive in June 1974, and 60 million dollars in 1975 for the release of two Bunge and Born heirs. These rich hauls completely dwarf the average gain for crimes of violence, and there is no doubt that many groups around the world have adopted political slogans and labels as a 'front' for purely private criminal gain. In other cases the terrorists, who may originally have embarked on revolutionary terrorism from motives of political idealism, begin to enjoy the unexpected fruits of their way of life, and live in a manner to which they have not been accustomed in expensive villas or jet setting in the Arab capitals. There is much evidence that the small élite of international 'hit-men' and professional terrorist organisers form a privileged 'aristocracy' whose affluent life-style has little in common with that of the oppressed humanity they claim to serve. Not all the proceeds of terrorist blackmail are ploughed back into arms and equipment. Moreover the plurality of currencies and banking systems makes it relatively easy for terrorists to transfer their funds, and difficult for the police to identify sources and financial backers.

Trained international terrorists are a scarce and expensive commodity for revolutionary organisations. Their training, expertise and experience makes them hard to replace. Not that they often need to be replaced. A RAND Corporation study of sixty-three major kidnapping and barricade operations between 1968 and 1974 found that terrorists had a 79 per cent chance of evading death or punishment, whether or not they successfully seized the hostages. And less than 10 per cent of the 127 terrorist attempts at aircraft hijacking between March 1968 and July 1974 resulted in the death or imprisonment of the terrorists. The RAND study found that even in cases where all concessions to the terrorists' demands were rejected there was a 67 per cent chance of the terrorists being able to escape with their lives either by accepting safe passage in lieu of original demands, or going underground, or by surrendering to a sympathetic government.[28]

Furthermore, the average international terrorist has been conditioned into believing that if he or she is captured it will be only for a short while before the government releases them out of sheer fright or their 'brothers and sisters' secure their release by further terrorist blackmail. According to Mr Robert A. Fearey, Special Assistant to the U.S. Secretary of State and Co-ordinator for Combating Terrorism, between 1971 and 1975 less than 50 per cent of captured international terrorists actually served out their prison sentences; the average sentence awarded to terrorists who stood trial was eighteen months.[29] Hence the terrorists' faith in their own release is grounded on an all too accurate assessment of the weakness and pliability of governments. Release of imprisoned comrades thus becomes a prime motivation for further acts of terrorism. It is a factor which is constantly under-rated by academic analysts. And once again the Western liberal states are more vulnerable in this regard than authoritarian régimes. The latter do not hesitate to use capital punishment to dispose of terrorists. The liberal state, with its more lenient penal code, clutches the captured terrorist like an asp to its bosom until he or she is freed by one means or another to re-embark on a career of systematic murder.

# XXXII
# EFFECTS OF INTERNATIONAL TERRORISM

How serious are the effects of international terrorism, and how grave are the potential dangers it poses for international order and the well-being of nations and individuals?

Compared to the sanguinary and catastrophic effects of international and internal wars, international terrorism has constituted a minor law and order problem in international relations, comparable in some ways to the phenomenon of piracy on the high seas in an earlier age. It is manifestly improbable that tiny bands of *francstireurs*, however desperate, could seriously threaten an international order dominated by super-powers with their vast military strength and global capabilities. The idea of a group such as the Japanese U.R.A. actually trying to bring about world revolution by terroristic means against all the centres of world military and economic power simultaneously is clearly ludicrous. The most they can hope to achieve is the sowing of disruption and alarm, or the temporary interruption or exacerbation of diplomatic relations between states. In some cases the effects may extend to provoking misunderstandings and diplomatic disputes involving third party states: for example, conflicts may arise over disputed jurisdictions, extradition requests, or allegations of covert aid or condonation of terrorist acts.

One must accept the remote possibility that, in combination with other factors, such as long-standing border disputes, economic rivalry or military ambition, such quarrels about terrorism could spark a border clash or even a war. It should not be forgotten that the assassination of the Austrian Archduke Francis Ferdinand and his wife at Sarajevo on 28 June 1914 by Gavrilo Princip, a member of *Mlada Bosna* ('Young Bosnia'), played its vital part in igniting the terrible conflict of 1914–18. There is no clear evidence that the Serbian government was directly involved, and indeed this seems highly unlikely, given the vulerability of Serbia at that time. It has been shown that senior Serbian army officers encouraged the plot, and that the Serbian terrorist organisation, Black Hand, provided the assassination weapons. Nevertheless the important point is that the action of the terrorist movement created a situation in which the Serbian government was drawn ineluctably into war.

More recently, at one point in 1976, it seemed highly likely that a conflict would break out between Kenya and Uganda in the wake of the Entebbe hijacking.[30] Generally speaking, however, it is concentrated and protracted internal terrorism which has by far the most serious repercussions. For if such internal campaigns contribute to grave internal strife and instability within an already weakened régime an ensuing power vacuum or change of régime may have profound effects on local balances, and may even provoke extensive intervention by the other powers. This was certainly the case in the Lebanon conflict in 1976.

It is clear that the number of deaths and injuries caused by international terrorism is small compared to the casualties from all forms of internal strife. In the Nigerian Civil War alone it is estimated that one million people were forced to starvation and death as a direct result of the conflict. One hundred thousand people were killed in the Indonesian Civil War of 1966.[31] Over 40,000 died in the Lebanese Civil War 1975–6. In the whole of the period 1968–76 deaths caused by acts of international terrorism total just below 1,000. This is considerably less than the total deaths caused by the Northern Ireland conflict in the same period, and is only 5 per cent of the *annual* homicide rate in the United States.

Yet there is a sense in which this whole debate about necrology numbs and distorts our sensibilities.[32] Have we become so indifferent to the value of an individual human life that we can no longer hear the cries of the victims, the suffering of the dying and injured, the anguish of the bereaved? Is it not a crime against God and humanity that these innocent lives have been taken by terrorist guns and bombs? Is is not an intolerable outrage that many of those who have massacred the innocent are still going scot free in foreign capitals? We are right to be shocked by the character of the victims of international terrorism: 'The immediate victims may have no organic connection to the political policy of the target state, and may indeed not even be a citizen of that state nor have any influence over its policy. . .'[33] So much for the claim that the terrorist weapon is a 'rational' or 'clinical' weapon of justice. It is sheer bloody murder, and no truly civilised society can tolerate or condone such an act. All liberal states have a clear duty to take every possible national and international measure to extirpate these crimes against humanity. It is a sad commentary on the moral weakness and cowardice of modern governments that many states have culpably failed to perform this duty. And this is a problem we must revert to shortly in considering specific measures to combat international terrorism.

# XXXIII
# POTENTIAL THREATS

International terrorism already poses a clear and present danger to the lives of innocent people and to social peace and order. But it would be naïve and shortsighted to assume that the destructive capacity and danger involved in international terrorism will remain at its present level. There are a number of extremely ominous trends which, taken together, render the terrorist danger daily more deadly, and which make the duty of governments continually to refine and improve their security all the more urgent. I do not believe it is helpful or desirable for analysts to indulge in exaggerated alarmism. As I have commented earlier, this in any case only plays into the terrorists' hands. There is also the real risk that, in speculating about potential terrorist threats one may be unwittingly providing terrorists with ideas for fresh targets or tactics. I am very conscious of the weighty responsibility incumbent upon the academic analyst to preserve a careful balance between over-imaginative sensationalism and foolish complacency.

I believe that four dangerous kinds of potential threat can be discerned. First, there is the distinct possibility of a formally organised international terrorist league emerging. This has not yet occurred (at the time of writing, 1976), but there have been clear intimations that, in addition to well-established bilateral contacts and co-operation between different terrorist movements, certain groups are now collaborating more closely on a regular basis. The OPEC conference hijack in 1975 was an international operation in more ways than one: its leader appears to have been a Venezuelan, 'Carlos' Ilich Ramirez Sanchez, and the group included both Arabs and recruits from Baader–Meinhof. There is, as yet, no evidence that such *ad hoc* collaborative operations have led to the establishment of any new transnational terrorist organ. However, to the extent that this type of multilateral co-operation enables the terrorists to pool their specialists, weaponry and resources it does appreciably increase the 'clout' available for a specific attack. On the other hand, such transnational collaboration brings severe additional difficulties and hazards for the terrorists which tend to cancel these gains. All terrorist groups are prone to factionalism and often to bitter in-fighting; these multilateral operations are particularly endangered by conflicts and jealousies between the different nationalities participating. Moreover if terrorists become too independent of national governments they risk losing the necessary tacit co-operation and sanctuaries of sympathiser states or sponsor régimes. A group that looked as if it was developing a genuinely 'autonomous' capability would be viewed with increasing suspicion by each and every state lest the terrorist group should be deployed against them. Hence while it is clear that governments need to be on their guard against a kind of transnational conspiracy by a non-state actor co-ordinating operations on a very wide scale, the chances are that governments would combine to snuff it out as soon as it revealed its hand.

Another somewhat more dangerous trend, which is increasing rapidly, is the use of terrorist groups as 'mercenaries' by sponsor régimes to conduct terrorist proxy war against an 'enemy' state. Some of the states most heavily involved in this proxy war activity have been mentioned earlier: they include the Soviet Union, China, East Germany, Czechoslovakia, Bulgaria, Romania, Cuba, Libya, Somalia, North Korea, Yemen and Vietnam. Even some of the smaller countries in this list have shown an amazing geographical range in their support of subversive and terrorist activities. Cuba, for instance, has been involved in aiding groups in practically every Latin American country, in Africa, and even the Middle East, in addition to those in Puerto Rico and the United States. In many cases there is competition between subversive régimes for the recruitment of groups and the launching of campaigns in specific countries.

There are a number of reasons why this constitutes a particularly grave source of escalating terrorism. Access to the armouries, training facilities and cash and logistic support of sponsor régimes vastly increases the fire-power of the terrorist groups. Sponsor states find proxy war remarkably cheap compared to conventional military attack, while at the same time terrorism carries none of the risks of open war. It is clandestine and undeclared, and therefore the sponsor state can simply disavow any involvement. The target state, especially if it is militarily weak and politically and economically unstable, will find it almost impossible to prevent external aid reaching terrorist groups. Meanwhile liberal states constrained by the moral scruples of public opinion will be unable to intervene covertly in sufficient strength to counter the enemy terrorists or subversives active in the target state. Thus there is not the restraining or checking element of force available to uphold the victim régime. Furthermore the 'sponsor' states engaging in terrorism and subversion have no problem in countering retaliatory guerrilla, terrorist or subversive attacks in their own backyards. The legal rectitude of Western public opinion would rule any such daring counter-strokes entirely out of the question for liberal democratic governments. Liberal states still labour under the illusion of peace and the norms of proper international conduct such as non-interference in the domestic affairs of other states.

Meanwhile the communist states and other aggressive authoritarian régimes find they can wage armed struggle, including proxy war by means of terrorist mercenaries, virtually unchecked and without fear of reprisal. The scenarios of those who seem to believe that surrogate war by terrorism could continue for long periods at a relatively low-intensity level seem to be totally unconvincing.[34] Those states most likely to employ it will regard it solely as a useful *auxiliary* weapon, purely an adjunct to soften up the target state or as an accompaniment to full-scale subversion or armed take-over. In the eyes of Marxist–Leninist movements and régimes all means of revolutionary struggle are both permissible and potentially useful. It is quite unreal to assume that they will be content to sustain conflict at some 'surrogate' level by means of terrorism alone. Revolutionary régimes would not be satisfied with this because what they want is revolutionary take-over. And Western states will not employ 'surrogate' or terrorist war simply because their traditions and publics would not permit them to. In sum, I conclude that the most probable development in the 1980s will be an escalation of proxy unconventional war in third party states. It is highly improbable that major powers would unleash covert attacks against each other's own territories. The fear of provoking a retaliatory war or punitive attack by a powerfully armed adversary is an effective deterrent against such adventures. The covert war in third party states is likely to be in many modes and combinations, with the use of terrorism figuring as an effective auxiliary in certain circumstances.

The increased opportunities for covert intervention by 'sponsor' subversive states are closely inter-connected with a third dangerous trend, the increasing availability of more potent portable weapons highly suited to offensive terrorist operations. Terrorists have already exploited such developments as plastic explosives (which are more difficult to detect in security searches) and miniaturised letter bombs, on a very wide scale. We have also noted instances where they have gained possession of Soviet SA–7s, hand-held, heat-seeking surface to air missiles.

What new weapon developments are terrorists, and sponsor states that may seek to exploit terrorism in the future, likely to be most interested in? It would be a mistake to assume that terrorists recognise some iron law of restraints or limits on the destructiveness and killing power of the weapons they employ. When engaged in offensive long-range operations deep into the territory of what they regard as a hostile state, they are not likely to allow any humanitarian concerns about number of casualties to impede their chances of gaining their objectives. Let us suppose that their aim is to attack a prestigious economically or militarily important target such as a power plant, a pipeline or a military headquarters. Terrorists planning such an attack will want to maximise the elements of surprise, destructive capacity and dramatic effect. Ideal terrorist weapons for such operations will be highly portable, easily concealable, and when fired will be as silent and invisible as possible (no smoke or flash). Terrorists will therefore be interested in acquiring weapons which are accurate, reliable and simple to operate at ranges which will facilitate the gang's rapid escape. They will be interested also in personal weapons with sufficient fire-power to overwhelm the small numbers of armed guards, police or troops that may be deployed to guard their targets.

It is well known that the latest developments in small weapons technology — in propellant fuels, metallurgy and design, for example — have provided many states with arsenals of weapons highly attractive to terrorist organisations. These include: the M.A.C. 11 revolver, which fires at the speed of 1,200 rounds per minute and is almost completely silent, lightweight grenade launchers and mortars, squirtless flame-throwers, short-range man-portable anti-tank weapons, and shoulder-fired multi-shot rocket launchers. Of particular advantage to terrorists would be a weapon such as the new disposable German anti-tank gun, which can be fired even from a small room without detection because it has no rear blast, muzzle flash or smoke. In the next few years we are likely to see determined attempts by terrorist groups to obtain such weapons either by arrangement with sponsor governments or by stealing them from military arsenals. These dangers are made all the more real because of the fact that governments engaging in proxy terrorism or aiding allied terrorist movements are unlikely to show any prudential restraint in releasing short-range disposable weapons to terrorists, for they will not feel threatened by such developments unless and until they are the victims of attacks by hostile terrorist groups deploying similar weapons against them. The ugly prospect is an ever-widening diffusion of these increasingly accurate and portable short-range weapons beyond any possible hope of governmental or inter-governmental arms control.

There is thus an urgent need for governments to strengthen the defences of vulnerable targets and to improve the weaponry of security guards and police with responsibilities for protecting them. It is an irony of the current situation that the gravest danger to the security of civil nuclear facilities may be posed by an armed terrorist group with the conventional weapons to outgun guards and police.

An equally serious danger is the proliferation of new generations of more accurate and reliable man-portable precision-guided munitions (P.G.M.). The leading military powers have developed a wide range of such weapons for battlefield use against tanks and air-craft. A wide range of guidance systems, ranging from radio and radar control to lasers and infrared heat-seeking wire control, has been developed. Such weapons will be produced in increasing quantities in the coming decade, and will find their way into the arsenals of both Warsaw Pact and NATO member—states. The likelihood of terrorist groups acquiring them will undoubtedly increase. The attractiveness of these weapons to terrorists is obvious: some of them have a hit probability approaching one, over a range of two or three kilometres. Thus, for example, a terrorist group could by this means assassinate a head of state and his entire entourage in a motorcade from a hiding place several kilometres distant and make good their escape in anonymity and ease.

There are already reports of P.G.M.s being 'lost' or stolen. It is in the interests of all responsible governments to tighten their security over this weaponry to reduce the possibilities of its acquisition by fanatical and desperate autonomous groups. I do not share the gloomy view that it is already too late for governments to act in this field. On the contrary, this constitutes one of the most vital problems which should be considered on the agenda for inter-governmental co-operation to combat international terrorism.

We shall revert to this matter in discussing general measures against international terrorism (see Part III, Chapter XXXVII).

The fourth and by far the gravest potential form of terrorist threat, in my view, is that of nuclear terrorism. Many analysts have endorsed the somewhat sanguine assessment of an American writer that 'The threat of nuclear action by terrorists appears to be exaggerated.'[35] In support of this optimistic view it has been argued that terrorists are not really interested in mass murder, but in gaining publicity and using propaganda to influence people. As I have argued earlier, I believe this to be a gross over-simplification of the nature of terrorist strategy and tactics. Of course publicity and propaganda are generally key tactical objectives. But in many cases their *cardinal* aim is to create a climate of fear and collapse, essentially by terrifying and demoralising their targets into capitulation. And what more potent weapon of psychological coercion can be conceived in the modern age than the threat to explode a nuclear device or to release lethal levels of radioactivity into the atmosphere?

It would be extraordinarily foolish to assume that all terrorist groups shared the same perceptions of rationality, humanity and prudence that inform the consciences of most of humanity. In the strange transcendentalist logic of the fanatical political terrorist, as we have earlier observed, the end is held to justify *any* means. If any individual life is expendable in the cause of 'Revolutionary Justice' or 'Liberation' so may hundreds, even thousands, of lives have to be 'sacrificed'. One has only to turn to the hysterical writings of Johannes Most, Pierre Vallières or the Weathermen, to find mass slaughter of 'bourgeois vermin' not only commended but proudly and enthusiastically advocated. As for the international terrorist, who may be operating in the heart of the territory of his hated enemy, there has been a similar readiness on his or her part to regard the 'enemy' civil population as expendable.

There are, however, major practical constraints which help to explain the relative rarity, to date, of terrorists 'going nuclear'. In the first place nuclear weapons, both strategic and tactical, are naturally closely guarded by governments. Their security is the prime responsibility of security forces and secret services in all the nuclear powers. Furthermore, by their very nature their operational use is controlled by a highly complex secret code of procedures for unlocking the weapon and preparing it for action—readiness. Unless they had confederates within the nuclear military forces of the state concerned, terrorists would therefore be unable to operate such weapons. The most they might hope to achieve would be to gravely damage or destroy them by sabotage. It is also very clear that no nuclear power, even one engaged in sponsoring proxy terrorism, would willingly allow part of its own nuclear armoury to fall into the hands of a terrorist movement. For the danger of the movement recklessly triggering a nuclear conflict or a major limited war, or of the sponsor state being blackmailed by the movement with threats of nuclear use, would discourage any such adventurism.

There are also, however, extremely grave dangers involved in the diffusion of civil nuclear facilities and technologies in many states. For these processes involve the use of substances which could be employed to make a nuclear explosive device. Plutonium for incorporation into reactor fuel has to be shipped and in some cases transported by road. It is clearly highly vulnerable to theft by terrorists while it is in transit. Still more dangerous is the practice which has developed in the nuclear power industry of transporting plutonium nitrate in liquid form by road. This is a particularly hazardous process. Plutonium transported as a pure compound, even in small quantities, is a particularly tempting target for terrorist theft or hijack because of the material's obvious value in constructing a nuclear weapon. And, because of its extreme toxicity, it could also be used by terrorists as a weapon of radiological extortion. A recent British report by the Royal Commission on Environmental Pollution underlined both these dangers, but this does not appear to have influenced the policy of the British Atomic Energy Authority regarding the transportation of nuclear fuels. Plutonium is also present in spent reactor fuel. It then has to be stored because there is to date no commercially viable system for reprocessing it. And in the special case of the liquid metal fast breeder reactor more plutonium is produced than is actually consumed, so that the problem of disposal is especially acute. Terrorists therefore might seek by various means, including infiltration of the nuclear industry workforce, to obtain regular small supplies of nuclear materials. The particularly vulnerable points for nuclear theft include; storage facilities for spent fuel, fuel reprocessing plants, and fabrication and uranium enrichment plants. There is little doubt that sufficient quantities of enriched uranium and plutonium could be obtained to make possible the manufacture of a primitive nuclear device.[36] In the United States a college student, using only textbooks and data available to the

general public, designed a workable atomic bomb.[37] When one
bears in mind that a major recruiting ground for terrorist groups is
the universities, it is certainly credible that a group of competent and
qualified scientists and engineers could be recruited for the special
purpose of building an atomic weapon or advising the group on
techniques of nuclear sabotage and extortion. A team of five or six
could probably accomplish this within the space of five or six weeks
without incurring any serious risk to their personal health or
safety.[38] Estimates of the financial costs involved vary between
£5000 – £15,000.[39]

A particularly difficult threat to counter would be the terrorist
group organising large-scale theft, sabotage, or the manufacture of
an explosive device with the skilled assistance of many collaborators
within the nuclear power industry. Also, by infiltrating terrorist activists into relatively unskilled work on nuclear power plants the
terrorist organisation could gain vital information and assistance in
planning a raid on the nuclear site. Even a relatively small group
with a very crude general knowledge of a civil nuclear plant and its
points of vulnerability could be tempted into seizing control of an
installation and threatening sabotage as a means of extorting concessions. This would appeal to certain groups because of the
dramatic publicity they would receive. And it would be an extremely difficult and hazardous situation for the authorities. With the
possibility of a major disaster which could result, for example, from
reactor core disassembly and fire in a commercial fast breeder reactor, it would be a dangerous business to assume that the terrorists
were simply bluffing. Prudent authorities would have to rapidly
effect a mass evacuation of the population in the surrounding area.

It is sometimes argued that terrorists would be effectively dis-
couraged from sabotage of nuclear installations because of the risks
involved to their own safety, lack of knowledge of safety
precautions and ignorance of nuclear technology. We have already
noted that these weaknesses could be overcome by certain terrorist
groups through the employment of their own 'expert' advisers on
nuclear technology, or alternatively by the use of employees in the
installation as agents and collaborators. Even groups which have
not acquired this technical assistance or knowledge should not be
discounted as potential nuclear saboteurs. For instance, a particularly
fanatical group such as the Japanese United Red Army with a strong
element of *Kamikaze* in its make-up may well decide to sacrifice the

lives of a whole terrorist squad for the purpose of triggering a despairing nihilistic catastrophe. Governments and security forces would be wise to plan for the 'worst possible' terrorist contingencies. Much as they may like to reassure themselves that anarchist fringe groups or 'crazy state' terrorists are a tiny minority, they cannot afford to discount the possibility of a small number of suicidal schizophrenics launching into nuclear terrorism. It is the duty of the authorities to do all they can to prevent any such attacks from succeeding. There is certainly no shortage of evidence that individuals and groups have been tempted into attacks and threats against nuclear installations. According to my own estimates, on the basis of press reports alone, there were at least ten cases of attacks (eight of them involving the placing of explosives) between 1969–75 in Western Europe, and in March 1976 American officials disclosed that since March 1969 there had been a total of 175 cases of acts of violence or threats against nuclear facilities in the United States.

Prudence and common sense, not alarmism, should be our guide in trying to anticipate the nature of future international or transnational terrorist threats. In my view the gravest of these possibilities fall under the heading of what George Quester has termed 'micro-proliferation'.[40] Terrorist capture or fabrication of a nuclear weapon, or seizure or extensive sabotage of a nuclear facility, could pose the threats of holding whole cities or regions to ransom, mass slaughter and irreparable damage to the environment. No government can afford to ignore the real dangers of nuclear terrorism by non-state actors. Somehow 'micro-proliferation' must be brought within any future machinery of arms limitation and control.

# XXXIV
## THE HIJACKING PROBLEM

Since 1968–9 civil airline passengers and crews have been subjected to a wave of aircraft hijackings. And although there is some encouraging evidence of decline in the overall incidence of this form of international terrorism and in the percentage of successful hijacks, this has been somewhat offset by a trend towards more in-discriminate attacks on grounded aircraft and airport facilities and larger casualty rates. The problem is still very much with us, and is deserving of closer analysis.

The term 'aerial piracy', though often used to describe this phenomenon, does not really convey its essential character. For the point of aircraft hijacking in the majority of cases is not simply seizure of the aircraft and its cargo for its own sake but the exploita-tion of control over the aircraft and its passengers as a weapon of psychological coercion and extortion directed against governments. It is a particularly hazardous and difficult form of hostage situation for governments to handle. For the authorities on the ground have no accurate means of knowing the exact situation of the captors and hostages within the flying prison, the precise weaponry and mental state of the hijackers, or even, for certain periods, the terrorists' precise demands or ultimate destination.

We should be in no doubt about the inherently terroristic effects of a hijack on its immediate victims, the passengers and crew. Passengers are subjected to torments of worry, often over many hours, constantly under threat from terrorist revolvers, grenades and plastic explosives. Pilot and co-pilot are confronted with the near in-tolerable burden of trying to safeguard their passengers while under orders from fanatical terrorists who may know little or nothing of the technical constraints and vulnerabilities of modern airliners. There are few margins for error when you are flying a jumbo jet with up to 400 passengers over vast distances. And we should not forget those instances where aircraft hijack attempts have led to large-scale loss of life. For example, in the Soviet hijacking of 25 May 1973 the pilot and hijacker were killed and 100 passengers died in the ensuing crash. And on 15 September 1974, an Air Viet-nam plane crashed killing all seventy passengers and crew after a hi-jacker reportedly exploded a hand grenade. Considering the obvious dangers of fire, damage to the controls or incapacitation of the pilot, it is a miracle that there have not been many more similar disasters. The fact that loss of life through hijackings has not been greater is in large part due to the skill and courage of the aircrew and the gradually improving skill of governments, airlines and airport authorities in hijack crisis—management.

It is, in practice, difficult to draw a hard and fast distinction between international and domestic hijacking incidents because a high proportion of domestic flight hijacks have inevitably involved foreign passengers. However, the hijack attempt on an international air route is the paradigmatic case of international terrorism: the passenger list is likely to be international if not multinational, foreign airport and government authorities are inevitably involved, and there are immediate implications for inter-governmental negotiation and co-operation concerning communications with the hijackers, landing permissions, problems of jurisdiction, and complex difficulties of extradition and punishment. Hijacking on international airlines naturally attracts immediate world-wide publicity.

It is quite untrue that either the media or the general public have become blasé about hijacks. There is an immediate surge of sympathy for the suffering passengers and crew, with whom the general public readily identifies. And the intrinsic drama and uncertainty of outcome make it a compulsive story for the mass media. The more difficult it becomes to mount international hijacks, and the less frequent they become, the greater their dramatic impact and fascination for media and public.

It would be foolish of governments and aviation authorities to assume that terrorist organisations will simply tire of hijacking attempts or that it is a passing fashion. For revolutionary and national liberation groups this form of terrorism offers enormous attractions of advertising their cause and demands to international opinion. Moreover aircraft hijacking has a proven record of efficacy in wringing important tactical gains for terrorists, such as huge ransoms or the release of terrorist colleagues from gaol. As we shall shortly consider, aircraft hijack may also become a tactical necessity for successful completion of certain other long-range international terrorist operations, as indeed it was for 'Carlos' and his colleagues in their mass kidnap of OPEC ministers in December 1975. Nor should we neglect the inherent appeal to the neo-Marxist groups of assaults on what they regard as prestigious symbols of the affluence and power of the international 'capitalist ruling class'. By proving that even the world's most technologically advanced international transport system is vulnerable to terrorist attack, they hope to send a shiver down the backs of even the most exalted and powerful of their designated 'enemies'. For all these reasons aircraft hijacking is likely to remain a popular mode of international terrorism for many groups. Hence, despite encouraging signs that better security and inter-governmental co-operation are beginning to bite, I do not believe that there are any firm grounds for assuming that this mode of international terrorism has been decisively beaten. It is vital that liberal states do not relax their guard against it.

It should be recalled that similar hopes have been cruelly dashed after every previous wave of hijack attempts. In the first wave, following the First World War, nearly all were committed by refugees escaping from communist countries. There was then a lull until the period 1958–62. In 1958 Raúl Castro, brother of the Cuban leader, began to exploit hijackings for political purposes and this was immediately followed by what Richard Clutterbuck has described as 'a brief see-saw by refugees of hijackings from Cuba to America and of American aircraft to Cuba'.[41] Between 1962 and 1967 there was a further lull when hijack attempts dropped to an average of four per year. Then in 1968–9 there was a veritable explosion of hijacking incidents. In 1969 there were no less than eighty-two recorded aircraft hijack attempts world-wide which was over twice the total hijack attempts for the whole period 1947–67. There were two major new breeds of hijacker active from 1968; (i) United States criminals seeking ransom or escape from the law, and (ii) Palestinians, possibly emulating Cuban examples, employing hijacks as a political weapon in desperation as a means of publicising their cause and avenging Arab defeat in the 1967 war. They initially struck at Israeli citizens and aircraft, and then at those of states supporting Israel. In 1968 their attacks were directed mainly at El Al aircraft at European airports. Their short-term aims were generally to gain publicity and to blackmail Israel and Western governments into releasing brother Palestinian terrorists from gaol.

Several useful histories of aircraft hijacking are available and it is not my purpose to attempt to cover similar ground.[42] However, Table 8 provides a summary of recorded hijack attempts between 1948 and 1976, showing the breakdown of regions of flight origin, region of attempted diversion, and the percentage of attempts in which the hijackers succeeded in gaining a ransom or reaching their desired destination. These figures provide very clear evidence of the cyclical character of hijacking, and suggest that it would be foolhardy to leap to the conclusion that hijacking is in permanent decline. It has been widely suggested that the decline in politically motivated hijackings is attributable to the increasing efficacy of boarding gate security searches and the screening of passengers. Whereas there is little doubt that these procedures have been extremely effective in

## Table 8
### Aircraft hijacks 1948–76

| | 1948–57 | 1958–67 | 1968 | 1969 | 1970 | 1971 | 1972 | 1973 | 1974 | 1975 | 1976 |
|---|---|---|---|---|---|---|---|---|---|---|---|
| Flight origin | | | | | | | | | | | |
| North America | – | 23 | 23 | 37 | 14 | 29 | 29 | 2 | 7 | 11 | 4 |
| Latin America* | – | 18 | 10 | 29 | 15 | 13 | 8 | 5 | 4 | 4 | 2 |
| Western Europe† | – | – | 1 | 4 | 4 | 4 | 10 | 7 | 3 | 2 | 3 |
| Warsaw Pact | 15 | – | – | 2 | 15 | 1 | 3 | 3 | – | 1 | 1 |
| Middle East‡ | – | – | 1 | 3 | 14 | 5 | 5 | 3 | 3 | 3 | 3 |
| Other§ | – | 7 | 3 | 7 | 10 | 9 | 9 | 2 | 12 | 5 | 4 |
| Diversion attempted to | | | | | | | | | | | |
| North America | – | – | – | – | – | 5 | 14 | 2 | 7 | 5 | – |
| Latin America* | – | 41 | 32 | 63 | 28 | 26 | 19 | 5 | 4 | 4 | – |
| (of which, Cuba) | – | (41) | (32) | (63) | (26) | (20) | (13) | (3) | (4) | (1) | – |
| Western Europe† | 15 | – | 1 | 7 | 15 | 7 | 12 | 3 | 3 | 3 | 4 |
| Warsaw Pact | – | – | – | – | – | – | 3 | – | – | – | – |
| Middle East‡ | – | – | – | 4 | 16 | 4 | 6 | 7 | 6 | 4 | 6 |
| Other§ | – | 7 | 5 | 8 | 13 | 19 | 10 | 5 | 9 | 10 | 6 |
| Total attempts | 15 | 48 | 38 | 82 | 72 | 61 | 64 | 22 | 29 | 26 | 17 |
| Successful** | 13 | 31 | 33 | 70 | 46 | 24 | 18 | 11 | 8 | 6 | 8 |
| % successful | 86.7 | 64.6 | 86.8 | 85.4 | 63.9 | 39.3 | 28.1 | 50.0 | 27.6 | 23.1 | 47.0 |

\* Including Caribbean countries.
† Including Austria, Turkey and Yugoslavia.
‡ Including North Africa.
§ Asia, Australasia, Sub-Saharan Africa and unknown.
** Success: hijackers reached desired destination or obtained ransom.

countering criminally motivated hijacking in the United States, it is unlikely that they have been a major factor in reducing hijacks by the P.F.L.P. and other political groups. In the Palestinian case, as we noted earlier, it is likely that the P.L.O.'s policy decision to adopt a primarily political and diplomatic strategy and to suppress hijacking and other forms of international terrorism favoured by some factions has made some impact. Above all, the effectiveness of the Arab oil weapon and the increasing diplomatic leverage exerted by Arab states has tended to make acts of terrorism appear increasingly irrelevant and unproductive for the Palestinian cause. The Palestinian hijack wave, however, may be followed by others, for there is no shortage of desperate and fanatical groups who may be attracted into exporting terrorism via international airways, and who can find sympathetic states willing to provide them sanctuary.

It is helpful to classify the main types of hijack in terms of underlying motivations. At least four main types can be distinguished: (i) the refugee escape; (ii) criminal ransom extortion and escape; (iii) political terrorist publicity and blackmail; and (iv) the getaway plane hijack as part of an overall land- or sea-based terrorist operation. A further closely allied problem we shall consider is terrorist attacks on aircraft on the ground, airport facilities, and attacks with bombs and missiles against aircraft in flight. The refugee escape, as we have noted, was the characteristic form of hijack from Eastern Europe between 1945–52. It again became important as an element in the spate of Cuban hijacks 1958–62. Since then it has been very much eclipsed by hijacks for very different motives, though there is likely to be a continual trickle of such incidents. Though these hijacks may undoubtedly be terroristic in their psychological effects on crews and passengers, their primary aim is not the extortion of concessions or publicity for political purposes. Very often the recipient countries welcome the hijackers with acclamation and tend to regard refugee escape, even where casualties have been caused, as perfectly legitimate. Inevitably this has made it difficult to establish universal agreement about extradition. Some states wish to reserve the right to accord political asylum in such circumstances. A most pertinent question which is often posed, because it highlights the moral dilemma, is: 'Would Israel turn back a planeload of Soviet Jews?'

The second category, criminal ransom extortion and escape, has had    important    implications    for    the    development    of counter-measures. The overwhelming majority of the hijackings that hit the United States almost like a craze in 1968–9 were committed by criminals or mentally unbalanced individuals. The vast number of domestic airports and air services, and the proximity of Cuba as a potential haven, undoubtedly made America a particularly vulnerable target. Yet, paradoxically, the clear lack of any political 'revolutionary' motivation in these cases ultimately made it much easier for Castro to negotiate the five-year bilateral hijack pact with the United States. Over half of the 121 aircraft diverted to Cuba between 1968–70 were from the United States. Clearly the Cuban authorities did not welcome this uninvited influx of armed criminals seeking ransoms, and of the mentally deranged. Criminal hijackers faced increasingly tough treatment from the Cuban authorities if they succeeded in reaching Havana, and most were handed over to the United States for trial, or arrested, convicted and imprisoned in Cuba.

Under the terms of the U.S.–Cuba Hijack Pact, signed in February 1973, both governments undertook either to return hijackers for trial or to try them in their own courts, and, if convicted, to mete out severe punishments. The agreement covers both aircraft and ship hijacking, and has been 100 per cent effective in achieving its objectives. However it is noteworthy that the pact still leaves the signatory governments free to exercise discretionary rights to grant political asylum. Hence it is not inconceivable that politically motivated hijackings, for example, by a Puerto Rican 'national liberation' group enjoying Cuban support, could still rely on a Cuban sanctuary.

In Western Europe, the Middle East, and increasingly in Africa and Asia, the major hijacking threat is posed by politically motivated groups using it as a means of publicising their cause, or of extorting concessions from governments such as the release of imprisoned terrorists or the payment of ransoms. Political hijackings in these regions are far more difficult to prevent for a number of reasons. An important factor has been the proximity of a number of Middle Eastern states prepared to give sanctuary to hijackers who claim to be working for the Palestinian cause. The complex international infra-structure and inter-connections of some of the terrorist groups involved has made it extremely difficult to identify possible hijack gangs and their intended targets. To take an extreme example of this, the three Japanese Red Army terrorists who carried out the

Lod Airport massacre on 30 May 1972 were initially trained in arms and explosives in Japan and North Korea, given further training under P.F.L.P. auspices in a camp in Lebanon, obtained forged passports in West Germany, and were provided with weapons in Rome, where they boarded an Air France aircraft bound for Tel Aviv. It was hardly surprising that their attack took the authorities completely by surprise.

Perhaps the most important of all the underlying reasons for the intractability of the political hijacking problem, however, is psychological. Fanatically determined revolutionary terrorists are prepared to take much higher personal risks for their cause, often to the point of sacrificing their own lives. Leon Trotsky once remarked 'What distinguishes a revolutionary is not so much his capacity to kill as his willingness to die.' Once again it is vital to caution against judging the terrorist by one's own standards of rationality and prudence. The more desperate a revolutionary group becomes for publicity or some tactical success, the more it will be tempted to throw caution to the winds and bring off a daring terrorist *coup*. Very often a fresh hijack or airport attack is undertaken as an act of vengeance for an earlier defeat or failure, and to show that the terrorists are still determined to wage war until final victory.

By far the most dramatic political extortion hijack of recent years was the P.F.L.P. seizure of an Air France airbus with 258 passengers just outside Athens while *en route* for Paris from Tel Aviv on Sunday 27 June 1976. It is now known that the whole operation was planned by Wadih Haddad, an experienced hijack terrorist who had been a key figure in organising the Dawsons Field multi-hijack in September 1970. Haddad based himself in Somalia, which has become a major launching base for subversion in East Africa and the Middle East, to concert the whole operation. There is also strong evidence that there was a prior arrangement between the Ugandan dictator Amin, and the P.F.L.P., to use Entebbe as a base for the terrorists to hold the hostages. The Air France pilot has testified that the leader of the P.F.L.P. hijack team (two Germans and two P.F.L.P. men) knew the plane's ultimate destination was Entebbe at the outset. And on their arrival at Entebbe the German woman hijacker was heard to declare: 'it is all right, the Army is waiting.' It has also become clear, from numerous testimonies of released hostages, that Amin was blatantly colluding with the hijackers and trying to exploit the situation to his own maximum advantage.[43]   Amin allowed the hijackers to bring in additional terrorists, arms and explosives to the airport. And it soon became clear that Ugandan soldiers were sharing the task of guarding the hostages with the hijackers. The hijackers threatened to execute the hostages unless fifty-three Palestinian terrorists were released from gaol — 12 p.m. on Thursday, 1 July was set as the deadline for the executions. At 11 a.m. Israel Radio announced that the Cabinet was willing to negotiate. In view of the enormous emotional pressure and angry protests of relatives in Israel, and given the immediate danger to the hostages' lives, it is easy to understand why Israel made this departure from its normal policy of no concessions.

What the rest of the world and the Israeli public did not know was that secret plans were already being prepared by the Israel Defence Forces to mount a daring commando rescue operation. This imaginative and brilliantly executed long-range rescue has been fully described and celebrated elsewhere. But what are its political implications for the future of politically motivated hijackings for the purposes of publicity and blackmail? There can be little doubt that the Israeli raid profoundly shook the P.F.L.P. and the various Middle Eastern states which had traditionally aided or succoured Palestinian terrorism. But it would be wrong to assume that Entebbe has totally eliminated this form of international terrorism. For Israel was only enabled to administer this salutary blow against terrorists and their backers by a very rare combination of circumstances. In the first place the hijackers provided both the incentive and the opportunity for direct Israeli intervention when they released all the non-Israeli passengers on 1 July. For thenceforward it was a primarily Israeli affair. Although the Israeli government and people felt increasingly isolated and deserted in their hour of crisis at least they could single-mindedly concentrate on getting the hostages out by a unilateral operation. What chance would there have been of mounting a combined military rescue operation in concert with the French and other Western governments involved? (The idea of the British Labour government lending any assistance to such an operation is truly laughable. It transpires that the British Foreign Office, not satisfied merely with failing to follow the American lead in congratulating Israel on her action, actually sent a message of condolence to Amin.)[44]  Who can doubt the considerable advantage accruing to the Israelis in having sole control over the whole operation?

In addition, there were a number of distinct strategic advantages inherent in the fact that the target was the Ugandan major airport. Firstly, Uganda is diplomatically relatively isolated. Its only consistent supporter, Libya, was too far away to offer any assistance. She has no alliance with powerful neighbours. If a Middle Eastern state had been harbouring the hijack there would have been a serious risk of the raid provoking international war with Israel. In the case of Uganda there was no such risk. A second major advantage resulted from Israel's earlier military and economic–advisory relations with Uganda. Israeli intelligence possessed an almost unrivalled bank of information on the state of Ugandan military preparedness, terrain and even detailed plans of Entebbe airport. Another colossal advantage lay in the almost legendary incompetence and unreliability of Ugandan armed forces and leadership. (Even so the Israelis were taking great risks because the Uganda army did actually possess the weaponry at Entebbe to have inflicted heavy casualties on the Israelis had the Ugandans stayed at their posts.)[45]

Finally, it should not be overlooked that Israeli transport aircraft were operating at the very limit of their range. Even so, the success of the operation depended upon the use of the Nairobi airport facilities, and these were only accessible because of the long-standing antipathy of the Kenyan government for the Amin régime.

In the context of international terrorist hijacking it would be unreasonable to expect such a conjunction of circumstances favourable to armed rescue to recur frequently. Terrorist organisations know this full well and have undoubtedly not abandoned the hijack weapon. They will seek to mount fresh operations applying some of the lessons they have learnt from the Entebbe defeat, and striving desperately to avenge it. At Entebbe the Israelis won an important battle against international terrorism. But it is going to take concerted action by many states on many fronts before we can claim that we have won the war. There were, it is important to remember, two very ominous facts about the Entebbe hijack that have tended to be lost sight of in the general euphoria. The first is that the team of four hijackers, all of them known members of terrorist organisations and armed with explosives and guns, were without any difficulty able to board aircraft *en route from Israel* at Athens international airport, an airport that had previously experienced several terrorist attacks. (In one of them in August 1973 two Arabs opened fire with machine-guns on passengers killing three, wounding fifty-five and seizing thirty-five hostages.) It is clear that when the Entebbe hijackers boarded the Air France plane at Athens on 27 June 1976 the airport ground services were in a state of complete disruption because of a strike. Search and screening procedures were not functioning properly. The terrorists probably could not believe their good luck. Nevertheless they should never have been allowed to board the plane. There should be an absolute rule that if strike action renders boarding gate checks impossible then no boarding should be permitted. It should be remembered that Athens is by no means the first airport to have fallen down on elementary security, nor is it by any means the worst offender in this regard.

The other ominous message of the Entebbe hijack was the inflation in the ransom price of the hostages. At Dawsons Field in September 1970 the terrorists demanded the release of seven terrorist prisoners in return for fifty-six hostages. At Entebbe the price demanded had quadrupled.

The fourth main type of aircraft hijacking, the political terrorist 'getaway' plane comandeered as part of a larger terrorist operation is beginning to overshadow the other types in importance. The type, by definition, cannot be effectively prevented by even the best airport security in the world. The escape aircraft and the prearranged landing facilities in a foreign state become, as it were, part of the ransom the state subjected to terrorist attack has to pay for the release of hostages. In a sense the government becomes a party to the hijack, and this was dramatically, though doubtless unintentionally, symbolised when the Austrian Minister of the Interior was seen to shake hands with the terrorist leader before the latter flew off with his cargo of hijacked OPEC Ministers to Algiers, and then on to Tripoli on 22 December 1975. Another dramatic example of this type of hijack occurred in August 1975, after five Japanese Red Army guerrillas had stormed the American Embassy in Kuala Lumpur, seizing fifty-three hostages, and forced the Japanese government to release five of their fellow terrorists from Japanese prisons. The terrorists were then provided with a Japanese Air Lines DC–8 which took them to Libya. While there are still states willing to provide sanctuary for hijackers, and governments prepared to bow to their demands, it is hard to see how this form of hijack can be prevented. It is likely to provide a major headache for governments in the next decade.

Other terrorist threats to air travellers and air facilities include attacks on grounded aircraft, airport buildings, and the potential threat of surface to air missile attack on an aircraft in flight. These forms of terror amount to nothing more or less than sheer random massacre of the innocent. Mass murder of unarmed civilians is a crime against humanity. Fellow-travelling revolutionaries and terrorists often boast of terror being a 'clinical' and 'precise' revolutionary weapon. Have they forgotten the massacres at Lod and Rome? Three Japanese United Red Army members attacked passengers at Lod Airport on 31 May 1972, killing twenty-five and wounding seventy-six. At Rome Airport on 17 December 1973 five Palestinian terrorists attacked a grounded Pan American World Airways plane, spraying it with machine-guns, throwing bombs and grenades, and setting the plane on fire. They killed thirty-two people and wounded eighteen. In this latter case the murderers were able to get away scot free to Kuwait.

It is quite clear that the combating of these particularly murderous forms of terrorism cannot be accomplished by improved airport security and intelligence alone. It is a physical impossibility for the authorities to provide round-the-clock blanket security for all airport runways and buildings. Far the most effective approach, as we shall consider under the heading of general measures against international terrorism, is to secure effective implementation of international agreements on the extradition and punishment of terrorists, and the introduction of the death penalty for such crimes, where it does not already apply.[46]

What specific counter-measures have been found most effective in combating aircraft hijacking and related forms of international terrorism? Among the most successful have been improved measures of prevention and defence on the ground with the object of stopping the potential hijacker getting through the boarding gates. One may hope that police intelligence will be good enough to pick up advance warning of an intended hijack, including even some clue as to the individuals likely to be involved. For reasons we have already examined, however, it is far more difficult to obtain and co-ordinate such intelligence on an international scale. Inter-governmental police co-operation is constantly being improved. Yet inevitably some intending hijackers, probably using forged documents and elaborate cover, will slip through the net and arrive, unknown to the authorities, at an international airport. Once there the only sure way of preventing him reaching his objective is to subject all the intending passengers to thorough body and baggage searches to ensure that anyone carrying a weapon of any kind is prevented from boarding.

The United States has been the world leader in this field. Following the multi-hijack to Dawson's Field in September 1970, President Nixon appointed Lieutenant General Benjamin O. Davis Director of Security and charged him with the task of co-ordinating anti-hijack measures on a nationwide basis. This was an enormous responsibility in a country which had over 150 million air passengers per year, over 300 international flights departing daily, and 15,000 domestic flights per day. General Davis decided that nothing less than 100 per cent searches at the boarding gates were required. All American airlines and airport authorities were consulted about the planning of this programme, and in 1973 it became obligatory for the airports to process every passenger through metal detecting machines (magnetic and electronic hand searches and magnetometer arches).

Davis was not merely content to persuade the airports to install and use the equipment, and to search every passenger. He also insisted on procedures providing enough equipment and personnel 'to ensure that the passengers and their baggage could be searched *faster* than they could check in after the search at the ticket counter in the boarding lobby'.[47] The queue had to be at the ticket counter rather than at the search barrier. This was the secret of making the scheme acceptable to the travelling public. And the scheme has been fully justified by its success. The figures in Table 8 reveal the sudden ending of successful hijack attempts on flights originating in the United States after 1973. In 1974 alone twenty-five potential hijackings were averted as the result of 2400 firearms being confiscated at various airports in the United States.

The enormous success of the American passenger search programme should encourage emulation by other states. Unfortunately the equipment required is very expensive and some countries have been slow to install it. Others have neglected to ensure conscientious and rigorous use of the equipment on all passengers. Hasty and superficial searches are unfortunately all too common in many international airports. One particularly grave problem arises where universal search procedures are not instituted for domestic flights. For it is then possible for a potential hijacker to seize an aircraft on an internal flight and divert it overseas. British vulnerability

in this respect was embarrassingly demonstrated in the hijacking of a
B.A.C. 1–11 on a flight from Manchester to London in January
1975. To be really 100 per cent effective against international hijacking the boarding gate control has to cover *every* flight in every
national aviation system. Now clearly we are a very long way from
achieving this. Even in many countries that could certainly afford
such a comprehensive system there are often political and
organisational obstacles imposed. And, as we have noted, there is
always the possibility of human error on the part of the search personnel, superficial or inefficient use of search procedures, and even
the bribery and connivance of ground personnel. Because of its lack
of universality and unavoidable margin of error it is therefore essential to combine boarding gate searches with a range of other
measures.

In the first year of the Palestinian aircraft hijacking wave
(1968–9) the main targets were El Al aircraft. El Al developed its
own very tough individual security system, and over eight years it
has proved remarkably effective. At great cost they installed armed
skymarshals on every flight and bullet-proof lockable doors dividing
the cockpit from the passenger cabins. These measures have proved
their worth time and again. One of the best known El Al successes
was the defeat of the hijack attempt by Leila Khaled and Patrick
Arguello on an El Al Boeing 707 en route from Amsterdam. The
Israeli skymarshals shot Arguello when he was in the act of releasing
his grenade. Fortunately for the passengers the grenade failed to explode. Khaled was overpowered. After this defeat Palestinian
terrorists turned their attention to trying to attack El Al aircraft on
the ground. They have had some spectacular near misses. For instance, in January 1975 the Black September Organisation
mounted an R.P.G.–7 portable non-precision rocket launcher at
Orly Airport in an attempt to hit an El Al Boeing with 136
passengers and a crew of eleven aboard just about to take off for
Montreal and New York. If the terrorists had been using the precision S.A. 7 missile it might well have been a tragedy. As it was, they
missed the Boeing and hit a Yugoslav Air Lines DC–9, injuring a
Yugoslav steward and a French gendarme.

One authority on the 'skyjack war' has pointed out that the El Al
methods of in-flight security seem to have paid dividends financially
as well as in political and security terms. '. . . since 1968 the airline
has expanded at an impressive rate. In 1967–8 its annual turnover

was $52,000,000, in 1972–3 $135,000,000. And in 1972 it had the highest load factor of any airline on the North Atlantic route – sixty-nine per cent.'[48] Yet despite this considerable success the security measures on El Al flights cannot totally suffice. As we have seen, the terrorists simply switch their methods of attack to the most vulnerable points. The greatest current dangers to their air passengers are from sabotage and ground attack. And for protection against such threats they are compelled to depend on the airport security and police work of national governments. There is no panacea for security in aviation.

It has already been shown that hijacking is an extremely complex and international problem bedevilled by political and ideological conflicts. For as long as some states are prepared to view certain hijackings and attacks on travellers as legitimate acts of 'freedom fighters', there is no possibility of obtaining universally agreed international legal norms and procedures for dealing with such acts. The harsh fact is that progress towards combating hijacking by means of international law conventions and general treaties has been extremely limited. The Tokyo (1963), Hague (1970) and Montreal (1971) conventions on civil aviation have done little more, one leading scholar concludes, than provide 'the first stage in the development of an international regime for the control of aircraft hijacking'.[49] These conventions' net result has been to establish a somewhat crude and monolithic framework for dealing with the problems of unlawful seizure of aircraft based on the principle *aut dedere aut punire*.

The Tokyo convention on Offences and Certain Other Acts Committed on Board Aircraft (1963) sets out the jurisdictional guiding principles requiring contracting states, (i) to make every effort to restore control of the aircraft to its lawful commander and, (ii) to make every effort to ensure the prompt onward passage or return of the hijacked aircraft together with its crew, passengers and cargo. Signed in September 1963, it did not come into force until six years later. By late 1975 only seventy-seven states had ratified the convention.

In December 1970 the Hague Convention for the Suppression of the Unlawful Seizure of Aircraft was signed. It requires contracting states to either extradite apprehended hijackers to their country of origin or to prosecute them under the judicial code of the recipient state. However, there are significant clauses allowing 'political offence' exceptions to the requirement of extradition. Contracting parties are free to exercise such latitude as they see fit in interpreting grounds for granting political exceptions and asylum.

The Montreal Convention for the Suppression of Unlawful Acts Against the Safety of Civil Aviation, signed in September 1971, attempted to extend the scope of international law to encompass sabotage and attacks on airports and grounded aircraft. Under this convention contracting states are required to extradite or prosecute for offences of this nature. It also lays down the principle that such offences be subject to severe penalties. The Convention came into force in January 1973, but by late 1975 only sixty-five states had ratified.

It is hard to escape the conclusion that these conventions do not provide much of an effective barrier to aircraft hijacks or attacks. All the states which have traditionally provided sanctuary, succour and condonation of air terrorism are notable for their absence from the list of ratifying states. Yet there is a still more fundamental weakness. The most serious deficiency of these conventions is that they fail to provide any effective system of enforcement sanctions to ensure that requirements to extradite, prosecute and punish hijackers are actually observed. What is needed to make such machinery effective, as one leading academic authority has argued, is enforcement sanctions 'that really do have some teeth in them'.[50] There must be a procedure for sanctions against a state failing to fulfil its obligation.[51]

There are at least five possible routes out of this impasse which, if taken in combination, would go far to strengthening international machinery to prevent and deter air terrorism. The first is the approach, cogently supported by McWhinney, of strengthening the application of the international legal doctrine of state responsibility. Diplomatic and political pressure should be brought to bear to press governments to toughen their own domestic procedures and penalties for air terrorism offences. There is a clear case for appealing to a state's natural self-interest in this regard. A reputation for softness greatly increases the likelihood of a state being chosen for a terrorist operation. A hijacker appearing before a court in 1974, for example, candidly admitted that Amsterdam Airport had been selected by the terrorists because sentences were known to be light in Holland. Moreover, as McWhinney points out, if states do not succeed in giving international accords real teeth, the temptation for certain states to take unilateral punitive or military retaliation against a sanctuary state will become all the greater. A second possible avenue is the development of more bilateral pacts, on the U.S.–Cuba Hijack Pact model. It would be a great advance if agreements could be secured with individual Arab states that have traditionally opposed general international conventions, but have now wearied of the ensuing complications of acting as a haven for terrorists. It is perhaps too much to hope that such pacts will follow the lead of the U.S.–Canada Hijack Treaty (1976) in dropping the political offence exception clause altogether. This would be a politically and ideologically impossible step for an Arab state. But even the wider adoption of bilateral pacts on the Cuba model would be a substantial deterrent to many types of hijacker.

There is also the possibility of obtaining regional treaties on extradition, punishment and enforcement. However, even in the European Community, which has a strong common interest in such efforts and a well-established organisational structure for co-ordination, progress in this field has been abysmally slow. A fourth, and perhaps even more long-term possibility is for states to reinforce the existing general international conventions on hijacking with the adoption of an enforcement sanctions convention. Some valiant efforts have been made along these lines by the United States, Canada, the Netherlands and the United Kingdom. For example, at the final International Civil Aviation Organisation (ICAO) meeting on the draft of the Hague Convention, the United States attempted unsuccessfully, to drastically restrict exceptions to the extradition and punishment of hijackers, to exclude the political offence exception defence against extradition, and to establish hijacking as a common crime. In summer 1973 a proposal by a number of Western states for a separate enforcement convention to back up the Tokyo, Hague and Montreal Conventions by means of punitive sanctions depriving offending states of the rights and services provided by international air service agreements was roundly defeated at the ICAO Assembly in Rome.

However, this last-mentioned approach may not after all have to depend upon prior agreement or adoption by an international organisation. As McWhinney has forcefully argued, in many ways the most practicable and potentially the most powerfully effective method of punishing states harbouring or aiding terrorists is for the trade unions and professional organisations within the international aviation industry to impose their own unilateral sanctions.

McWhinney rightly recalls the remarkable speed with which an El
Al aircraft hijacked to Algiers was released in 1968 when the International Federation of Airline Pilots threatened to boycott all flights
in or out of Algeria.[52] The piloting skills and indeed the technical
services required by modern airliners are so complex that they simply could not be substituted by any boycotted régime. Moreover,
other states would not dare to break the ban for fear of incurring the
boycott themselves. One must agree that the threat of such a
boycott

> against a delinquent state remains a reserve control, to be used, if
> need be, in default of affirmative and effective control by the
> organised community... Its potential effects are immense and
> relatively immediate. And if there be argued the extra weight of
> much larger and financially far more powerful organisations such
> as the International Transport Workers' Federation ... then the
> chances of applying effective, if informal, community sanctions
> against delinquent States seem very real and also immediate.[53]

One other form of international response to air terrorism has been
widely discussed by analysts. This is the possibility of establishing a
kind of supranational Air Crimes Commission with its own court,
code and international prison. The scheme proposed by Peter
Clyne[54] would depend on member–states being prepared to hand
over apprehended hijackers to the commission for trial, regardless of
country of origin. All member–states of the commission would be
obliged to boycott any member–state that failed to meet its
obligations, thus cutting off all air communications with the
offender. Clyne goes further and argues that any state refusing to
join the commission scheme should also be boycotted. The
difficulties of creating such an organisation in the present climate of
international relations look insuperable. When one considers the
obstacles confronting even those modest attempts to strengthen the
international conventions on hijacking described earlier, the Clyne
proposals appear totally impracticable.

In conclusion, Western governments should continue to develop
tougher measures of the kind outlined above in order to combat international air terrorism more effectively. It would be irresponsibly
complacent to assume that hijacking and attacks on aviation
facilities will simply go out of fashion. We need to be vigilant

against newer and often more sanguinary forms of terrorist action against air travellers. And if states do not show the political will and courage required to take really effective international action we are likely to see an increasing recourse to unilateral military actions by aggrieved states, with all the risks to life and peace that such methods imply.

# XXXV
# DIPLOMATIC KIDNAPPINGS AND ATTACKS

It has been an almost universally accepted convention of international relations since the age of the Greek city states that ambassadors and other diplomatic representatives of foreign states should enjoy special privileges of immunity and protection within host states. Grotius refers to this tradition in asserting confidently

> that the common rule, that he who is in foreign territory is subject to that territory, does, by the common consent of nations, suffer an exception in the case of ambassadors; they being, by a certain fiction, in the place of those who send them: and by a similar fiction they are, as it were, *extra territorium*; and thus, are not bound by the Civil Law of the people among whom they live."

The doctrine of the Right of Legation, and the principles of diplomatic rights to immunity and protection were expressed in the norms of diplomatic reciprocity that emerged from the Peace of Westphalia (1684). The practice of diplomacy between modern sovereign states is indeed founded on these essential Westphalian norms.

The terrorist tactic of diplomatic kidnapping, developed primarily by Latin American revolutionary movements in the mid-1960s, constitutes a threat to this aspect of the international order, disrupts normal diplomatic relations, and provides the terrorists with a powerful weapon of publicity and political extortion. It has proved an increasingly popular tactic with terrorists of all nationalities and ideological colours following the initial wave of Latin American kidnaps between 1968 and 1971. The reasons for its popularity are not hard to find. Statistics show that kidnapping has become the single most effective terrorist method of extorting ransoms and releases of prisoners. Between 1971 and 1975 in Latin America alone kidnappers gained $80 million in ransoms for hostages. Yet while the rewards are high, the risks are extraordinarily low. Recent studies have shown that, despite tougher measures by many governments, the kidnappers have in most countries an 80 per cent chance of escaping capture or death. By the same token, however, it is also a relatively low-risk form of terrorism for the victims. Only about 4 per cent of all kidnap victims are actually killed by the terrorists.[56] A special study of diplomatic kidnappings found that 33 per cent of kidnap victims are released without payment of a ransom while 50 per cent are released on payment of the ransom demand.[57]

The present status of accredited diplomats under international law is that of specially protected persons. By virtue of their position they are accorded more privileges and protection than private individuals or other aliens. Hence kidnapping of a diplomat is an offence not only against domestic law, but against international law. In broad terms states can only be held directly responsible for the violation of diplomatic rights and privileges if such violation can be shown to have resulted from clear negligence or lack of diligence in the duties of protection. The host state can only be held indirectly responsible for failure to protect aliens when it can be shown that the state, through its agents, has failed to prevent, punish or remedy any offence against international law by private persons which results in the injury of an alien. It is generally recognised international law that the duty of protection of foreign envoys should be taken to include special vigilance in guarding their safety, the prosecution and punishment of those guilty of offences against their persons or property, and where applicable, official apology and restitution. It is allowed, however, that in times of civil war or mass disturbances some of these obligations may in effect be temporarily inoperable, though the obligation to show due diligence in the prevention and punishment of such crimes still applies.

In the wake of the spate of twenty-one diplomatic kidnappings between 1968 and 1971, of which no less than seventeen took place in Latin America, the Organisation of American States (O.A.S.) formulated a Convention to Prevent and Punish Acts of

Terrorism Taking the Form of Crimes Against Persons and Related Extortion that are of International Significance. This convention was a precursor of the U.N. Convention on the protection of diplomats. In terms of Latin American legal tradition the convention was a remarkably bold innovation, for it has always been the case that Latin American states have held very strictly to the principle of extra-territorial political asylum. They did not follow the U.S. practice of refusing to recognise the political offence exception. Hence the O.A.S. Treaty was in danger of being wrecked in similar fashion to many draft measures against hijacking, that is through failure to agree that the *aut dedere aut punire* principle be applied. The O.A.S. Convention, signed in 1971, circumvents this difficulty by asserting, in Article 2:

> For the purposes of this convention, kidnapping, murder, and other assaults against the life or personal integrity of those persons to whom the state has the duty to give special protection according to international law, as well as extortion in connection with those crimes, shall be considered common crimes of international significance, regardless of motive.[58]

Thus, by making diplomatic kidnapping a common crime, the convention made it possible for contracting parties to extradite or prosecute in all such cases. While this may provide a useful model for other regional organisations it has not been wholly successful in Latin America. Only four of the thirteen signatory states had actually ratified the convention by the end of 1975. It is difficult to overcome the deadweight of legal conservatism even in a region which has unrivalled experience of this form of terrorism throughout the continent.

The United Nations Convention on the Prevention and Punishment of Crimes Against Internationally Protected Persons Including Diplomatic Agents was signed in December 1973. It lays down the duty of contracting states to establish certain acts against protected persons as common crimes, and adopts the familiar 'extradite or prosecute' formula. By late 1975 only nine member states had ratified. Both these measures poignantly underline the difficulty of securing effective international legal machinery to deal with international terrorism.

In the absence of effective international action it is up to national governments to carry the main burden of combating this particularly cowardly form of international terrorism. The battle has to be waged on two fronts. Firstly, all governments of states prone or vulnerable to terrorist attack should, as part of the overall security measures described in Part II of this study, make it their business to provide adequate protection for the diplomatic community and other likely foreign targets. There have been many cases in which a diplomatic kidnapping provided the stimulus for the introduction of sweeping emergency powers to deal with terrorism. The *Front de Libération du Québec* (F.L.Q.) kidnapping of James Cross, British Trade Commissioner in Montreal, in October 1970, is a case in point. Following the kidnap of Cross and the Minister of Labour in the Quebec Provincial Government, Pierre Laporte, the Canadian government took the extreme step of invoking the War Measures Act. This Act was in force for six months, and it enabled the federal government to saturate the Montreal region with troops, leaving the police as free as possible to get on with the job of tracking down the kidnap cells. The security forces were given sweeping powers to search and hold for questioning, and in the course of the emergency the authorities rounded up 340 suspected F.L.Q. activists for questioning. Nevertheless it was almost nine weeks before the kidnappers were located. Cross was only released after a deal had been agreed by Premier Trudeau under which three of the kidnappers and four of their relatives were flown to Cuba in a Canadian Forces aircraft. Cross was freed on 3 December 1970, but the unfortunate Pierre Laporte was murdered by the more ruthless and desperate cell which had seized him.

Security measures alone, however thorough, are not enough to combat this form of terrorist attack. Moreover we must remember that in many of the countries where terrorism is rife the security forces are already hopelessly overstretched and cannot possibly perform their tasks of diplomatic protection effectively. Under these circumstances, as Richard Clutterbuck has rightly emphasised,[59] it is vital that the government accrediting diplomats should make adequate plans for the contingency of kidnap.

Many practical aspects of a kidnap incident can be anticipated and to some degree prepared for — machinery for co-operation with the host government concerning siege tactics if and when the kidnappers and their hostage are surrounded, regarding the safeguarding of the kidnap victim's family and possessions, and possibly even agreement on code words to be employed in any written or spoken communications permitted by the terrorists.

However by far the most agonising yet significant decision that the accrediting government must take is whether or not to accede to ransom demands. It will already be clear from the argument in Part II on the general principles of anti-terrorist strategy that I favour a firm policy of minimising rewards: no deals, no concessions — however callous and inflexible this may seem to the hostage and those intimately involved. As Baumann argues[60] such a policy is consistent with the aim of maximising the possibility of deterring the rational kidnapper. Over time, terrorists will discover that certain governments repeatedly refuse to concede their demands. Thus, at least in the case of some potential kidnappers, 'if ransom will be denied or if the desired asylum will not be granted, there will be no rewards and no reason to attempt a kidnapping'.[61] There is, of course, still the problem of deterring the kidnapper whose main purpose is publicity. However the second half of Baumann's formula, the maximisation of punishment, does provide a weapon for dealing with this form of kidnapping as well as those aiming at extortion. One implication of this part of the solution for governments is that they must constantly seek to extend and strengthen the application of the *aut dedere aut punire* principle to cover this kind of international terrorist crime wherever it occurs. The other very clear implication must surely be that the penalties for this kind of offence should be made far more severe. Could it not be argued that the appropriate penalty for terrorist murder, whether of a diplomat, or of a private alien, whether of a head of state or the most humble citizen, is capital punishment?

Diplomats are still extremely vulnerable to both assassination and kidnapping attempts, though it is possible that improved security measures by certain states, and the firm 'no ransom' policy upheld by other states, such as the United States and Britain, have combined to reduce the kidnap risk to some extent.

# XXXVI
# BARRICADE AND HOSTAGE
# SITUATIONS

Diplomats are by no means the only group in the front-line for kidnapping attempts by international terrorists. If the diplomats become a harder and more inaccessible target there are many other potential target groups such as alien businessmen, missionaries, doctors and tourists, offering the terrorist attractive possibilities of extortion and publicity. Moreover in many countries such groups are too numerous to be adequately protected by the host state.

It is by no means a recent innovation in international terrorism. An American historian has provided a fascinating analysis of the kidnapping of a private U.S. citizen, Mr Perdicaris, by the bandit Raisuli near Tangiers in May 1904.[62] (The release of Perdicaris was eventually achieved through the threat of U.S. military intervention.) Roberta Wohlstetter has argued that it was Raúl and Fidel Castro who pioneered the modern wave of political kidnappings which 'used foreign nationals . . . as pawns in a domestic struggle for power'.[63] And she points out that: 'They violated not only internal rules of internal political order, but also the meagre international rules that lend stability to relations among states.'[64] It is clear that the sensational publicity gained from the rash of kidnaps of U.S. citizens in the American and Canadian press considerably aided Castro in his campaign to intimidate America into withdrawing or withholding assistance to the Batista régime. (By late June 1958, the Castro guerrillas had kidnapped at least forty-seven U.S. citizens, including thirty servicemen. Castro even used the U.S. captives as a weapon to make the United States force the Cuban air force to cease the bombing of the rebel zone in Sierra Cristal. Raúl Castro told the United States that the guerrillas would hold the U.S. captives in the bombing zone.) In the late 1960s and early 1970s the political kidnapping of foreigners (especially Americans) in Latin America, South East Asia and the Middle East, reached epidemic proportions.

In countering this threat to its private citizens abroad the liberal state must again have recourse to the guiding principles of seeking to minimise rewards and maximise the chances of punishment for the terrorist. It would be totally irresponsible and unjust for a liberal democracy to treat some of its citizens as more deserving of strenuous efforts at release. All foreign citizens kidnapped abroad must be given equal attention, energy and support by government to secure their earliest possible release. But at the same time release must not be bought at the price of the long-term safety and well-being of other travellers abroad. Every time a ransom demand is paid it makes fresh acts of extortion at ever higher prices more likely. Yet this firm 'no ransom' approach is perfectly compatible with the energetic pursuit of negotiations for the release of the hostage via the mediation of either the state in which the abduction has occurred or a trusted third party.

There is another line of approach of some practical value open to governments. They should identify personnel who are likely to be employed in a high-vulnerability area for terrorism, and devise some briefing for them before they take up the post, both on the general political background and conflicts within their specific region, and on useful practical lessons of hostage survival in case of need. For while it is true that every kidnap or barricade-and-hostage situation is unique, and that every individual terrorist personality poses different problems to the hostage, it is possible to distil some relevant ground rules that may greatly increase the individual's chances of surviving in the event of kidnap. McClure observes: 'It is difficult to exaggerate the shock effect of a kidnapping. From a state of total well-being, the victim in seconds finds himself in mortal peril. At first he cannot believe what is happening; he is stunned, disorientated, often paralyzed with fear — but then, he may also reflexively try to defend himself or to escape.'[65]

To overcome this position of weakness and psychological disorientation obviously requires enormous reserves of mental and physical stamina, and coolness. And these resources are more likely to be brought fully into play if there is adequate psychological preparation by the potential victim. The hostage should learn to study his captors' personalities, behaviour, motivations and beliefs, for this may help him to understand his situation more fully and to predict likely developments. It is also vital that the victim should be vigilant against his captors' attempts at influencing him by mental conditioning and against the dangers of over-empathising or over-identifying with the captors.

A magnificent example of the way in which an intelligent and brave individual can cope with a protracted imprisonment is offered by Sir Geoffrey Jackson. Sir Geoffrey was kidnapped by the Tupamaros in Uruguay in January 1971 and held for nine months in a so-called 'People's Prison' in the most unspeakable conditions. [66] Faced with the hazards of disorientation, isolation, claustrophobia and rather clumsy attempts to break down his moral resistance, Sir Geoffrey proved that it was possible to break through the communication barrier and to reduce, if only marginally in some cases, the hostility of the captors towards him. He attempted, rationally and objectively, to assess the ideological commitments, attitudes and emotional characteristics of all the guerrillas he met. Somehow he managed to preserve his dignity, sanity and sense of humour through his ordeal. What his experience proves above all is that high leadership qualities, emotional stability, and calm stoicism are even more important than physical stamina in hostage survival.

# XXXVII
# GENERAL MEASURES AGAINST INTERNATIONAL TERRORISM

Contemporary terrorism, as has already been shown, has an increasingly international dimension. Some terrorist organisations have acquired the resources, tactics and skills to operate internationally. Others even have vaguely defined international aims and have developed the rudiments of transnational or, at any rate, multilateral collaboration with like-minded organisations. A properly synchronised programme of international and national measures is clearly required if these organisations are to be countered effectively. Sadly, however, the record to date of international collaboration against terrorisms is one of abysmal failure.

The United Nations has proved a broken reed on the whole subject of terrorism. It has proved as useless in countering terrorism as the League of Nations before it. It is not hard to see why this should have been so. Member–states of the U.N. are unable to agree even on a basic working definition of terrorism, for they are deeply ideologically divided in their attitudes towards violence in general. To the Third World state enjoying the first flush of 'national liberation', terrorism is the essential handmaiden of revolt against oppression, and all forms of revolutionary violence except those directed against one's own state are viewed as *ipso facto* morally legitimate. Communist states regard political terrorism as 'legitimate armed struggle' when it succeeds and as 'adventurism' when it fails. For liberal states terrorism is anathema, a blatant denial of individual rights and a violation of the doctrines of democracy and constitutionalism. We have earlier observed that a number of member–states of the U.N. have sponsored, promoted and condoned terrorism as a weapon of coercive diplomacy.

A clear example of the contradiction at the heart of the United Nations is provided by the General Assembly Declaration of Principles of International Law Concerning Friendly Relations and Co-operation Among States in Accordance with the Charter of the U.N. In this document it is asserted that: 'Every state has the duty to refrain from organizing, instigating, or participating in acts of civil strife or terrorist acts in another state or acquiescing in organized activities within its territory directed toward the commission of such acts.' This appears to be an absolute prohibition of such acts. But the document then proceeds to declare that member–states have an obligation to assist peoples struggling for their right to self-determination and freedom and independence. The U.N.'s adherence to the doctrine of armed struggle was forcefully restated in the 1976 session of the General Assembly, when, for the first time, an overwhelming majority of members supported it.

In 1972, in the shadow of the Munich Olympics massacre and the international wave of letter-bombings, the United States proposed a general convention on the export or international spread of terroristic violence 'from countries involved in civil or international conflict to countries not a party to such conflict'. This draft Convention for the Punishment of Certain Acts of International Terrorism aimed to apply the *aut dedere aut punire* principle of the Hague Convention to a far wider category of crimes, including; kidnapping, assassination and serious bodily harm where such acts are aimed at civilians outside the target state. Hence, for example, it would have covered an act such as the Munich Olympics terrorist attack because it was a violent act by Palestinians against Israelis committed on the soil of a third party state. The American draft convention had the laudable aim of trying to concentrate on limiting the *spread* of international terrorism. It left the business of prosecution and punishment for *internal* acts of terrorism to the domestic jurisdiction of individual states. Yet even this relatively cautious and practical step was opposed and ultimately defeated by the clamorous objections of the so-called 'non-aligned group' of U.N. member–states. The General Assembly refused to take any action on the U.S. Draft Convention other than to refer it to a 35-member *ad hoc* Committee on Terrorism to study the subject. As a result of the pressure of the fourteen non-aligned members of this committee, 'terrorism' was completely redefined as: 'Acts of violence and other repressive acts by colonial, racist, and alien regimes against peoples struggling for their liberation.' Once again the U.N. had become bogged down in a discussion of the ends and purposes of national liberation struggles, the problems of ending racial discrimination and apartheid, etc. In view of this ideologically deep-rooted impasse, attempts at an internationally agreed definition of terrorist crimes, and a generally accepted machinery for extradition and punishment of terrorists, will remain beyond reach. Sadly, it is unlikely that the West German government's 1976 initiative in attempting to obtain a U.N. convention prohibiting the taking of hostages will escape a similar fate.

Are the prospects for action at the level of regional international organisations any better? Until 1975 there was much optimism expressed about the prospects of achieving some effective machinery at the European Community level, an optimism which was shared by the present writer. I must confess, however, that developments in late 1976 and early 1977 have led me to a much more despondent view. Reviewing overall progress in the field of combating terrorism in the last decade one is impressed by the fact that informal co-operation at the top levels of police and security services has progressed much more rapidly than judicial and political co-ordination. The high hopes placed on the new European Convention for the Suppression of Terrorism are likely to be sorely disappointed unless the high-minded sentiments on extradition, prosecution and punishment expressed therein are given the real teeth of enforcement machinery. At present this agreement and the draft Community code on terrorism look dangerously out of touch with reality. Early in 1977 it was made cruelly obvious that at least one major European state, France, was prepared to subordinate its obligations under any international treaty or convention to the exigencies of national interest. Moreover the Strasbourg European Convention was already running into quicksands as the result of the strong reservations expressed by France, Italy, Portugal and Norway. It was objected that the Convention failed to include provision for the political offence exception clause or for grant of political asylum.

Prospects of securing greater constraints against terrorism by means of changes in international law receded in 1977. The Diplomatic Conference on Laws of War adopted a proposal which would, in effect, provide a measure of legal protection for terrorist attacks. Under this proposal national liberation movements, many of which practise terrorism extensively, are accorded lawful belligerent and prisoner-of-war status *as of right*. No attempt is made to outlaw terrorist acts, and even the well-established requirement that combatants distinguish themselves from civilians during hostilities would be swept away. The new proposal only requires that a lawful combatant carry arms openly 'during such time as he is visible to the adversary while he is engaged in a military deployment preceding the launching of an attack'. In a classic understatement the Swiss delegate observed that the proposed article was ambiguous, legally unclear, and liable to put the civilian population at risk.

We are forced back to where we began our discussion. Ultimately the liberal state has no *deus ex machina* it can rely upon to rescue it from the agonising political and moral dilemmas of waging war on terrorism. In the end each sovereign liberal state is left to shift as best it can in the constant struggle to uphold the rule of law and to protect the life and limb of its citizens. Contemporary terrorism in its severe forms constitutes what is arguably the most testing and immediate challenge to the will and courage of liberal democracies. It would, I believe, be disastrous if we failed to meet that test. Courage and a determined will to uphold liberal values and institutions, far from being irrelevant qualities more suited to the heroic past, are now more than ever needed if liberty is to survive, and contemporary barbarisms are to be vanquished.

# NOTES AND REFERENCES

PREFATORY NOTE

1. For instance, there have been numerous academic seminars and symposia on the theme of terrorism in the United States and Western Europe, and a new journal on the subject is being developed in the United States.
2. For example, recorded international terrorist incidents alone increased from below 50 per year in the period 1965–8 to over 100 per year in 1969–70, to 200 per year in 1973.
3. For example, see Anthony R. Wilkinson's dismissal of the term in B. Davidson, J. Slovo and A. R. Wilkinson, *Southern Africa: The New Politics of Revolution* (Harmondsworth: Penguin Books, 1976) p. 219.
4. See Paul Wilkinson, *Political Terrorism* (London: Macmillan, 1974) for a general survey and a bibliography of historical studies, and Lester A. Sobel (ed.), *Political Terrorism* (New York: Facts on File, 1975) for a narrative survey of terrorist activity as reported in the world Press from 1968 through 1974.


PART I

I

1. Aristotle, *The Politics*, III 3.
2. Locke, *Second Treatise on Civil Government*, VI 57.
3. Madison, *Federalist Paper No. 51*.
4. Aristotle, op cit., III 4.
5. Ibid., IV 2.
6. Aquinas, *Summa of Theology*, II–II, q.42,a.2,c.
7. Ibid.
8. Locke, op. cit. XVIII 199, 202.
9. See C.B. Macpherson, *The Political Theory of Possessive Individualism* (Oxford: Clarendon Press, 1962) and Introduction to *Leviathan* (Harmondsworth: Penguin Books, 1968).

10. Hobbes, *Leviathan*, XXIV 2.
11. See for example, Michael Oakeshott, *Hobbes on Civil Association* (Oxford: Blackwell, 1975) pp. 63 ff.
12. Hobbes, op. cit. XVII 2.
13. Ibid., XXI 2.
14. Ibid.
15. Oakeshott, op. cit., p.63.
16. Hobbes, op. cit., XXIX 2.
17. Ibid., 'A Review, and Conclusion'.
18. Locke, op. cit., XVIII 204.
19. Ibid., XIX 228.
20. Ibid., 229.
21. Madison, op. cit.

II

22. See, for example, Richard A. Falk and Saul H. Mendlovitz, *The Strategy of World Order*, vol. 3 (New York: The U.N. World Law Fund, 1966) and Grenville Clark and Louis B. Sohn, *World Peace through World Law* (Harvard University Press, 1966).
23. Locke, op. cit., VIII 97.
24. John Stuart Mill, *On Liberty*, IV.

III

25. Locke, op. cit., XI 135.
26. Ibid., 142.
27. Montesquieu, *L'Esprit des Lois*, 181.

V

28. Hamilton, *Federalist Paper No. 15*.
29. See Ernest van den Haag's superb argument, *Punishing Criminals: Concerning a Very Old and Painful Question* (New York: Basic Books, 1976).
30. See for example, Winifred A. Elkin, *The English Penal System* (Harmondsworth: Penguin Books, 1957) especially ch.11 and 12.

VI

31. Raymond Williams, *Keywords: A Vocabulary of Culture and Society* (London: Fontana, 1976).

VII

32. Madison, *Federalist Paper No. 10*.

33. Ibid.
34. Adam Roberts (ed.), The Strategy of Civilian Defence (London: Faber, 1967); Gene Sharp, The Politics of Non-violent Action (Boston: Porter-Sargent, 1973); Mohandas K. Gandhi, Satygraha: Nonviolent Resistance (Ahmedabad: Navajivan, 1958).
35. Ernest van den Haag, Political Violence and Civil Disobedience (New York: Harper and Row, 1972) pp. 29–31.
36. Ibid., p. 31.
37. Ibid., p. 28.

VIII

38. Edmund Leach, Culture and Communication (Cambridge University Press, 1976) p. 9.
39. See Konrad Lorenz, On Aggression (New York: Harcourt Brace, 1966) and for his critics see: Ashley Montague, The Nature of Human Aggression (London: OUP, 1976) and Erich Fromm, The Anatomy of Human Destructiveness (London: Cape, 1974).
40. Fromm, op. cit., pp. 96–7.
41. Gerald Priestland, The Future of Violence (London: Hamish Hamilton, 1974) p. 6.
42. Samuel P. Huntington, 'Civil Violence and the Process of Development', in Adelphi Paper No. 83 (London: IISS, 1971) pp. 1–15, and Political Order in Changing Societies (New Haven: Yale University Press, 1968).

IX

43. Ted Gurr, 'Psychological Factors in Civil Violence', World Politics, vol. 20, no. 2 (Jan 1968) pp. 252–3.
44. Alexis de Tocqueville, L'Ancien Régime et la Revolution, trans. Henry Reeve (London: John Murray, 1856) pp. 322–3.
45. Ted. R. Gurr, Why Men Rebel (Princeton: Princeton University Press, 1970); James C. Davies, 'Towards a Theory of Revolution', American Sociological Review, vol. 27 (Feb 1962) pp. 5–19; W. G. Runciman, Relative Deprivation and Social Justice (London: Routledge & Kegan Paul, 1966).
46. Feliks Gross, The Seizure of Political Power (New York: Philosophical Library, 1958) pp. 388–90, and 'Political Violence and Terror in 19th and 20th Century Russia and Eastern Europe', in vol. 8 of A Report to the National Commission on the Causes and Prevention of Violence (eds.), James F. Kirkham, Sheldon G. Levy and William J. Crotty (Washington, D.C.: U.S. Govt. Printing Office, 1969) pp. 421–76.

47. T. A. Critchley, *The Conquest of Violence* (London: Constable, 1970) p. 26.
48. On this aspect see Huntington 'Civil Violence and the Process of Development'.
49. A point stressed by Feliks Gross, 'Political Violence and Terror', op. cit.
50. See L. Trotsky, *The History of the Russian Revolution*, I 86–8.


XI

51. A Solzhenitsyn, *The Gulag Archipelago, 1918–1956*, trans. Thomas P. Whitney (London: Book Club Associates, 1974) p. 28.
52. See for example, F. Kitson, *Low Intensity Operations: Subversion, Insurgency and Peacekeeping* (London: Faber, 1971).
53. Critchley, op. cit., pp. 203–4.
54. Ibid., pp. 202–3.
55. See A. J. Deane-Drummond, *Riot Control* (London: RUSI Defence Studies, 1975).
56. Milton, *Paradise Lost*, I 648.
57. Morris Fraser, *Children in Conflict* (Harmondsworth: Penguin Books, 1974), and James L. Russell, *Civic Education in Northern Ireland* (Belfast: Report of the Northern Ireland Community Relations Commission, 1972).


XII

58. For example, see Richard Cobb, *Terreur et Subsistances 1793–1795* (Paris: Librairie Clavreuil, 1964); Robert Conquest, *The Great Terror* (London: Macmillan, 1968); Donald Greer, *The Incidence of Terror during the French Revolution* (Cambridge, Mass.: Harvard University Press, 1935); and Colin Lucas, *The Structure of Terror: the Example of Javogues and the Loire* (Oxford University Press, 1972).
59. Eugene V. Walter, *Terror and Resistance: A Study of Political Violence with Case Studies of Some Primitive African Communities* (New York: OUP, 1969).
60. Raymond Aron, *Peace and War* (London: Weidenfeld and Nicolson, 1966) p. 170.
61. Cited in an unpublished talk by Dr Richard Clutterbuck.
62. Brian Jenkins, 'International Terrorism: A Balance Sheet', *Survival*, vol. 17, no. 4 (Jul/Aug 1975) p. 158.
63. See discussion in *Report on Torture* (London: Amnesty International and Duckworth, 1973).

64. Paul Wilkinson, *Political Terrorism* (London: Macmillan, 1974) p. 80.
65. Raymond Aron, op. cit., p. 170.
66. S. Andreski, 'Terror', in *A Dictionary of the Social Sciences* (Glencoe: UNESCO and Free Press, 1964).
67. This is a reference to the clamour of the Hébertists and the Jacobin Club in 1793 that 'terror be made the order of the day'.
68. See Chalmers Johnson, *Revolution and the Social System* (Stanford University Press, 1964) and *Revolutionary Change* (University of London Press, 1968) and Peter Calvert, *Revolution* (London: Macmillan, 1970) and *A Study of Revolution* (Oxford University Press, 1970).
69. Che Guevara, *Guerrilla Warfare* (Harmondsworth: Penguin Books, 1969) p. 26.
70. Ibid., p. 105.
71. Regis Debray, *Revolution in the Revolution?* (Harmondsworth: Penguin Books, 1968) p. 74.
72. Carlos Marighela, *Minimanual of the Urban Guerrilla* (reprinted in IISS *Adelphi Paper No. 79*) p. 36.
73. Ibid.
74. See Bernard Lewis, *The Assassins: A Radical Sect in Islam* (London: Wiedenfeld and Nicolson, 1967).
75. Walter Laqueur, 'Coming to Terms with Terror', *Times Literary Supplement* (2 April 1976) pp. 362–3.
76. Carlos Marighela, 'On the Organizational Function of Revolutionary Violence', in *For the Liberation of Brazil*, trans. John Butt and Rosemary Sheed (Harmondsworth: Penguin Books, 1971) p. 44.

XIII

77. Michael Confino (ed.), *Daughter of a Revolutionary, Natalie Herzen and the Bakunin/Nechayev Circle* (London: Alcove Press, 1974) pp. 306–7.
78. Ibid., p. 257.
79. Ibid., pp. 257–8.

PART II

XIV

1. Jean-Paul Sartre, *Critique de la raison dialectique* (Paris: Gallimard, 1960).
2. Ibid., p. 208.
3. Maurice Cranston, 'Sartre and Violence', *Encounter*, vol. XXIX, no. 1 (July 1967) p. 23.

4. Raymond Aron, *History and the Dialectic of Violence: an analysis of Sartre's 'Critique de la Raison Dialectique'*, trans. Barry Cooper (Oxford: Blackwell, 1975).
5. Georges Sorel, *Reflections on Violence*, trans. T. E. Hulme and J. Roth (New York: Collier Books, 1961) p. 126.
6. Jean-Paul Sartre, Preface to Frantz Fanon, *The Wretched of the Earth* (Harmondsworth: Penguin Books, 1967) pp. 18–19.
7. Hannah Arendt, 'On Violence', collected in *Crises of the Republic* (Harmondsworth: Penguin Books, 1972) pp. 90–91, 97–8: also Raymond Aron, *History and the Dialectic of Violence*.
8. Feliks Gross, 'Political Violence and Terror in 19th and 20th Century Russia and Eastern Europe', in vol. 8 of *A Report to the National Commission on the Causes and Prevention of Violence*, (eds) James F. Kirkham, Sheldon G. Levy and William J. Crotty (Washington D.C.: U.S. Govt. Printing Office, 1969) pp. 421–76.
9. Hannah Arendt, *On Revolution* (Harmondsworth: Penguin Books, 1973) p. 19.

XV

10. See Carlos Marighela, 'Handbook of Urban Guerrilla Warfare' in *For the Liberation of Brazil* (Harmondsworth: Penguin Books, 1971) pp. 61–97.
11. For instance, by mid-1976, the estimated costs to the British taxpayer of maintaining the army's presence in Northern Ireland were running at over £80 million per annum, and the costs of compensation for damage and injury incurred in the 'troubles' at over £90 million per annum. In Stuttgart in the German Federal Republic an estimated two and a quarter million pounds was spent on the specially built bomb-proof courtroom used for the trial of members of the Baader–Meinhof group alone.
12. Richard Rose, *Northern Ireland: A Time of Choice* (London: Macmillan, 1976) pp. 24–5.
13. Richard Rose, *Governing without Consensus: an Irish Perspective* (London: Faber, 1971).

XVII

14. Feliks Gross, 'Political Violence and Terror in 19th and 20th Century Russia and Eastern Europe', in vol. 8 of *A Report to the National Commission on the Causes and Prevention of Violence* (eds) James F. Kirkham, Sheldon G. Levy and William J. Crotty (Washington D.C.: U.S. Govt. Printing Office, 1969).
15. Emile Durkheim, *The Rules of Sociological Method*, trans. S. A.

Solovay and J. H. Mueller (New York: The Free Press, 1964) p. 108.

16. Sergey Nechayev, 'Catechism of the Revolutionist' (1869) in Michael Confino (ed.), *Daughter of a Revolutionary, Natalie Herzen and the Bakunin/Nechayev Circle* (London: Alcove Press, 1974) pp. 224–5.
17. Karl Mannheim, *Ideology and Utopia* (London: Routledge and Kegan Paul, 1936) pp. 219–23.
18. Ibid, pp. 177–9.
19. Ibid, p. 36.
20. Pierre Vallières, *White Niggers of America* (New York: Monthly Review Press, 1971) p. 60.
21. Dr Andre Lassier, article in *Le Devoir*, 5 May 1963.
22. Letter from German Lopatin to Natalie Herzen, August 1970, in Confino, op. cit., pp. 314–15.

XVIII

23. For a discussion of this aspect of Soviet activity see *The Annual of Power and Conflict*, 5th ed. (London: Institute for the Study of Conflict, 1976).

XIX

24. See, for example, David Fromkin, 'The Strategy of Terrorism', *Foreign Affairs*, vol. 53, no.4 (Jul 1975) pp. 683–98.
25. Reported in *The Times*, 13 Dec 1976. The Los Angeles County sheriff claimed that an eight ton munitions cache found in the desert area sixty miles north of Los Angeles and in townships east of the city was 'the largest of its type ever found in California and probably the nation'. Also found with the arms were anti-black, anti-semitic and anti-Mexican literature, and food, medical supplies and chemicals for making napalm and poison gas. The police have linked the arms cache with an extreme right-wing paramilitary group.
26. Carlos Marighela, 'On the Organizational Function of Revolutionary Violence' in *For The Liberation of Brazil*, trans. John Butt and Rosemary Sheed (Harmondsworth: Penguin Books, 1971) p. 44.
27. Thomas Perry Thornton, 'Terror as a Weapon of Political Agitation' in H. Eckstein (ed.), *Internal War* (New York: Free Press, 1964) p. 73.
28. Ibid., p. 75.
29. From the *Concise Oxford Dictionary* definition of propaganda.
30. Charles Roetter, *Psychological Warfare* (London: Faber, 1974).
31. From the testimony of Okamoto quoted in Peter Clyne *An Anatomy*

    *of Skyjacking* (London: Abelard Schuman, 1973).
32. Brian Crozier, *A Theory of Conflict* (London: Hamish Hamilton, 1974) p. 129.
33. As argued in Frank Kitson, *Low Intensity Operations* (London: Faber, 1971).

XX

34. Paul Wilkinson, *Political Terrorism* (London: Macmillan, 1974) pp. 138–43 and *Terrorism versus Liberal Democracy: the Problems of Response* (London: Institute for the Study of Conflict, 1976).
35. Alexis de Tocqueville, *L'Ancien Régime et la Revolution*, trans. Henry Reeve (London: John Murray, 1856) pp. 322–3.
36. Wilkinson, *Terrorism versus Liberal Democracy*.

XXI

37. Alexander Solzhenitsyn, *The Gulag Archipelago 1918–1956* (London: Book Club Associates, 1974) p. 144.

XXII

38. Brian Crozier, *A Theory of Conflict* (London: Hamish Hamilton, 1974) p. 143.
39. Ibid., p. 205.
40. Feliks Gross, 'Political Violence and Terror in 19th and 20th Century Russia and Eastern Europe, in vol. 8 of *A Report to the National Commission on the Causes and Prevention of Violence* (Washington, D.C.: U.S. Govt. Printing Office, 1969) pp. 421–76.

XXIII

41. See for example, the anti-police propaganda in *Time Out*, and *The Workers' Press*, and in T. Bunyan, *The Police State in Britain* (London: Friedman, 1976).
42. See William L. Tafoya, 'SWAT – Special Weapons and Tactics: Part I', *PWC Bulletin*, vol. LXXV, no. 8 (Feb 1975).
43. For useful discussions of police responses and organisation to deal with terrorism see T. Bowden, *Men in the Middle – the U.K. Police,* Conflict Studies No. 68 (London, 1976) and F. Gregory, *Protest and Violence: The Police Response,* Conflict Studies No. 75 (London, 1976).
44. Reports in *Daily Telegraph*, 8 Nov 1976, and *Boston Globe*, 7 Nov 1976.
45. Chief Inspector Charles Clarkson of West Yorkshire Constabulary,

quoted in an article in *The Times* headed 'Police train to tackle the armed criminal', 23 April 1975.

46. *Hansard*, 15 Jan 1976, Commons reply by the Home Secretary to a question by Mr Toby Jessel, M.P., on present trends in Metropolitan Police recruitment.

47. Peter Evans, *The Police Revolution* (London: Pitman, 1973) pp. 97–8.

48. Ibid., p. 185.

XXIV

49. Report of speech by Sir Robert Mark delivered in Leicester, 11 Mar 1976, as reported in *Daily Telegraph*, 13 Mar 1976.

50. *Daily Telegraph*, op. cit., reports on NCCL spokesman's comment on Sir Robert's speech: 'Sir Robert is playing with fire.'

XXV

51. Speech to the Federation of Conservative Students, Brighton, 7 Oct 1976, reported in *The Times*, 8 Oct 1976.

52. Brigadier W. F. K. Thompson, 'Ulster: when the kidding has to stop', *Daily Telegraph*, 14 Jan 1975.

53. For the record of the Loyalist terrorist groups down to 1972 see Martin Dillon and Dennis Lehane, *Political Murder in Northern Ireland* (Harmondsworth: Penguin Books, 1973).

54. It is even reported that the two Provisional I.R.A. men responsible for the kidnap and murder of Mr Thomas Niedermayer, the West German consul, in December 1973, are known to the police. Yet they are allowed to go free because witnesses are too frightened to give evidence against them (see the remarkably detailed report by Chris Ryder in the *Sunday Times*, 2 Jan 1977).

55. *Economist*, 30 Nov 1974.

56. Explanatory Memorandum, *Prevention of Terrorism (Temporary Provisions) Bill,* 1974.

57. Frank Zimring, 'Is Gun Control Likely to Reduce Violent Killings?', *University of Chicago Law Review*, vol. 35, no. 4 (Summer 1968) pp. 721–37.

58. Statement by Dr O'Brien, reported in *The Times*, 20 Oct 1976.

PART III

XXXVI

1. See Brian Jenkins, 'Chronology of Recent Incidents in International Terrorism' in David Carlton and Carlo Schaerf (eds), *International*

*Terrorism and World Security* (London: Croom Helm, 1975) pp. 35–49.

2. U.N. Information Centre report BR/73/37 (Sept 1975) pp. 3–4.
3. Martha Crenshaw Hutchinson, 'Transnational Terrorism and World Politics', *The Jerusalem Journal of International Relations*, vol.1, no.2 (Winter 1975) p. 110.

XXVII

4. For detailed evidence see International Institute for Strategic Studies, *The Military Balance 1976–77* (London, 1976).
5. *Annual Survey* (New York: Freedom House Institute, 1976).

XXVIII

6. The data on which these generalisations are based is available in the annual publications of the Institute for the Study of Conflict, the International Institute for Strategic Studies and the U.S. Department of Defense.
7. Sir B. H. Liddell-Hart, *Strategy: The Indirect Approach* rev.ed. (London: Faber, 1967) p. 375.
8. Ibid.
9. See Melvin J. Lasky, 'Ulrike Meinhof and The Baader Meinhof Gang', *Encounter*, vol. XLIV, no. 6 (June 1975) pp. 9–23.
10. See especially Brian Jenkins, 'International Terrorism: A Balance Sheet', *Survival*, vol. 17, no. 4 (July/Aug 1975) pp. 158–64, and *International Terrorism: A New Mode of Conflict*, Research Paper no. 48, California Seminar on Arms Control and Foreign Policy (Los Angeles: Crescent Publications, 1975).
11. Martha Hutchinson, 'Transnational Terrorism in World Politics', *The Jerusalem Journal of International Relations*, vol.1, no.2 (Winter 1975) p. 120.
12. Ibid.
13. Frank Kitson, *Low Intensity Operations* (London: Faber, 1971), p.8.
14. David Milbank, *International and Transnational Terrorism: Diagnosis and Prognosis* (Washington D.C.: Central Intelligence Agency Research Study, April 1976).

XXIX

15. Bernard Brodie, *War and Politics* (London: Cassell, 1974) p. 274.
16. Geoffrey Fairbairn, *Revolutionary Guerrilla Warfare: The Countryside Version* (Harmondsworth: Penguin Books, 1974) p. 20.
17. Brian Crozier, in an unpublished paper 'Terrorism: The Problem in Perspective'.

18. In December 1974, for example, it was reported that the P.L.O. claimed to have arrested twenty-eight activists in Palestinian dissident cadres, and to be holding them in guerrilla prisons pending trial by a 'revolutionary court': see report by Joseph Fitchett, *Observer*, 1 Dec 1974. However, there is no clearly authenticated report of dissident Palestinian activists receiving anything more severe than brief 'corrective' detention under P.L.O. guard.

XXX

19. Richard Clutterbuck, *Living with Terrorism* (London: Faber, 1975).
20. On the weekend of 8–9 Jan 1977, Moscow experienced its first terrorist bomb attack near Perovmayskaya metro station to the north-east of the city. It is reported that six passengers were killed and many seriously injured. The explosion was reported by the official news agency, Tass, as 'small'. No group has claimed responsibility. Was it a nationalist or separatist movement? Was it a K.G.B. attempt to discredit the dissident movement? Some Soviet sources indicated widespread concern that the greater flow of information concerning political violence and terrorism in the West may have led to emulation by a protest group in Russia.
21. For instance, according to Solzhenitsyn's third volume of *Gulag*, the Soviet authorities tried to keep secret a popular uprising in Novocherkassk, Ukraine, that occurred in June 1962. Swingeing price increases coinciding with severe wage cuts affecting workers at the Novocherkassk electric locomotive plant caused a strike at the plant, and demonstrators marched on local militia and party headquarters. Army units with tanks sent in to restore order ended up firing into the crowd. Solzhenitsyn quotes eyewitness accounts reporting between seventy and eighty killed and many wounded. The régime tried to stifle all news of these events by spiriting away survivors and observed participants to prison and to Siberia. Yet, even so, word-of-mouth accounts still survive, and Solzhenitsyn's careful reconstruction of the events has ensured that it is no longer a secret.
23. An example of this form of weakness was the decision by a French court, on 11 January 1977, to allow Muhammad Daoud Audeh to go free. This followed his arrest under an INTERPOL warrant initiated by West Germany, as a result of a tip off to the French police by the Israelis. Daoud was wanted for questioning in connection with the Black September Organisation massacre of Israeli athletes at Munich in 1972. The Israelis claim that Daoud Audeh planned the Munich attack and many others, including terrorist raids in Israel. The West German and Israeli governments which had both expressed a desire for Daoud's extradition, expressed strong protests at the

release. But it was too late. The damage had been done, and the new European convention on the suppression of terrorism was blatantly ignored.

XXXI

24. The 'phenotype' hypothesis is proposed by D. V. Segre and J. H. Adler in 'The Ecology of Terrorism', *Encounter'*, vol. XL, no. 2 (Feb 1973) pp. 17–24.
25. As suggested by Eugene Methvin in an unpublished paper, 'Modern Terrorism and the Rise of Megamedia in "The Global Village" ', March 1976.
26. See Segre and Adler, op. cit.
27. As reported in *The Times*, 30 November 1972.
28. *Terroristic Activity – International Terrorism:* Hearings before the Subcommittee to Investigate the Administration of the Internal Security Act and Other Internal Security Laws of the Committee on the Judiciary, United States Senate, Ninety-Fourth Congress, First Session; Part 4; 14 May 1975 (Washington: U.S. Government Printing Office, 1975).
29. 'Terrorism: "Growing and Increasingly Dangerous" ' (Interview with Robert A. Fearey), *U.S. News and World Report*, 29 Sept 1975, p. 79.

XXXII

30. For an account of the significance of Sarajevo see Barbara Tuchman's splendid *The Guns of August* (London: Hamish Hamilton, 1962).
31. On this whole subject, see the brilliant discussion by Gil Elliot, *Twentieth Century Book of the Dead* (London: Allen Lane, 1972).
32. Ibid., pp. 13 ff.
33. Steven J. Rosen and Robert Frank, 'Measures against International Terorism', in Carlton and Shaerf (eds), *International Terrorism and World Security*, p. 60.

XXXIII

34. The main proponent of the simplistic surrogate war hypothesis is Brian Jenkins: see his *International Terrorism: A New Mode of Conflict*, Research Paper no. 48, California Seminar on Arms Control and Foreign Policy (Los Angeles: Crescent Publications, 1975) pp. 20 ff.
35. Brian Jenkins, 'International Terrorism': Trends and Potentialities: A Summary of Conclusions', unpublished mimeographed paper (March 1976) p. 3. But note that the contrary view has been cogently argued

by Martha Crenshaw Hutchinson in 'Defining Future Threat: Terrorists and Nuclear Proliferation', paper delivered to the Conference on International Terrorism: National, Regional, and Global Ramifications, organised by the Ralph Bunche Institute and City University of New York, June 1976.

36. See Mason Willrich and Theodore B. Taylor, *Nuclear Theft: Risks and Safeguards* (Cambridge, Mass.: Ballinger, 1974).
37. See report, *New York Times*, 27 Feb 1975.
38. See E. M. Kinderman, 'Plutonium: Home Made Bombs?', paper presented to the Conference on Nuclear Public Information organised by the Atomic Industrial Forum, March 1972, in *Peaceful Nuclear Exports and Weapons Proliferation* (Washington, D.C.: U.S. Govt. Printing Office, 1975) pp. 25–6.
39. *New York Times*, 27 Feb 1975, p. 12.
40. George Quester, 'What's New on Nuclear Proliferation?', paper presented to the Aspen Workshop on Arms Control, 1975; reprinted in U.S. Congress, House Committee on International Relations, Subcommitte on International Security and Scientific Affairs, *Nuclear Proliferation: Future U.S. Foreign Policy Implications:* Hearings, Ninety-fourth Congress, First Session (Washington, D.C.: U.S. Govt. Printing Office, 1975), pp. 476–99.

XXXIV

41. Richard Clutterbuck, *Living with Terrorism*, p. 95.
42. See for example: Peter Clyne, *An Anatomy of Skyjacking* (London: Abelard–Schuman, 1973); David Phillips, *Skyjack* (London: Harrap, 1973); and Richard Clutterbuck, ibid., pp. 95–114 for an excellent synopsis.
43. See the vivid account in Ze'ev Schiff, Eitan Haber and Yeshayahu Ben-Porat, *Entebbe Rescue* (New York: Dell, 1977).
44. Reported *Sunday Telegraph*, 11 July 1976.
45. See Schiff, Haber and Ben-Porat, op. cit.
46. For fuller discussion of this approach, see Part III, ch. XXXVII 'General Measures'.
47. Richard Clutterbuck, op. cit., p. 118.
48. David Phillips, *Skyjack* (London: Harrap, 1973) p. 173.
49. Alona Evans, 'Aerial Hijacking' in *International Terrorism and Political Crimes*, ed. M. Cherif Bassiouni (Springfield, Illinois: Charles C. Thomas, 1974) p. 247.
50. Edward McWhinney, *The Illegal Diversion of Aircraft and International Law* (Leiden: Sijthoff, 1975) p. 97.
51. Ibid., p. 48.
52. Ibid., p. 74.

53. Ibid., p. 76.
54. Clyne, op. cit., p. 166.

XXXV

55. Grotius, *De Jure Belli et Pacis*, II, XVIII 5.
56. Brooks McClure, 'Hostage Survival', paper presented to the conference organised by Glassboro State College on 'Terrorism in the Contemporary World', April 1976.
57. Edler Baumann, *The Diplomatic Kidnappings* (The Hague: Martinus Nijhoff, 1973) p. 167.
58. O.A.S. Official Records/Ser. P./English. Third Special Session, General Assembly, AG/doc. 88 rev. 1. corr. 1., 2 Feb 1971.
59. Clutterbuck, op. cit., pp. 66–7.
60. Baumann, op. cit., 'Summary'.
61. Ibid.

XXXVI

62. See Barbara Tuchman, 'Perdicaris Alive or Raisuli Dead', *American Heritage*, vol. X, no. 5 (Aug 1959).
63. Roberta Wohlstetter, 'Kidnapping to Win Friends and Influence People', *Survey*, vol. XX, no. 4 (93) p. 2.
64. Ibid.
65. McClure, op. cit., p. 5.
66. See Sir Geoffrey's own vivid account in *People's Prison* (London: Faber, 1973).

# INDEX

Acton, Lord 159
Ad-hoc Committee on Terrorism
  (U.N.) 233
aerial piracy 207; *see also* hijacking
Agathocles 8
Air Crimes Commission 223
airport security 217–19
Aldergrove Airport 163
Al Fatah 184–5
Algeria 60, 223
Allende, Salvador 127
Ambonese 182–3
American–Irish community 167
American Purposive Psychology
  School 35–6
Amin, President 213–14
amnesty, general 118, 128, 155
Amsterdam 132, 219, 221
anarchism 58, 78, 83, 97, 98, 106,
  107, 112
Andreski, S. 53
Angola 177
Angry Brigade 83, 93, 135, 139
*anomie* 96
anti-tank gun 201
Anti-Terrorist Squad 141–2
anti-Vietnam war campaign 26
Aquinas 5, 7–8
Arafat, Yasser 186–7
Arendt, Hannah 76, 79
Argentina xii, 62, 183, 189, 194
Arguello, Patrick 219
Aristotle 4–5, 7
'armed liberation struggles' 177–9,
  231–3
Armed Proletarian Nuclei 135
Army, British 89, 91–2, 136–7,
  147–64
Army, Israeli 152–3

Aron, Raymond 74, 76
arrest and questioning powers 164
assassination 181, 196, 232
Assassin sect 59, 76
asylum, political 192, 211, 226, 234
Athens 6, 129, 215–16
Atomic Energy Authority (British) 204
Austria 216
autonomist movements 85–6, 107, 122,
  182
*Avanguardia Nazionale* 141

Baader–Meinhof gang 76, 93, 97–8,
  139–40, 143, 179, 184, 198
Baddawi Conference (1972) 194
Bakunin, Michael 66–8, 98, 111, 174
Bakuninist International 174, 180
Balcombe Street siege 132, 142
Bangladesh 123, 159
B.A.O.R. 137
Baumann, Edler 228
Bay of Pigs 126
Begin, Menachem 109
Beilen 132, 182
Biafrans 183
Birmingham bombings (1974) 162
Bismarck, Otto von 130
Black Cross 98
Black Hand 196
blackmail 129–32
Black September 219
boarding-gate searches 209, 211,
  217–19
Bolivia 183
Bomb Disposal Squads (Police) 142
bomb-planters 95
Bomb Squad 142
border security 165–6
Bosch, Orlando 127

Brazil xii, 62, 63, 130, 183, 189
Broadcasting Authority Act
(Ireland) 168–9
Brodie, Bernard 182
Bucher, Giovanni 130
Bulgaria 199

Callaghan, James 150
Calvert, Peter 55
Canada 138, 227, 229
*Carabinieri* 141
'Carlos' (Ilich Ramirez Sanchez) 184,
198, 208
Castro, Fidel 126–7, 212, 229
Castro, Raúl 209, 229
*Catechism of the Revolutionist* 98
Central Intelligence Agency 126–7
Chartists 44
Cheka, the 42
China 21, 61, 103, 199
Church Committee (U.S.) 42, 125
civil disobedience 21, 26–8
civil rights movement (U.S.) 26, 112
Clausewitz, General Carl von 49
Clyne, Peter 223
Collingwood, R. G. 97
Collins, Michael 114, 164
Colombia 62
colonial independence struggles 51, 60,
167, 182
communal violence 96
communism 71
community, political 47, 86, 90–1,
118–19
*Compagnies Républicaines de Sécurité*
(C.R.S.) 149
concessions to terrorists 128–32
conscientious objection 26–7
consensus, political 44, 91
consent 14–17, 78
constabulary role 43, 143–4, 150–1,
157
constitutional rule 6–8, 118–19, 160
Corrigan, Mairead 90
Cosgrave, Liam 166
counter-terrorist strategy and tactics
xiii–xiv, 81–2, 104, 114–33,
139–70, 205–6, 209, 217–24,
227–34
*coups,* military 20, 159
Coyle, Marian 131–2
Cranston, Maurice 73
crime and criminality 21–2, 38, 49,

65–8, 94–5, 126, 194, 212
Criminal Jurisdiction Act (U.K.) 166
Criminal Justice Amendment Act
(Ireland) 166
criminal ransom extortion and es-
cape 211–12
Critchley, T. A. 1, 19, 37, 44–5
*Critique de la raison dialectique* 72–4,
76–7
Clutterbuck, Richard 189, 190, 209,
227
Cross, James 227
Crozier, Brian 113, 135
Cuba 61, 62, 85, 125, 126–7, 177,
183, 199, 209, 211–12, 227, 229
Cyprus 60
Czechoslovakia 166, 179, 199

D 11 squad 142
Davis, Lieutenant-General
Benjamin O. 218
Dawsons Field 213, 216, 218
Debray, Régis 58, 60, 100, 108
deportation 163
despotism 6, 8, 9, 122–3
détente 177
detention and internment 155–6, 160–1
deterrence 21–2
detonators 168
dictatorship 20, 50–1, 122–3
diplomatic kidnappings and
attacks 224–8
Diplomatic Protection Group 142
Dollard, John 35
Dostoevsky, Fyodor 101
Dugdale, Rose 131
Durkheim, Emile 96

East Africa 213–16
East Germany 199
Easter rising, Dublin (1916) 61, 86
economic problems 86, 89, 91, 153,
159, 181–2
*économistes* 13
Egypt 187
El Al 209, 219–20, 223
Elbrick, Charles 130
*embourgeoisement* 71
emergency powers 45, 50, 80, 122–3,
154, 158–9, 159–65, 227
English utilitarians 12
Entebbe hijack and rescue 129, 188,
196, 213–16

entry controls 163
EOKA 51, 85
equality 6–7
E.R.P. (Ejercito Revolucionario del
    Pueblo) 194
espionage 164–5
ethics xii, 65–8, 106, 175
Eugenie, Empress 180
European Convention for the Suppression
    of Terrorism 233–4
European Economic Community 13,
    120, 222, 233–4
existentialists 72
explosives, control of 146–7
extradition 192–3, 196, 208, 222, 226

Fairbairn, Geoffrey 182–3
Fanon, Frantz 54, 62, 100
fascism 51, 58, 71, 75, 106–7
Faulkner, Brian (Lord) 153, 158–9,
    165
F.B.I. 127, 140–1
Fearey, Robert A. 195
Fedayeen 185
Federal Border Guard 140
Federal Criminal Office 140
Federal German Republic 83–5, 139,
    140, 143, 213, 233
Federalist Papers 17, 24–5
Ferdinand, Archduke Francis 196
Ferrer, Francisco 98
F.L.N. (Front National de
    Libération) 98
Florida 126–7
F.L.Q. (Front de Libération du
    Québec) 59, 85, 99, 170, 227
foco, guerrilla 61, 100
force
    as necessary sanction of law 21
    defined 19
    international relations 175–6
    proper use in liberal state 41–7, 79,
        117
    role of in liberal state 18–20
foreign workers 192
France 19, 71, 149, 159, 214, 233–4
francs-tireurs 196
Frankfurt school 72, 76
Fraser, Morris 47
freedom 7, 102–3, 122–3
Freiheit 62
Fromm, Erich 30
frustration–aggression theory 35–6

Futurist movement 107

Gaddafi, Colonel 166
Gagnon, Charles 85
Gallagher, Eddie 131–2
gaol-releases 60
Garda 165
Gardiner Committee 128
Gaza 152–3
Georgia (U.S.S.R.) 122
ghettos 61–2
Giap, General vo Nguyen 108
Golan Heights 185
government, role of in anti-terrorist
    policy 124, 129–33, 150–1
Great Britain 19, 44–5, 88–92, 105,
    107, 150–70, 214, 228
Great Scotland Yard 162
Green, T. H. 38–9
grenade launchers 201
Gross, Feliks xiv, 37, 79, 96, 135
Grotius, Hugo 224
Guardia di Finanza 141
Guardia di Pubblica Sicurezza 141
guerrillas 52, 60–4, 108, 180
guerrilla warfare 60–4, 100, 108, 113,
    137, 157, 178–9, 183–4, 191
Guevara, Che 58, 71, 100
Guildford 162

Haag, E. van den 27–8
habeas corpus 160
Haddad, Wadih 213
Hague 182
Hague Convention (1970) 220–1, 232
Hamilton, Alexander 17
Heath, Edward 158
Heathrow Airport 148
Herrema, Tiede 131–2, 142
Herzen, Natalie 101
hijacking 148, 181, 187, 195, 206–24,
    226
Hitler, A. xi
Hobbes, Thomas 8–11, 18, 72, 74
Ho Chi Minh 71
Holland 182
Holleben, Ehrenfried von 130
Home Office 144, 148
hostages 128–32, 190, 195, 207, 216,
    229–31, 233
housing 90, 116, 152
Huntington, Samuel 31
Hussein, King 185

I.C.A.O. (International Civil Aviation
    Organisation)  222
ideology  96–102
imprisonment  127–8
incipient civil war  150–70
India  123, 159
indicators (of impending insur-
    gency)  134–6, 139
Indonesia  182–3, 197
industrial confrontation  45
injustice  35–8, 62, 65, 115–16
insurrection, mass  55, 108
intelligence, security  51, 87, 114,
    125–7, 132–41, 154, 156, 161–2,
    217
inter-communal relations and conflict  33,
    59, 86, 90, 91, 117–18, 150, 167
Internal Macedonian Revolutionary
    Organisation (I.M.R.O.)  181
international cooperation in countering
    terrorism  138, 166, 202, 208,
    217, 220–2, 231–4
International Federation of Airline
    Pilots  223
international relations  xii, 87, 119, 138,
    175–81, 182–234
INTERPOL  138
intervention, foreign  177–81, 199–201
I.R.A.
    Official  93, 167
    Provisional  19, 53, 85, 88, 90, 93,
        97, 131–2, 142, 153, 154–7,
        160–2, 167, 168–9, 173, 179
Iraq  105, 187
Ireland  60, 85, 86–92, 114, 116, 119,
    131–2, 150–70, 188
Irgun Zvai Leumi  51
Irish Government  165
Israel  91, 105, 129, 152–3, 185–8,
    209, 211, 213–16, 232
Italy  xii, 71, 106, 135, 159, 234

Jackson, Sir Geoffrey  231
Japan  216
Japanese United Red Army  53, 59, 93,
    174, 184, 196, 205, 212–13, 216,
    217
J-curve  37
Jenkins, Roy  162
Jerusalem  185
Johnson, Chalmers  55
Jordan  184–5
judicial review  160–1

judiciary  17–18, 66, 86, 124–5,
    153–4, 156, 160, 233
jurisdiction  192–3, 196
just rebellion doctrine  39, 65
just war doctrine  65

Kamikaze  205
Kenya  196, 215
K.G.B.  125, 166
Khaled, Leila  219
kidnapping  129–32, 181, 224–31, 232
King, Martin Luther  112
Kitson, Major-General Frank  114, 180
Kropotkin, Peter  66–7, 98
Kuala Lumpur  216
Kurds  183
Kuwait  217

Lander police  140
landing permissions  208
Laporte, Pierre  227
Laqueur, Walter  62
Lassier, André  99–100
latifúndio  63
Latin America  62, 63, 181, 224–5,
    225–6
law  4–5, 7, 16–18, 21–3, 86, 118,
    123, 124–5, 127, 128, 138, 151,
    154, 176
    international  176, 220–3, 225–6
    martial  154
    rule of  7, 16–18, 42, 66, 86, 118,
        121, 123, 127, 138, 156, 234
Law Enforcement Intelligence Unit
    (L.E.I.U.)  140
laws of war  see rules and laws of war
Leach, Edmund  30
Lebanon  104–5, 123, 159, 187, 197,
    213
legality  42–3, 151, 153–4
legation, right of  224
legislature  160
legitimacy  41, 78, 118, 120, 232
Lenin, Vladimir Ilyich  58, 177, 184
Les Mots  74
Letelier, Orlando  127
lex talionis  22
liberal democracy  13
    and majority principle  39, 71, 78–9
    and modern pluralism  25
    capacity for peaceful internal
        change  25–9
    external threats  176–81

general principles of counter-terrorist
  strategy 121–32
measures against incipient civil
  war 150–70
measures against spasm terrorism in
  liberal democracy 139–49
measures against terrorism 114–21
participation, representation and
  obligation 15
terrorist threats 80–92, 86, 94, 105
vulnerabilities of 188–92, 200, 234
liberalism 6, 7, 19, 71, 234
liberal tradition and philosophy 3–6, 21,
  77–8, 119, 122–3, 234
liberties 18, 19, 103, 114, 119, 122,
  125, 175, 189–90, 234
Libya 105, 166, 179, 199, 215, 216
Liddell-Hart, Sir B. H. 178
Lisburn 154
Locke, John 4–5, 8, 11–12, 14, 16–17,
  19–20
Lod Airport massacre 53, 112, 212–13,
  217
Long Kesh 154
Lopatin, German 101–2
Lorenz, Konrad 30
'Loyalist' paramilitary and terrorist
  groups 156, 158

Machiavelli, Niccolo 8, 116
Madison, James 4, 5, 7, 12, 24
majority 39
Malatesta, Errico 98
Malaysia 117
Mannheim, Karl 97–9
manpower, police 145–6
Maoists 97
Mao Tse-tung 71, 108
Marcuse, Herbert 71, 76, 78
Marighela, Carlos 58, 61, 63, 80–1,
  100, 108–9
Mark, Sir Robert 147
Marx, Karl 73, 74, 76
Marxism 58, 71, 78, 83, 97, 100, 107,
  123, 177, 200, 208
Matthews, Mr and Mrs 142
McClure, Brooks 230
McWhinney, Edward 221, 222–3
McWhirter, Ross 105
media, mass 59, 79–80, 103, 122, 130,
  146, 153, 167, 168–70, 190,
  193–4, 208
Meinhof, Ulrike 93

Metropolitan Police 142
'micro-proliferation' 204–6
Middle East 213
militarisation of politics 109
military 20, 41–2, 43, 81, 83, 89, 105,
  109–10, 136–8, 147–70, 183
Military Aid to the Civil Power
  (M.A.C.P.) 147–9
Mill, John Stuart 4, 7, 14–15, 19
miniaturised letter bombs 201
minimal force, doctrine of 43–7, 143–4
Ministry of Defence (British) 148
Ministry of the Interior (Italian) 141
minorities 28–9, 40, 104, 114–16, 117
missiles 201
Mlada Bosnia 196
Monasterevin 131
Montesquieu, Baron 9, 17
Montreal Convention (1971) 221
mortars 201
Most, Johannes 49, 62–3, 203
'Motorman' operation 154
Munich massacre (1972) 140, 174, 232
Mussolini, B. xi

Napoleon III 180
Narodnaya Volya 76
National Council for Civil Liberties 147
National Defence College 162
nationalism 85–6, 97, 107
'national liberation' ideology 90
NATO 137
natural law 5, 16
Nazis 143
Nechayev, Sergey 58, 67–8, 98, 101–2
necrology 197
New Left 79, 179
New York Police Hostage Negotiating
  Team 141
nihilism 58, 66, 97–8, 106, 107
Nixon, Richard 218
'no-go' areas 154
NORAID 167
Northern Ireland 44, 47, 80, 85,
  87–92, 109, 116, 118, 119, 121,
  128, 136, 137, 139–40, 146,
  150–70, 197
Northern Ireland (Emergency Provisions)
  Act (1973) 134, 165
Northern Ireland (Emergency Provisions)
  (Amendment) Act (1975) 160–1,
  165
Northern Ireland Executive 158–9

North Korea    184, 199, 213
Norway    234
nuclear facilities, civil    202, 204–6
nuclear weapons    177–8, 181–2, 189,
    203–5

O'Brien, Conor Cruise    165, 169
oil rigs and pipelines    149
oil weapon    185, 186, 211
Okamoto, Kozo    112
Old Bailey    162
O'Neill, Lord    118
OPEC Conference, December
    1975    174, 198, 208, 216
opposition and protest, peaceful    24–9,
    115, 124, 126
oppression    37, 121–2
order, civil    18–19, 122–3, 159
Ordine Nuovo    141
Organistion of American States (O.A.S.)
    Convention (1971)    255–6
Orly airport    219
Orsini, Felice    180

Palestine    51, 129, 174, 184–8, 209,
    211
Palestinian terrorists    148, 170, 184–8,
    194, 209, 211, 212, 219–20, 232
parties, political    24–5, 40
P.D.F.L.P. (Popular Democratic Front for
    the Liberation of Palestine)    187–8
peace    175, 198
'peace-offensive'    177
Peace of Westphalia (1684)    224
peasantry    61
'People's Prison'    231
Perdicaris kidnap (1904)    229
P.F.L.P. (Popular Front for the Liberation
    of Palestine)    174, 185, 187,
    213–16
philosophes    13
Pike, Douglas    191
plastic explosives    201
pledged group, Sartre's concept of    73
P.L.O. (Palestine Liberation
    Organisation)    97, 179, 185–8,
    211
plutonium    204
police    20, 41–6, 87, 92, 110, 126,
    131–2, 134, 135–6, 139–49, 160,
    161–4, 233
    British    139, 141–8, 149, 161–4
police–army cooperation    148–9

polis    6
political hijacking    212–16
political objectives (of
    government)    158–9
political obligation    5, 12–16, 39, 41
political offence exception clauses    220–2,
    234
political terrorist 'getaway' hijack    216
Politics (Aristotle)    6
Portugal    108, 234
practico-inert, Sartre's concept of    72
Praetorian violence    33
praxis    72
precision-guided munitions
    (P.G.M.s)    202
press, the    169–70, 190
Prevention of Terrorism (Temporary
    Provisions) Act, 1974    162–3
Prevention of Terrorism Supplemental
    Temporary Provisions, Northern
    Ireland Order, 1976    163
Princip, Gavrilo    196
propaganda    66, 79–80, 81–2, 95,
    111–12, 124, 128, 135, 139, 161,
    165, 167, 168–70, 190–1, 203
propellant fuels    201
protest    28–9, 40
Protestant Action Force    156
Provisional Sinn Fein    168–9
psychological techniques (for combating
    terrorism)    131–2, 140, 230–1
psychopathology    66, 93
publicity    80–2, 95, 111–12, 190,
    193–4, 203, 208
public order    43–6
public support and cooperation in anti-
    terrorist measures    146–7, 190–1,
    200, 208
Puerto Rico    199, 212
punishment    21–3, 27, 113, 127–8,
    134, 152, 191, 195, 208, 221, 226,
    228
putsch    109

Quebec    85, 119, 138, 227
Quester, George    206

Raisuli    229
RAND    194–5
ransoms    60, 112, 129–32, 194, 216,
    225, 228
reactor fuel    204
reason    7, 13

Red Army Fraction 83
Rees, Merlyn 156
reform 115–16, 133
Reform Bill (1832) 44
refugee escape 211
Rejectionist Front 187–8
relative deprivation theory 35–7, 96
religious conflict 90, 116, 158–9
remonstrative violence 24–8, 33
resistance 26–7, 33, 39–40, 119, 122
revolution 6, 27, 48, 54, 55, 58–64, 97, 107
*Revolutionäre Kreigwissenschaft* 62
rights 7, 18, 103, 119, 122, 126
riots 44–6
rocket-launchers 201, 219
Romania 199
Rome 141, 213, 217
Rose, Richard 88–9, 91, 158
Rousseau 7
Royal Canadian Mounted Police 138
Royal Commission on Environmental Pollution 204
Royalty Protection Group 142
Royal Ulster Constabulary (R.U.C.) 165
rules and laws of war 53, 79, 201, 234

Sadat, President 187
sanctuary 212, 222
Sarajevo 196
Sartre, Jean-Paul 54, 71–8, 100
Schiphol Airport 167, 179
Scotland 137
Scottish philosophical radicals 13
search powers 163
Sendic, Raoul 183
separatist movements 85–6, 107, 119–20, 182
Serbia 196
series, Sartre's concept of 73
siege situations 130–2, 227–31
signals of impending insurgency 134–6, 139
situationists 72, 76, 78, 112
Six Day War 185, 186, 209
skymarshals 219
S.L.A. (Symbionese Liberation Army) 98
slavery 6, 39
'sleepers' 134
Social Democratic and Labour Party (S.D.L.P.) 158
socialism 7
Solzhenitsyn, A. xi, 42, 121–3

Somalia 177, 199, 213
Sorel, Georges 74–5, 97, 107
South Africa 39
South Armagh 157
South Moluccans 132, 182
Soviet Union xi, 62, 71, 92, 97, 103–4, 121–2, 137, 166–7, 176–9, 184, 186, 190, 199, 211
Spain xi, 106
Spanish Civil War 61
Spartacists 61
Special Air Service (S.A.S.) Regiment 148–9
Special Branch 136, 142
Special Constabulary 45
Special Patrol Group (S.P.G.) 142
special powers legislation 159–65; *see also* emergency powers
special status and privileges (in gaol) 127–8
Special Weapons and Tactics squads (SWAT) 141
spies 67–8, 122
Stansted Airport 148
state
    abuses of state power and dereliction by 40, 74, 78–9
    and importance of intelligence 136–8
    and peaceful opposition and protest 24–9
    and political obligation 13
    and problems of internal defence 114–21
    concept 3
    liberal 3–5, 7
    punishment and deterrence in 20–23
    relevance and significance 14
    role of force in 18–20
    rule of law in 16–18
    sponsors (in international terrorism) 199–201
    targets (in international terrorism) 199–201, 232–3
    terrorist threats to 80–92, 94–5
    under internal attack 150–70, 175, 234
    unselective nature 21
    vulnerability to terrorist attack 102–6
Stern Gang 51
student revolt 71, 179
subversion 47, 135, 180, 199–200
Suharto, President 182
Sunningdale Agreement 158

Sydenham Airport 163
Syria 105, 187

tabun 143
Talandier, Alfred 67
target audience or group, terrorists' 50,
    52, 110–12
Technical Support Branch (New Scotland
    Yard) 142
technology 103, 188–9
    and weaponry 200–6, 208
Tel Aviv 213
Tel-el-Zaatar 187
television 153, 167, 168–70; see also
    media, mass
terror
    concepts, characteristics,
        typology 47–64
    epiphenomenal 48–55
    régimes and processes 48
    philosophy and ideology of 71–80
    Sartre on the role of 73–4
    totalitarian terror apparat 121–2, 177
terrorism
    and criminality 65–8
    causes of 93–102
    concepts, characteristics,
        typology 47–64
    definition of political terrorism 49
    international and transnational xiv,
        82, 104, 138, 173–234; causes
        181–95; defined 173–4;
        effects 195–7; nuclear
        203–6; threats posed by 198–
        206, 231
    its dangers and threats to liberal
        states 80–92
    repressive 33, 55, 57, 113, 121–2
    revolutionary and sub-revolutionary
        xiii, 19, 33, 55, 56; causes
        93–102; counter-measures to
        combat 139–47; ideologies
        96–102; spasm 121; strategy
        and tactics 106–14
    theories of 93–102
terrorists
    funds 166–7, 194
    ideologies and beliefs 96–102, 107,
        231
    organisational structure and
        recruitment 133–4, 166–7, 194
    personality 95, 230–1
Thameside 18

'third force' 41, 149
Third Republic 159
Thornton, T. P. 111
Thrasymachus 8
Tocqueville, Alexis de 4, 36, 97, 117
Tokyo Convention (1963) 220
torture 50, 121–2
totalitarianism 122, 190
Tower of London 162
Troilus and Cressida 18
Trotsky, Leon 213
Trotter, Wilfred 30
Trudeau, Pierre 227
Tupamaros 61, 107, 170, 183, 194,
    231
'two wars' strategy 117–18
tyranny 3–4, 7–8, 11–12, 18, 20, 53,
    115, 119, 122

Uganda 129, 196, 213–16
Ukraine 122
Ulster Freedom Fighters (U.F.F.) 156
Ulster Peace Movement 90
Ulster Volunteer Force (U.V.F.) 156
Ulster Workers' Council strike 109,
    158–9
unemployment 153
United Nations 13, 71, 175, 176, 185,
    186, 226, 231–3
    Convention (1973) 226
    General Assembly 232–3
United States of America 39, 40, 87–8,
    107, 125–7, 130, 137, 140–41,
    167–8, 181, 186, 187, 189, 197,
    204, 206, 209, 210–12, 218, 226,
    228, 229, 232
urban guerrillas 29, 58, 60–4, 100, 117,
    150, 152–3, 183–4
urbanisation 61–2, 183
Uruguay 107, 183, 231
U.S.–Canada Hijack Treaty (1976) 222
U.S.–Cuba Hijack Pact (1973) 127,
    212, 222
U.S. National Commission on Prevention
    of Violence 23
utopian mentality 98–9

Vallières, Pierre 85, 99, 203
Venezuela 62, 183
victims 39, 48, 52–3, 64, 88, 100–1,
    129–32, 139, 162, 197, 207,
    230–1
Vietcong 194

Vietnam  61, 177
violence
    causes of in liberal states  34–8
    characteristics and typology  30–4
    civil  19
    collective  30–1
    defined  19, 23
    escalation  32
    general theories  30–1
    in international relations  175–81
    intensity  32
    meaning  31
    Sartre's philosophy of  74–7, 79
    scale  32
    whether morally justified in a liberal
        state  39–40

Walter, Eugene V.  48
war  182
    civil  18–19, 55, 86–7, 92, 105, 137,
        150–70, 177–9, 197
    international  33, 55, 175–6
    proxy  179, 199–200

psychological  48–9, 81, 110, 191,
    203
suppressed civil  121, 150–70
surrogate  179
unconventional  49, 58–64, 105,
    110–11, 114, 133, 137, 177–81
War Measures Act (1970)  227
Warsaw  125
Warsaw Pact  71, 137
Watergate  18, 126
weaponry  39, 103, 112, 134
    for police anti-terrorist units  142–4
    government measures to regulate
        availability of firearms and ex-
        plosives  168, 201–6
    in terrorist hands  166
Weathermen  83, 93, 139, 203
Weber, Max  53
Weimar Republic  159
West Bank  152, 185, 187–8
Western Europe  181
Whitelaw, William  158
Williams, Betty  90
Williams, Raymond  23